The New Corporate Frontier

The Big Move to Small Town, U.S.A.

David A. Heenan

McGraw-Hill, Inc.

New York St. Louis San Francisco Auckland Bogotá
Caracas Hamburg Lisbon London Madrid
Mexico Milan Montreal New Delhi Paris
San Juan São Paulo Singapore
Sydney Tokyo Toronto

To Doris, the ultimate frontiersmom,
with love and thanks

HC
110
.D5
H44
1991
c.1

Library of Congress Cataloging-in-Publication Data

Heenan, David A.
  The new corporate frontier : the big move to Small Town, USA /
David A. Heenan.
     p.   cm.
  Includes bibliographical references and index.
  ISBN 0-07-027770-2
  1. United States—Industries—Location. 2. United States—
Economic conditions—1981—Regional disparities. 3. United
States—Rural conditions. I. The New Corporate Frontier.
HC110.D5H44   1991
338.6'042'0973—dc20   91-3165
                                                                 CIP

1 2 3 4 5 6 7 8 9 0   DOC/DOC   9 7 6 5 4 3 2 1

ISBN   0-07-027770-2

*The editors for this book were Theodore C. Nardin and Barbara Toniolo, the editing
supervisor was Olive H. Collen, and the production supervisor was Don Schmidt.
This book was set in Baskerville by Carol Woolverton, Lexington, Mass.*

Printed and bound by R. R. Donnelley & Sons Company.

Contents

About the Author

David A. Heenan is chairman and CEO of Theo. H. Davies
& Co., Ltd., one of Hawaii's original Big Five companies and
the North American holding arm for Jardine Matheson, the
worldwide British trading company based in Hong Kong.
Mr. Heenan has served on the faculties of The Wharton
School and the Columbia Graduate School of Business, and
holds a Ph.D. from the University of Pennsylvania. He is also
the author of *The Re-United States of America* and has contributed articles to the *Harvard Business Review, The Wall
Street Journal, The New York Times,* and the *Christian Science
Monitor.*

Preface

April 18, 1987. That was the day when the seeds of the idea for this book were sown. Over lunch at the beautiful Kapalua Bay Club on Maui, I was introduced to Randall Fields, chairman of Mrs. Fields Cookies Inc., probably the world's preeminent maker of chocolate chip cookies. Randy explained how, a few years earlier, he and his vivacious wife, Debbi, had moved their company from the congested San Francisco Bay area to the high mountain country of Park City, Utah. The reason: a superior lifestyle. To the Fields, their new home meant cleaner air, better schools, more time for family, fewer hassles—all with considerable cost savings.

A big-city boy at heart (Boston, New York, Tokyo, and Sydney had been my favorite haunts), I was skeptical at first about running a major business from the American Alps. After all, the high frontier—in its most pejorative form, the "boondocks" (from *bundok*, the word for "mountain" in Tagalog, the main language of the Philippines)—was synonymous with "remoteness." It was "out of it," literally and figuratively. Besides, my image of small-town America was clouded by the mythical Peyton Place, Bedford Falls, and Twin Peaks of fiction and television. How, I wondered, could a company have access to its customers, bankers, lawyers, and accountants from a primitive outback location? How could it lure talented professionals from the cultural amenities of major metropolitan centers?

My skepticism vanished after several visits to Mrs. Fields' headquarters in the Wasatch Mountains. Park City, I soon discovered, is much more than a popular year-round resort nestled in a magnificent landscape of forested hills and grassy vales. Large-town facilities and services exist hand in hand with the "everybody knows everybody" atmosphere and civic pride of a smallish burg. Although life in this former mining town of 5000 people proceeds at a leisurely pace, a sophistication and a cultural awareness unusual for a community its size are also present. Mrs. Fields' Cookies convinced me that a location off the beaten path can, indeed, be good for business.

With the aid of modern technology, Debbi and Randy Fields are able to more than compensate for the size limitations of Park City and the remoteness of the Utah highlands. Today, their $130-million business boasts a dominant share (roughly 30 percent) of the U.S. market for specialty cookies—and, on the international scene, is booming. Randy, a highly acclaimed computer guru, has linked the company's 520-plus units to the head office with a variety of software packages—packages so advanced that the cookie maker markets them to other multiunit companies. The computer network is, however, no panacea. Despite voluminous reports that hit her desk every day, Debbi Fields, president of Mrs. Fields, logs up to 350,000 miles a year to oversee the firm's day-to-day operations.

In the end, though, space age telecommunications is the key to managerial success at Mrs. Fields. By redefining the concept of distance, the talented husband-and-wife team have reaped the benefits of a publicly traded, global business while enjoying the lifestyle advantages of the ultimate picture postcard setting.

Is Mrs. Fields Cookies a fortuitous corporate anomaly? Is the call of the wild reaching other U.S. businesses? To evaluate the viability of a nontraditional headquarters, I crisscrossed the country—focusing on both established and embryonic firms based in Small Town, U.S.A., as well as businesses that had recently relocated or were contemplating a move to the new frontier. My conclusion—and the central theme of this book—is that U.S. corporations are demonstrating a clear and growing preference to domicile in smaller, relatively remote townships. As we shall demonstrate, this preference is part of a prevailing national trend to redistribute power—organizationally as well as geographically.

In my travels, I also found that the corporate culture that evolves in firms headquartered away from the metropolis incorporates features well established in Japanese companies—features of loyalty and commitment glamorized a decade ago by William Ouchi, Ezra Vogel, and other scholars. In this regard, frontier-based businesses may be well worth emulating.

The New Corporate Frontier is not a treatise on urban planning or relocation strategy. It is a book about power—about how and where power will best be exerted in the coming years. We argue that command has shifted from, and will continue to shift from, the center (traditional, monolithic headquarters and large cities) to the periphery (so-called miniheadquarters and small- to medium-sized communities). U.S. companies that partake in this important trend will be better equipped to face the competitive realities of the 1990s and beyond.

Acknowledgments

Many people helped make this book possible. My deepest gratitude goes to Marie E. MacCord. Her painstaking research and far-flung travels contributed much of the information upon which *The New Corporate Frontier* is based. Reginald B. Worthley and Mona Nakayama also assisted with selected research assignments. Staff at public libraries across the country were most helpful, none more so than the staff at the University of Hawaii's Hamilton Library.

In the academic community, Peter F. Drucker's profound understanding of the new realities confronting American companies and communities was extremely helpful, as was his overall encouragement of this project. Howard V. Perlmutter contributed significantly to my understanding of strategic partnering and power sharing in today's organizations; several segments on these subjects draw upon our previous articles.

Other scholars who offered important insights included Charles E. Summer, Jr., William G. Ouchi, Warren Bennis, Harold J. Leavitt, Paul Berman, Warren J. Keegan, Edwin J. Perkins, Jerry I. Porras, Edgar Schein, Larry Greiner, Tom Stitzel, Tom Cummings, Stanley Davis, Daniel B. Boylan, Michael Marsden, Russell Taussig, Sidney Robbins, William Hamilton, Richard R. West, Amos A. Jordan, Gale Merseth, and Lloyd R. Vasey.

Many business executives and public officials played a vital role in articulating the special features—the pluses and minuses—of Small Town, U.S.A. Of course, Debbi and Randy Fields deserve special recognition. Others who offered important contributions included Arthur C. Clarke, Gary Hamlin, Frank P. Popoff, Rich Long, Ian Bund, Ted Doan, Joseph Stewart, John V. Evans, Sr., R. V. Hansberger, Dirk Kempthorne, James B. Greene, Samuel H. Crossland, Shirl C. Boyce, Phillip M. Barber, Bill Bridenbaugh, Brian M. Powers, Gerald R. Rudd, Gary Michael, Velma Morrison, Mary Schofield, Jon Miller, J. Duncan Muir, Trudy Morris, Robert Sutton, Susan Barnes Piegza, Robert Ady, Robert Matsui, Jadene Anderson, Karen Clark, Angie Dorsey, Peter Brockett, Anthony Nightingale, Calvin Reynolds, James Makaweo, Jim Morris, Martin Jackot, Kem Lowry, Bill Grant, Fred Sexton, Charles M. Leighton, Hiroshi Yasuda,

Beverly Nagy, Jay Pilon, Al Neufeldt, Richard Dahl, Ken Smith, James Maloof, Ivan West, Gill Butler, Donald Fites, David Lewis, Ronald Bonati, Ronald Schild, Charles Jett, Steve Waldhorn, Loren Romano, James Strachan, Vincent Yano, John McGrath, David Pellegrin, Paul Sturm, Herbert Cornvelle, David Bess, Gerald Coffee, James Johnston, Michael Schmicker, Kipling Adams, Jr., Kenneth Bentley, Phil Norris, Harriet Yamamoto, and Marion Morimoto. My heartfelt thanks goes to this special group of people.

Parts of this book appeared in the *Journal of Business Strategy*. My thanks go to Nancy Pratt and her colleagues for permitting me to incorporate these earlier pieces. My efforts were also influenced by a number of excellent writers who allowed me to cite their work with appropriate attribution. They include Jack Lessinger, John Herbers, Robert Fishman, Kenneth T. Jackson, David L. Birch, Alan Farnham, Donald L. Kanter, Philip H. Mirvis, John Naisbitt, Patricia Aburdene, Roberta Brandes Gratz, Bernard Wysocki, Jr., Anthony DePalma, George D. Hack, William Dunn, Anita Manning, Rushworth M. Kidder, Jane Jacobs, William H. Whyte, Robert Reinhold, Frederick Rose, Anne Taylor Fleming, Spencer Rich, David C. Walters, Louis H. Masotti, L. J. Davis, Rebecca LaVally, Charles C. Mann, John S. McClenahen, William Safire, Rosabeth Moss Kanter, Tom Peters, Cindy Skrzycki, Daniel H. Kehrer, Thomas A. Stewart, Claudia H. Deutsch, James O'Toole, Max DePree, Kenneth Labich, Marj Charlier, Dennis Farney, Griffin Smith, Jr., Sue Shellenbarger, Susan Chira, Hugh Sidey, Ross Atkin, Robert Levering, Jody Keen, Lori Sharn, Michael J. Weiss, Tom Furlong, Raymond C. Miles, Steve Lohr, and Michael J. Weiss.

For his editorial assistance, I am particularly indebted to William Sabin. His keen interest in the subject boosted a flagging writer with renewed enthusiasm. Ted Nardin, Barbara Toniolo, Alison Spalding, Wayne Smith, Charles Love, Kathy Gilligan, Olive Collen, and Jane Palmieri were also most helpful. My longtime friend Joseph Poindexter clarified and polished my early ideas and offered considerable support. Sandy Bodner helped bring the book to market. Sharon Kamada's competence, diligence, and unfailing good cheer through successive typings of the manuscript contributed greatly to its completion.

Finally, I am most grateful to my wife, Nery, and our sons, Eric and Marc, for their continued support and personal sacrifice during the past four years. Their patience and perseverance during my periodic bouts of hibernation enabled me to finish this book.

David A. Heenan

1
Overview

To Sinclair Lewis, Sherwood Anderson, and other early twentieth-century observers of the American scene, small towns were spelled "hicktown," "the sticks," or "the burgs." They were insular places, provincial, boring, and small-minded places, from which any youth with ambition absolutely had to escape. Serious careers, the argument went, could be forged only in boisterous urban centers smugly nicknamed "the Big Apple," "the Hub," or "the Windy City."

Today, however, these ideas are absurdly outdated. Executives are discovering that dynamic businesses can be run from relatively remote hamlets. My research of several hundred U.S. corporations shows that location does not have a negative impact on earnings. In fact, many of this country's most famous corporate names built their reputations in "the sticks." To illustrate:

- Wal-Mart Stores Inc. (Bentonville, Arkansas), the nation's biggest retailer, has consistently been ranked the best managed in its industry by several major business publications. The company has made its cofounder, Sam M. Walton, one of the wealthiest people in the United States.

- J. M. Smucker Company (Orrville, Ohio) commands an impressive 38 percent market share of the jams and jelly business, far ahead of its next competitor, Welch's, which has 12 percent. The 94-year-old company has parlayed a small family-run business into a $407-million-a-year public company.

- Caterpillar Inc. (Peoria, Illinois) dominates the world market for earth-moving equipment. From its home base in the heartlands, Cat has successfully rebuffed the competitive forays of Komatsu, Fiat, and

1

other foreign multinationals. The $11-billion giant consistently appears among the nation's top 10 exporters.

- Herman Miller Inc. (Zeeland, Michigan), repeatedly named by *Fortune* magazine as one of the "10 most admired U.S. companies," is an industry leader in design—the Eames chair and Chadwick modular seating are Miller products. Despite spending twice the furniture industry average on research and development, it has ranked seventh among major U.S. firms in total return to investors over the past 10 years.

- L. L. Bean Inc. (Freeport, Maine), the legendary mail-order retailer of hunting and camping equipment, generated sales of approximately $600 million in 1990. So successful has its catalog business been that the 79-year-old company boasts its own zip code.

These companies are proof that businesses can thrive in the boonies. Increasingly, small towns are serving as fertile environments for U.S. industry. How and why this phenomenon is unfolding as well as its implications for corporate America are the subjects of this book.

Outward Bound

Glorification of big cities prevailed for the better part of this century. Even as recently as 30 years ago the notion that small cities and towns might evolve into serious commercial centers was considered unthinkable, even heretical. Entering the 1960s, however, managers began to question the conventional wisdom that wedded companies and careers to the metropolis.

Not surprisingly, rising costs were the impetus for this reappraisal. The economic burdens of big cities had begun to take their toll on corporate America where it hurt most: the bottom line. Pressured by rising global competition, U.S. companies operating in big cities were faced with some hard questions: Can we afford to pay $50 a square foot for office rent and $11 an hour to people who clean floors? Can we continue to attract top-notch employees if up to 40 percent of their gross incomes will be devoted to housing? Can we compete in the world economy with workers who have graduated from substandard high schools where dropout rates often exceed 35 percent? For more and more businesses, the answer was "No."

Solutions to the difficulty posed by cities seemed close at hand. By fleeing just beyond the city's limits, firms could secure the advantages of metropolitan living without its costs. From 1960 to 1990, an astonishing two-thirds of U.S. *Fortune* 500 companies headquartered in New York City left town. Typically, their destination was the neighboring greenbelt of upstate New York, New Jersey, and Connecticut. Similar migrations took place in Chicago, Philadelphia, Detroit, and San Francisco.

Suburbs, for their part, welcomed these industrial migrants. Corporate headquarters not only replenished a community's tax coffers but also provided precious white-collar jobs. So town fathers across the country went on fishing expeditions for corporations. Their bait: industrial revenue bonds, tax abatements, and zoning changes.

Their efforts helped spawn the corporate boomtowns that border America's principal cities. Lower Fairfield County, Connecticut, was the first headquarters community to result from urban flight. At one time, it was the third-largest seat of *Fortune* 500 headquarters. Other locales followed: Tysons Corner, Virginia, west of Washington; King of Prussia, Pennsylvania, northwest of Philadelphia; Plano, Texas, on Dallas's northern outskirts; and Oak Brook, Illinois, near Chicago's O'Hare Airport. These and other suburbs have evolved into burgeoning communities, gleaming with contemporary architecture, that rival and often surpass traditional inner cities as centers of economic power and vitality.

They have not gained their new stature without cost, however. Companies and their employees are experiencing many of the frustrations they thought they had left behind. "It's not a big city, but it's beginning to feel like one," is a frequent lament of those who have moved to suburbia. As populations bulge, local roads become congested, landfills overflow, and once-superior schools lose their luster. The demands on public services give rise to an infuriating string of tax hikes. Affordable housing, too, quickly dries up.

Ironically, the cost advantages that originally spurred the move to the suburbs have also almost disappeared. Recent surveys by the Metropolitan Consulting Group, a relocation and real estate affiliate of the Metropolitan Life Insurance Company, found that the office operating costs of 20 major cities were not even 10 percent higher than those of their suburbs—so a savings in operating costs would probably be offset by the expense of a relocation. "Generally, you can no longer justify moving out to the suburbs for cost alone," says L. Clinton Hoch, Metropolitan's president.

Disenchantment has emerged on both sides of the bargain. As living costs soar and public services suffer, the suburbs have turned from friendly to frosty toward incoming businesses. Many local governments are calling for a halt—or a sharp limitation—on economic development.

Corporate America's next frontier? Out of town, all the way! Look for more and more farsighted businesses to leapfrog the megalopolis—and in one dramatic move settle in grass-roots America.

Greener Pastures

During the past 20 years, the United States has experienced a historic shift in population trends. The nation is seeing more people move to semirural areas than to urban areas. In the Northwest, West, Midwest, and Southwest, Americans are seeking more space and affordable housing, less congestion and pollution, reduced crime rates, better public schools, and stronger community values by moving away from the highly populated metropolises to smaller cities and towns.

Between one-third and one-half of the American middle class will live outside metropolitan and suburban areas by 2010, according to Jack Lessinger, professor emeritus of real estate and urban development at the University of Washington. "The first migration," he says, "was north and south with the first colonies, between 1735 and 1846; the second was west to the Mississippi–Ohio River valley towns, between 1789 and 1900; the third was from the country to the cities, between 1846 and 1958; the fourth, beginning around 1900, was from the cities to the post-World War II suburbs." The fifth migration is to what Professor Lessinger terms "penturbia": "small cities and towns, and subdivisions, homesteads, industrial and commercial districts interspersed with farms, forests, lakes and rivers." These outback areas, lying beyond the normal commuting range of the nation's central cities, represent the new American dream.

Penturbia carries many names. Some label the next wave of cities and towns with various adjectives: *new, free-form, edge, spread,* or *fringe.* Others call them *exurbs, slurbs,* or *ruburbs.* Although each moniker has its own subtle differences, urbanologists generally agree on three points. First, penturban communities have personalities of their own; they don't depend on a major city for jobs, shopping, or entertainment. In that regard, traditional definitions of "metropolitan" and "nonmetropolitan" are not helpful in explaining this phenomenon. According to most official census takers, a *metropolitan area* includes a central city of at least 50,000 people, with other cities and towns economically tied to it. Nonmetropolitan areas are rural, beyond the suburbs. However, distinctions between "metropolitan" and "nonmetropolitan" are hollow. What's more, the Census Bureau has changed the definitions of these terms with little regard to their characteristics. *Penturbia,* the experts agree, embraces metropolitan, nonmetropolitan, rural, and semirural communities.

Second, demographers believe that penturban growth will not result in the urban and suburban creep that typifies today's metropolitan areas. For these reasons, John Herbers, author of *The New Heartland,* describes the penturban phenomenon as "anticity, quite different from that of the established suburbs, which for all their sprawl, grew in close relation to the cities."

Third, urban watchers contend that penturbia represents the next wave of population growth. Recent U.S. Census Bureau data confirm that Americans are spilling out from traditional cities into the penturbs, as young people seek affordable housing or older folks migrate toward retirement communities near the mountains or seashore areas. "One of the great national stories of the 1980s is the continuing development of exurban areas," says Alan Heslop, a professor of government at California's Claremont McKenna College. This trend, he predicts, will extend well into the next century.

Two misconceptions about the present trend should be cleared up. First, it is not a repopulation of the hinterlands. The so-called rural renaissance of the 1970s was definitely misnamed. It reached its zenith about 15 years ago but never significantly changed the mix of city and small-town residents in this country. Today, many rural areas are bleeding. In 1950, about 44 percent of Americans lived on farms and tiny towns. That number has declined to about 23 percent. Consequently, backwaters with names synonymous with "Nowheresville" are not about to take off. The Great Plains has been abandoned; little remains of the twentieth-century homesteaders gone bust. "America's Ethiopia" is how some observers describe the Mississippi Delta country. Equally sad are the decimated mining and lumber towns in the West and the bankrupt textile communities in the South. Much of rural America remains in a rut, with large chunks of it resembling a kind of domestic third world.

Second, the flight to penturbia should not be confused with the back-to-the-land movement of the 1960s and 1970s, when many Americans sought solace in the cozy confines of rural living. The current revolution is being instigated by ambitious, career-oriented professionals. They are searching for a serious business environment where the daily tasks of living—work, getting to work, and leisure—can be simple, easy, and fun. They want it all: the stimulation of a first-class job with the ambience of a simpler lifestyle.

The ability to control lifestyle environments is a major driving force behind the appeal of the new corporate frontier. People desperately want to influence the quality of their public schools, the character of the open spaces, the caliber of local services, and more. They believe that small, low-density cities and towns offer the best potential for making a difference. Therefore, many Americans are *downshifting*—heading for the hills, the plains, the exurbs in search of communities where they can have an impact.

What we are seeing unfold is the selective preference for penturbia, particularly for those medium- and small-sized communities capable of providing the career opportunities and social amenities normally associated with big cities and suburbs. The most favored frontier towns are often linked to a major university, a state capital, a research park, or a similar institution that tends to provide the diversity and cultural spark sought by young professionals.

Typically, these cities are outlying townships of 200,000 or fewer people that are located at least 50 miles from a major city. We used to derisively call them the "boondocks," but any definition is highly personalized. It is largely a matter of perspective, measured more in terms of attitude than size or distance.

To die-hard San Franciscans, Oakland is miles away—spatially and economically. "It's in the boonies," many Bay Area loyalists would argue. By the same token, Staten Island might as well be on the far side of the moon to sophisticates from Manhattan Island. Staunch Back Bay Bostonians speak derisively of the Cradle of Liberty communities of Concord and Lexington as "the sticks." Southern California's car cultists, on the other hand, consider any Podunk town that is within driving range of a full tank of gas to be part of the Los Angeles galaxy.

Our frontier cities and towns carry a small "f." Independent of the nation's metropolises and large enough to have evolved a cultural identity of their own, they are places more akin to Colorado Springs (Colorado), Santa Fe (New Mexico), and Charlottesville (Virginia) than to Big Arm (Montana), Big Foot (Illinois), and Bow Legs (Oklahoma). They are locales where the best restaurant in town is not named McDonalds; where bingo, choir practice, and snipe hunts are not the high points of the day; where the one-room schoolhouse and the country doctor have long since disappeared; and where diversity is not only tolerated, but encouraged. Cities and towns small and somewhat isolated? Definitely. But hickish and clannish? Absolutely not.

Winds of Change

From a commercial wasteland a few decades ago, many midtier locales are winning the respect of big business. The odds makers had all but counted them out. It would take a miracle, the experts said, to reverse the steady decline of the hinterlands. But miracles, on occasion, do happen. Those miracles are the result of sweeping societal changes in the direction of the decentralization and demassing. They include the democratic revolution, the technological revolution, the minimalist revolution, and the revolution of corporate culture.

The Democratic Revolution

A revolution is sweeping the world—a revolution of democracy. There is a global loathing of centralized control, from the city streets of New York to Moscow. "Out" are closed, centralized, monolithic bureaucracies; "in" are open, decentralized, sleek organizations.

From Budapest to Beijing, socialist countries—starved for technology, capital, and goods from their capitalist peers—are becoming unlikely laboratories for free markets. Ideology has given way to pragmatism. Contempt for democratic capitalism has been replaced by envy. No longer do socialist hard-liners associate open democracies with trigger-happy imperialists or repressive dictatorships. Consequently, grand notions of a class struggle with the bourgeois have been eclipsed by a new set of concerns: creativity and innovation, access to the latest technology and training, and efficient business enterprises. To an increasing number of nations, the future lies in democratic reforms.

The force of this democratic revolution has shaken the communist world to its foundations. Eastern Europe and, more begrudgingly, the Soviet Union are discovering that economic and political freedom are closely connected. Despite its stops and starts, the manifesto of *perestroika* continues to wrest basic authority for economic management and decision making away from Moscow's central planning organs and hand it over to the 48,000 enterprises that make up the Soviet economy.

An American version of *perestroika* has been unfolding for some time. Since the early 1970s, U.S. presidents have favored the dispersal of influence and power away from Washington toward the states and cities. Revenue sharing was a major part of Richard Nixon's New Federalism, which in the early 1970s gave states the money to carry out their new authority. Every subsequent administration, Republican and Democrat alike, has reaffirmed its belief that local government is better equipped than Washington to assess needs and draw up programs on grass-roots issues. While pundits often disagree on how much of the federal pie, in fact, has been redistributed to states and municipalities, they concede that the axis of political power is tilting toward local government. Witness the rising number of congressional leaders abandoning Capitol Hill for gubernatorial or mayoral careers.

In 1990, former U.S. Senator Lawton Chiles and Senator Pete Wilson won the governorships of Florida and California, respectively. A few years earlier, Judd Gregg (R-N.H.), John R. McKernan, Jr. (R-Maine), and Carroll A. Campbell, Jr. (R-S.C.) retired from the House of Representatives to run for governor, while Congressmen Parren J. Mitchell (D-Md.) and Stan Ludine (D-N.Y.) set their sights on the lieutenant governorship. Another Capitol Hill expat: Bill Bonner, a five-term Democratic congressman, who gave up that seat in 1987 to become the mayor of Nashville, Tennessee.

What's more, the caliber of leadership in state capitals and city halls often outshines that in Washington. "Who are today's stars?" asks Congressman Robert Matsui, a California Democrat. "They're the governors—go-getters like Bill Clinton [Arkansas], Mario Cuomo [New York], and before them, James Blanchard [Michigan], Charles Robb [Virginia], and Bruce Babbitt [Arizona]—plus recent gubernatorial aspirant Diane Feinstein [California]." Besides, a governor or mayor "must take action," Matsui adds. "By the very nature of the job, there's nowhere to hide."

The imperative for action is paying dividends at the local level. No longer passive nebbishes, governors and mayors today are more innovative in their approaches to governing and raising revenues. They have taken the lead in trying to attract foreign investment, creating environmental and health programs, bringing in private concerns to help deliver public services, and raising money through lotteries and new taxes.

The democratic revolution carries over to America's public schools. The foundations of the current debate on educational reform emphasize the dispersal of power. Choice, school-based decision making, schools within schools, postsecondary school options, and decentralization are the watchwords of the new era. From Minnesota to Hawaii, Americans are dedicated to transferring power to those closest to children: parents, teachers, and principals.

People around the world are sensing that political, social, and economic issues are too difficult to resolve at center stage. Rather than crafting grand solutions at the traditional hub, government leaders are addressing these issues at the lowest possible level. They are diffusing power—institutionally, organizationally, geographically. This shift strengthens the case for smaller cities and towns—more so, when state-of-the-art technology is considered.

The Technological Revolution

Technology is the lubricant of the postindustrial machine, and its transfer to a widening band of nations has wrought some astonishing transformations. Take, for instance, technology's profound impact on the Tiananmen Square uprising. That revolt probably would not have occurred without facsimile machines and cellular telephones. Students in the People's Republic of China were constantly being bombarded with information and support from campuses across the United States. Reporters armed with mobile phones and satellite hookups informed the world of the tragic events of June 4, 1989. So worried was Beijing about the power and potential of this equipment that the government ordered its offices to intercept and hand over to authorities "reactionary propaganda" sent via fax.

Besides inciting democratic reform, the free flow of technology is permitting countries once excluded from the global economy to enter the fray. The tiny island state of Mauritius is a case in point. Remotely situated 500 miles east of Madagascar in the Indian Ocean, it is the boondocks personified. Nevertheless, this ministate has joined the economic big leagues. Aided by tax incentives and other enticements, Mauritius has attracted more than 200 foreign investors from Taiwan, India, France, West Germany, and many other nations. Hong Kong companies alone employ about 5000 Mauritians in 28 textile plants and represent the largest foreign investment in the country. The influx of foreign technology and know-how has made this tiny speck of land the world's third-largest exporter of knitwear—quite an achievement when you consider that there are no sheep on the island. As Mauritius demonstrates, no nation, city, or town with access to modern technology need be written off as an economic backwater.

Closer to home, technology is helping distribute economic power throughout the American landscape. Major advances in telecommunications are creating a footloose economy that permits firms to locate where they want to be, not where the traditional centers of finance and commerce dictate they have to be. In short, the economic deck is being reshuffled.

The nerve center of the new frontier corporation is an invisible web of advanced technology and telecommunications, including voice and video technology and video conferencing, that takes the place of the face-to-face contact typical in big-city businesses. What futurists John Naisbitt and Patricia Aburdene call "the new electronic heartlands" makes it possible for people to have the best of both worlds—a bucolic home in the outback with a technological link to major business centers. "For the first time in history," they contend, "the [geographical] link between a person's place of work and his or her home is being broken."

So taken with the merits of the new electronic heartlands were the two futurists that 5 years ago they purchased a palatial log cabin home in tiny Telluride, Colorado, in the southwest corner of the state. "Although we are 6 hours from Denver, with our computers, telephones, fax machine, and Federal Express, we are as in touch with the rest of the world as if we were in downtown London or Tokyo," argue the principals.

Indeed, this rustic mountain village of 1200 is setting its sights on becoming a high-tech haven. Local planners are laying the groundwork for a sort of space age community, known as "Mesa Z," which is expected to be twice the size of the existing town. "A fiber-optic network and a regional microwave system will be the components of a sophisticated information utility at Mesa Z," says Richard Lowenberg, an architect who is building a home in Telluride while he spends periodic bouts of time in an office in Sonoma County, California. "It may sound far out, but we think of it [the information utility] as like the sewer system of the future." To date, trendy Telluride claims to have the world's highest concentration of Apple and Macintosh computer users. Like other high-tech penturbs, it is the direct descendant of the decentralized "biotechnic city"—a place where nature and the machine live in harmony—that Lewis Mumford idealized 50 years ago.

In addition, the technological revolution has triggered an "atomization" of the U.S. economy that bodes well for the new corporate frontier. What David L. Birch, president of Cognetics, Inc., a management consulting firm based in Cambridge, Massachusetts, calls "the hidden economy" consists of over 7 million companies, approximately 90 percent of which employ fewer than 20 workers. These minnows of American industry, he asserts, have "created virtually all our new jobs since 1980, have grown rapidly, shown adaptability, and produced a large number of new products."

Penturbia is the preferred address for the many denizens of the hidden economy. Small, entrepreneurial firms tend "to flourish not around harbors, rail lines or interstate highways, but near universities, skilled labor pools, excellent telecommunications, and aesthetically beautiful places to live," says Birch. Consequently, the hidden economy is scattered across the countryside. "These rapidly growing companies are often located far from the declining companies they are replacing," he adds.

The Minimalist Revolution

For the better part of this century, corporate America worshipped at the altar of hierarchy. Verticality, scale, and power were all-important. After all, it was big business—Singer, Woolworth, Chrysler, and Sears, Roebuck—not a corps of idealistic architects, that commissioned the towering skyscrapers in the center city that still bear their names. These emblems of corporate might publicized American industry's lust for centralized command and control. Headquarters was the manor, the seat of ultimate wisdom and authority; operating companies, the lowly serfs.

By the 1960s, several factors began to signal the demise of the bigger-than-life head office. Foremost was the rise of global competition. With foreign products, well-made and well-priced, infiltrating U.S. markets, how many American companies could afford Pentagonlike bureaucracies? Very few.

Enter the minimalist corporation. Its basic tenet was that big was bad, especially at the head office. For a decade, U.S. firms slashed away at their headquarters staffs and cut deeply into middle management, at times eliminating entire levels. This bloodletting accelerated as companies discovered that they didn't have to provide a full range of staff services—or even line activities. When self-sufficiency came at too high a price, executives began to embrace the notion of "hollowing," "unbundling," or "disaggregating." American business rushed off to purchase such vital functions as manufacturing and marketing—and even the mundane tasks of typing and report production.

Efficiencies were also sought by forging strategic partnerships with other firms to share the costs of research and development, new product introduction, and other expensive staff functions. Corporations were willing to yield a degree of independence to reap the benefits of burden sharing. In addition, alternative employment concepts—job sharing, leasing, temporary help, telecommuting, and off-premises work—enabled firms to eliminate or transfer the weighty expenses of their central staffs.

The recent wave of mergers and acquisitions, takeovers, and leveraged buy-outs (called "LBOs") further stimulated the minimalist movement. Breakup prices of a diversified conglomerate were directly tied to the autonomy of its operating companies. Since stand-alone subsidiaries tended to enhance the value of the parent, there was added incentive to shift power and staff away from the head office to the business units.

Finally, dramatic improvements in information technology made the omnipotent command post obsolete. Commercial fax machines, cellular phones, overnight mail, teleconferencing, and corporate jets made communications so efficient that the full-blown headquarters became an industrial dinosaur. The evolution of the United States to an information-based society in which computer networks integrate teams of knowledge-oriented workers not only trimmed the corporate hierarchy, it flattened it. "The typical business 20 years hence will have fewer than half the levels of management as its counterpart today, and no more than a third of the managers," predicts management guru Peter F. Drucker.

Minimalizing, however, is misleading since it suggests a change in the quantity, not quality, of business organizations. Firms have discovered that "leaner and meaner" is not enough. To be successful, minimalist companies must encourage a radiation of power away from their "miniheadquarters" to the operating companies. This means recasting the headquarters-subsidiary relationships in terms of a partnership.

In the new organizational galaxy, management by trust replaces management by control. There is no divisible quantum of power in the minimalist enterprise. Losses on one side do not represent gains for the other. The shift in the nature of command simply lessens the head office's traditional condescension toward its operating companies. No longer is the center viewed as Rome; the periphery, as Pompeii.

Taken together, these forces gave rise to corporate America's love affair with minimalism. Who can argue with the benefits: lower overhead expenses, less bureaucracy, faster decision making, smoother communications, and greater entrepreneurship? With so much to gain, it is no wonder that hierarchy and size are the newest villains of U.S. industry. Small is beautiful, at least where headquarters is concerned.

Naturally, as firms streamline, their head offices become far more footloose. Minimalist employers know that it is far easier to transfer 200 people than 2000. In a poll by *Fortune* magazine, 73 percent of chief executives of the "500" said that they had relocated some facilities between 1985 and 1990, and 81 percent expected to relocate facilities in the future. One in seven said that they planned to move home base itself. Looking ahead, we should expect more, not fewer, corporate defections. And the penturbs are well-positioned to attract these wandering souls.

A decade ago, frontier cities and towns were an idea whose time had not come. Proximity, concentration, and size were everything. Under minimalism, all that is changing. "Something big is going on in the real America that most Americans who live inside urban beltways are missing: proximity is losing power," says celebrated columnist William Safire. With the new minimalist mindset, faster communications, and better market information, firms can operate effectively outside the mainstream. Witness the recent record of companies that fled New York City for supposedly isolated suburban locations. There has been little or no falloff in vital information or supporting services.

There is another benefit in locating the corporate headquarters away from major metropolitan areas. Distance reduces the risk that the head office will become overly immersed in the day-to-day affairs of the operating units. In today's decentralist world, companies prefer to take a hands-off approach with their local operations and to retain control of strategic issues at the miniheadquarters.

The Revolution of Corporate Culture

Ironically, business's rush to downsize and compress the organizational pyramid unleashed another powerful set of incentives for frontier living. What corporate America viewed as a vital process in the restoration of its global competitiveness was interpreted by others as the ruthless elimination of thousands of dedicated and hardworking careerists. Undoubtedly, the minimalist revolution stirred up deep-seated feelings of hostility and contempt for U.S. business. As a sign of the times, Donald L. Kanter and Philip H. Mirvis, authors of *The Cynical Americans*, found a dramatic rise in skepticism and cynicism toward private enterprise, particularly among the younger generation. Several other studies reached similar conclusions.

Enlightened employers must counter this cynicism and discontent. This means drafting a new social contract that regains the trust and confidence of the work force. The challenge of the 1990s is to forge a new kind of corporate culture—one that combines the efficiencies and flexibility of minimalism with important collective values: teamwork, participation, egalitarianism, and caring.

In our opinion, the cultural revolution that is unfolding is decidedly paternalistic. However, it should not be likened to the bygone era of the company town. Gone are the days when a supposedly benevolent employer could dominate every aspect of employee life—from shopping at the infamous company store to living in substandard company housing. The neopaternalism of the 1990s is far less intrusive. It seeks to redefine a proper balance between work, family, and community needs while regaining the trust and confidence of a shell-shocked work force.

Historically, small-town employers have been pacesetters in forging this kind of culture. Firms like Wal-Mart, Caterpillar, and Cummins Engine have spawned a communitarian ethos in which cooperation and caring are in everyone's best interests. Indeed, most penturban companies blend the strength of family ownership with the loyalty and trust of a committed work force. In many respects, these companies closely resemble the much-heralded Japanese corporation. They deserve close attention.

To sum up, the winds of change in the direction of demassing and decentralizing are stimulating the new corporate frontier. These winds signal a major transformation in both the nature and the location of corporate power. They are galvanizing the business community to reappraise its traditional habits and habitats—and to search for better alternatives.

The American Odyssey

The portrait, then, is of America in transition, in the middle of an odyssey—an odyssey that began 3 decades ago with corporate flight from the center city to the suburbs and that continues today to the penturbs. A steady trickle, not a cascade, best describes the out-migration process. Typically, it starts with small branch offices, research and development labs, and management training centers; next, come regional offices; and finally, prestigious corporate headquarters join the move. These newcomers, in turn, buffer the ranks of established enterprises as well as the recent start-ups that already call penturbia home.

As a practical matter, the gestation period to mold a solid nucleus of corporate luminaries is about 10 years—roughly the same amount of time it took Odysseus to reach Ithaca. To understand more fully the American odyssey, let us begin at the urban center.

PART 1
The American Odyssey

2
Bright Lights, Dim Prospects

Today, nearly three of every four Americans live in metropolitan areas—a percentage slightly less than Germany's (82 percent) and the United Kingdom's (80 percent) but somewhat more than France's (70 percent) and Spain's (59 percent). Still, urbanologists are divided over the future direction of America's cities. Some predict an economic resurgence of inner cities and the corporate commitment to them. Others, seemingly in the majority, forecast a steady exodus from the traditional cities and observe that, for the first time in American history, cities have been growing at a slower rate than the suburbs and some rural areas; these experts even suggest that the United States is destined to become the first postindustrial country without important cities.

Litany of Woes

What has been happening to the metropolis might best be described as the longest deathbed scene in history. "Taken individually, America's cities have been stagnating for a long time now," says famed urbanologist Jane Jacobs. However, the plight of urban America worsened considerably in mid-1980s. As a result, the present litany of big city woes includes:

High Costs

Many metropolitan areas have priced themselves out of business. In today's competitive world environment, U.S. firms must explore every possible avenue to reduce their overheads. J. C. Penney Company, Inc., the nation's third-largest retailer, had this in mind when it relocated 3000 employees from New York City to Plano, a suburb of 128,700 that is 19 miles north of Dallas. Costs were a major factor. Plano office space rents for $17 per square foot a year versus $47 in midtown Manhattan or $28 in Los Angeles. Consequently, Penney expects to save $60 to $70 million a year. Mobil Corporation, for its part, projected a $40-million saving by trading 42d Street for suburban Fairfax, Virginia, a few years ago. Other big-city expatriates report similar benefits.

Equally daunting are the costs, financial and psychic, for employees. According to a recent survey of the nation's 278 largest cities by the National League of Cities, affordable housing is their number one concern. In New York, Los Angeles, San Francisco, and Boston, a two-bedroom home typically costs double or triple the national average. So companies must fork out big bonuses and housing subsidies to persuade their employees to remain in or to relocate to these high-cost areas.

Crime and Drugs

Despite President Bush's $10.2-billion war on drugs, fewer than 10 percent of the nation's cities report making headway. Public officials in 58 percent of U.S. cities claim that drug problems have actually worsened in their areas. Besides, over half the murders committed in America's five biggest metropolitan areas are drug-related. The vicious cycle of what National Institute of Justice's former director James K. Stewart calls "crime causing poverty" is responsible for the gigantic increase in urban drug sales, burglaries, auto thefts, and—ultimately—murder, which now stands at an all-time high. In 1990, for instance, more than a dozen large cities broke their serious crime records.

What unnerves people most is "the unpredictable randomness of urban crime," says Adele Harrell of the Urban Institute in Washington, D.C., citing "the unexpected victims of drug wars and the random hostility of the homeless." Intoxicated by crack and crystal methamphetamine, youth gangs—the Bloods and Crips in Los Angeles, Chicago's Black Gangster Disciples, Miami's Peoples Nation—wage war in Beirutlike combat zones. Vandalism and rowdyism are not confined to the ghetto, as they were in former times. Even the best addresses fall prey to this insidious strand of urban terrorism.

Health Care

The eighties also introduced the epidemic of acquired immune deficiency syndrome (AIDS). The deadly virus severely strains the caseload burden of most inner-city health-care facilities, which are disproportionately saddled with the costs of AIDS patients. Approximately 10 percent of U.S. hospitals treated 58 percent of AIDS victims in 1987, according to a report of the National Public Health and Hospital Institute of Washington, D.C. Downtown hospitals today are barely able to provide general care for the burgeoning number of AIDS sufferers and drug-related emergency cases—a distinct worry for any company headquartered in the central business district.

The Homeless

Another predominantly 1980s phenomenon is homelessness. Big cities are unable to cope with the legions of folk who have come to their bosoms for food and shelter. The U.S. Conference of Mayors reported that three-fourths of 27 cities surveyed turned away hungry people and homeless families because of the growing demand and meager resources. The mayors further noted that incidence of alcohol and drug abuse in the homeless population jumped to 44 percent in 1989, from 34 percent the previous year.

Education

In New York, Los Angeles, Chicago, Detroit, and many other metropolitan areas, between one-third and three-fifths of students fail to complete high school. Furthermore, according to a recent study of the Carnegie Foundation for the Advancement of Teaching, 5 years of educational reform in the United States "have largely passed by our most deeply troubled school systems in large cities." Illiteracy, drugs, pregnancy, and violence continue to reduce high schools in the inner city to the vast wasteland depicted more than 30 years ago in the movie *Blackboard Jungle*.

Unfortunately, big-city firms must draw on the graduates of this ill-prepared labor pool for their sustenance. The results are tragic and could worsen. Metropolitan banks, for instance, are able to accept only one of every 25 to 40 recruits, while big-city telephone companies find that fewer than 5 percent of job applicants are able to pass the most basic prescreening test. This may explain why only one in three urban teenagers is in the labor force—half the national average. Unless inner-city schools change their ways, U.S. industry will continue to give the metropolis a failing grade.

Traffic and Smog

In 1975, 40 percent of urban roads were congested; today, close to 75 percent are. The worst commutes? Houston, New Orleans, New York,

Detroit, and San Francisco—in that order, says the U.S. Department of Transportation. Every day, travelers to and from most big cities confront clogged freeways and grueling delays. Many commuters report that they are exhausted by the time they get to work—and that their productivity suffers because of it.

Poor air quality is the sorry companion of urban gridlock. Americans today are more environmentally active than earlier generations. They are legitimately troubled by the threat that air pollution poses to their health. Sensing these concerns, the federal government has imposed strict limits on smog-causing pollutants, to be in place before the year 2000. But as a practical matter, an estimated 30 to 45 major cities will be unable to comply with these standards, according to the U.S. Office of Technology Assistance. Hence, the prospect of continued coughing and wheezing is pushing more and more people to clean-air locations beyond the urban fringe.

Fiscal Troubles

More than half the cities in the United States are spending more than they are taking in, according to a National League of Cities survey. A score of municipalities are too impoverished to repair their run-down subway systems, roads, bridges, and schools. Many downtown areas are experiencing a hemorrhaging of companies, jobs, and tax revenues. This depresses residential and commercial property values, which further erodes the tax base. Nervous bankers, in turn, tighten their lending limits, while tough-minded credit agencies downgrade the bond ratings of budget-troubled cities. Eventually, public officials must either reduce spending or raise taxes—or do both.

Will city hall confront these tough choices, or will urban America become the oil patch of the 1990s? The outcome affects all our lives. "Today, so many American cities are stagnant and in economic decline that stagnation and decline are acknowledged to be 'national problems,'" bemoans Jane Jacobs. To gain further insight into the myriad of these socioeconomic ills as well as the future of the big city as a business hub, let us examine urban America's twin towers: New York and Los Angeles.

Not Mad about Manhattan

New York City remains the nation's largest city, a title it has held since the first census in 1790, when it had 49,401 residents. The city that novelist B. J. Chute once called "a constantly changing extravaganza" now reflects the collective depression of 8 million souls. For Harry Smith, cohost of CBS's *This Morning*, the situation is so bad that he recently warned viewers to stay away from New York City, calling it a "Calcutta without cows." National news organizations like *Time* magazine also highlighted the city's decline with a widely circulated cover story on "the rotting of the Big Apple."

For many, the fiscal crisis that troubled the city in the 1970s was the touchstone of the urban crisis. New York was barely able to claw its way back to financial recovery—thanks to modest federal support and the robust economic conditions of the early 1980s. However, 17 years after its near bankruptcy, the Big Apple faces a new financial crisis. Gone are the job growth and real estate development that triggered a 12-year economic comeback. Gotham's official budget gap is projected to be $3 billion, and rating agencies are downgrading the city's creditworthiness. Estimates range up to $5 trillion as the amount of money it would take to bring the Big Apple back up to par.

The financial community is short-selling New York City—with good reason. Almost every corner of Gotham shows evidence of decay and upheaval: crime, illiteracy, and homelessness; drug abuse and AIDS; crumbling public facilities and substandard schools; at-risk youth and gang wars; racial intolerance and hostility; and exorbitant costs of living and doing business. A *Time*-CNN poll of 1009 New Yorkers found that 59 percent would live elsewhere if they could; 37 percent would stay. The city is dangerous, said 73 percent, and 50 percent agreed that you "must be a little crazy" to live in New York.

The most famous Big Apple boosters openly concede the city's steady deterioration. "There's a qualitative difference today," laments investment banker Felix G. Rohatyn, who, as chairman of the Municipal Assistance Corporation during the 1970s, helped rescue New York City from bankruptcy. "There is no part of the city where the quality of life is acceptable. It's not civilized to consider yourself lucky when you've been mugged but haven't been killed." Rohatyn's remarks were made shortly after his wife encountered a crazed purse snatcher. Even William H. Whyte, a man in love with New York, admits: "I am very scared of the city. I've been mugged twice." Echoing the *Time*-CNN results, he adds: "You've got to be crazy to live in Manhattan."

Drug-related crime is pushing the nation's largest city toward anarchy. The average age of first drug use by New York addicts is 12, and drugs infect the overwhelming majority of criminal offenders. In 83 percent of arrests, suspects tested positive for drugs. The Big Apple had a record 1905 homicides in 1989, and its murder rate for the first 6 months of 1990 was exceeded only by Washington's. "The streets have turned into shooting galleries," says Thomas Reppetto, president of the Citizens Crime Commission of New York. "Crime is tearing at the vitals of this city and has completely altered ordinary life. Worst of all, it is destroying the morale of our citizens." Indeed, some Gothamites are dressing their children in clothes made of bullet-resistant Kevilar. Also available: bulletproof schoolbags, clipboards, and briefcases.

Seeking a respite from this modern-day Dodge City, writer and television journalist Barbara Howar recently fled to Shotwell, North Carolina. "Every New Yorker, native or otherwise, knows to look over a shoulder at all times," she recalls. "Dead bolts have become a way of life." The dead bolt mentality is most pronounced in the ghettos that seem to invade more parts of the city daily. In Harlem, the black and Hispanic quarter of Manhattan, 70 percent of high school–age youths are dropouts, 80 percent of babies are illegitimate, and young black males in New York City have a lower life expectancy than the general population of Bangladesh does.

"Hell in a very tall place" is how Camilo Jose Vergara described a subset of the permanent underclass living on New York City rooftops. "Contrasting with the panorama of the city are the sights that greet a manager who told me that he visits those roofs in the early morning: he sees a line of men defecating alongside a wall and others sleeping nearby," Vergara wrote in the *Atlantic Monthly*. "In this, the richest of cities in the richest of countries, in buildings of advanced late-twentieth-century technology, men who own nothing sleep under the open sky on a windswept roof 300 feet above the ground."

This social maelstrom is souring corporate America on the Big Apple. A joint study by Louis Harris & Associates and Cushman & Wakefield, Inc., found that New York ranked dead last among 36 cities when measured by the top five factors influencing a head office move: large or more functional space, more room to expand, favorable image, occupancy costs, and proximity to homes of senior corporate executives. According to a recent survey of Runzheimer International, Gotham is the hardest location to sell to businesspeople—by almost a 2 to 1 margin over the next city (Los Angeles). In addition, one-half of all transfers to New York City are rejected, compared to 25 percent 2 years ago. For those who can afford it, the preferred choice is to leave town. According to the Household Goods Carriers' Bureau, which tracks the business of the city's six largest moving companies, 12,000 more customers moved out during 1988–1990 than moved in. Obviously, Americans are not mad about Manhattan.

Nor is the future outlook rosy. "Cities are going to experience increasing difficulties because of drugs, crime, and the aging of the population," predicts Kenneth Rosen, director of the Center for Real Estate and Urban Economics at University of California at Berkeley. The real loser of the 1990s will be greater New York, he adds.

Trouble in Paradise

For years, Los Angeles was America's sunrise; New York, its sunset. The only big city in the industrial world that is still growing rapidly, L.A. is expected to challenge the Big Apple for population supremacy by 2010. "Greater Los Angeles has become America's true 'second city,'" claim Charles Lockwood and Christopher B. Leinberger. "If present trends continue, and if nagging problems don't overwhelm the metropolitan area, Los Angeles might even emerge as the Western Hemisphere's leading city in the early twenty-first century."

From the start, America's first "suburban metropolis" violated the traditional pattern of metropolitan growth—a high-density central business district surrounded by leafy suburbs. In Los Angeles, "the single-family detached house escaped from the periphery to become, paradoxically, the central element in the structure of the whole city," says Rutgers urban historian Robert Fishman. Indeed, the outward sprawl of the metropolis, which began 40 years ago with the suburban development of the San Fernando Valley, may soon embrace townships over a hundred miles away.

L.A.'s assault on verticality carried over to its business organizations. Southern California's frontier spirit and wide open spaces have encouraged the formation of small, entrepreneurial companies rather than bulky corporate hierarchies. Los Angeles remains, first and foremost, a haven of "burgeoning entrepreneurship and confident self-expression," write David L. Kirp and Douglas S. Rice in the *Harvard Business Review*.

From Rodeo Drive to Jefferson Boulevard, wheeler-dealers flit around town doing deals from Porsches equipped with cellular telephones and fax machines. Their labors have made L.A. the home of more of the nation's fastest-growing businesses than any other metropolitan area. The relatively staid business practices of the East and Midwest would not be at home here; play-it-safe strategies don't work in "Lotus Land." The heroes of this center of glitz and glamour are the entrepreneurs, who live and die on their ability to innovate and market new ideas to the world. For years, these values protected Angelinos from the economic entropy and urban decay of New York and many other older cities. Paradoxically, the qualities of toughness, innovativeness, and risk taking may be why only 17 *Fortune* 500 industrial companies have built their headquarters in the greater Los Angeles area.

To be sure, the City of Angels surpassed San Francisco as the West Coast's financial center a decade or so ago. Even banks that still have their head offices in the bay area, like the Bank of America and Wells Fargo, have shifted many of their operations to the L.A. region. Today, the city houses 18 *Fortune* 100 diversified financial institutions (mostly savings and loans). In addition, there are about 130 foreign banks in Los Angeles (second only to New York), while eight of the nine biggest Japanese car manufacturers have their North American headquarters in the area. But by and large, L.A. evolved as a small business mecca: 95 percent of its firms have fewer than 50 employees.

Until recently, the L.A. business climate was almost as sunny and mild as its Santa Monica beaches. During the 1980s, however, Southern California's golden image became tarnished by a series of spiraling problems: overcrowding, poor schools, warring gangs, high-cost housing, polluted air, and overcrowded freeways. In large part, the automania that nurtured Southern California's sprawling growth gave rise to its recent decline.

When it comes to cars and parking, Los Angeles is a veritable *Guinness Book of World Records*. The freeway capital of the United States has 36,000 parking meters, 250,000 parking signs, 40,000 intersections, 3700 traffic lights, and 6500 miles of streets. The yearly traffic toll in Los Angeles County, where there are 6.5 million vehicles for 8.6 million residents: 485,000 hours of wasted time; $507 million in lost productivity; and 72 million squandered gallons of gasoline. Assuming continued road construction delays, the average commuting time will hit 2 hours by the year 2010, up from 45 minutes now. By then, the average travel speeds will slow from 35 to 19 miles per hour; more than half of daily travel time will be spent at a dead stop.

Angelenos sometimes go to ridiculous extremes to avoid the city's infamous traffic snarls. A number of hassled business travelers plop on board American Airlines' regularly scheduled, 17-mile flight from Long Beach to L.A. International Airport. The intracounty hop, which takes less than 10 minutes, avoids the toil of heavy freeway traffic. The fare: $85 for a round-trip ticket.

For less adventurous souls, Los Angeles's overcrowded roadways bring another danger: the most polluted air in the country. On two out of three days, at least part of the metropolitan area violates federal air quality standards. Smog hovering around the San Gabriel Mountains is killing once-profuse gardens of oleander and jasmine. As a result, city legislators are introducing a series of tough antipollution laws. One such law requires employers of more than 100 workers to introduce plans to have only two of every three people drive to work. Another mandates that 70 percent of the trucks and 40 percent of the cars in the area convert to such cleaner fuels as natural gas, methanol, or electricity. Despite these new measures, L.A.'s air quality is expected to deteriorate further over the balance of this century.

Then, there is the shambles of public schooling. In the 1960s, the Golden State was one of the top spenders on education. Today, it ranks in the bottom decile. Only 32 percent of California's tenth graders go on to graduate in their senior year. But unlike most big cities, L.A. is experiencing an increase in its school-age population—at a rate of 14,000 students per year. Because of overcrowding and a shortage of classrooms, area children must attend classes year-round—many in facilities that are not air-conditioned.

A related dilemma: the assimilation of ethnic minorities. In 1960, whites made up 90.3 percent of the population of Los Angeles County; in 1980, 53 percent; and in 1990, 41.6 percent. New Americans, primarily Hispanics and Asians, will continue to assume a greater role in the city's future. "Los Angeles," predicts Richard Weinstein, dean of architecture and urban planning at UCLA, "will be the first American metropolis of the third world."

To date, the integration process could hardly be described as smooth. "Los Angeles really isn't a melting pot," says Jack Kyser, chief economist of the L.A. Chamber of Commerce, "It's more of a stir-fry wok, a mosaic of dozens of ethnic communities that don't assimilate." This wave of immigration strains an already sorry school system: Eighty-two languages must be taught in the Los Angeles Unified School District. According to UCLA researchers, L.A. is the second-most-segregated metropolitan area (after Chicago) in the nation.

This pattern of segregation, isolation, and alienation is largely responsible for the crumbling, graffiti-plagued infrastructure that characterizes many Los Angeles neighborhoods. The result is a core of poverty that is common to so many American cities. "Increasingly, the sociological skyline of Los Angeles looks like a nighttime vista from a police helicopter: a glow of wealth on the horizon and poverty beneath," writes Frederick Rose of *The Wall Street Journal*. Contemplating the city's future, Allen J. Scott, a UCLA geographer, says: "It could be a Dickensonian hell."

Angelenos have a keen sense of this hell. A 1988 Rand Corporation report on local attitudes found that 58 percent of area residents believed that the quality of life had eroded over the past 15 years. A majority of respondents were concerned that there would be a further deterioration in the 1990s, and nearly half of those surveyed dreamed of moving somewhere else. Indeed, some experts predict that 860,000 people will leave the metropolitan area during the next 20 years.

Today, in fact, more Americans are moving out of greater Los Angeles than into it. Statistics show that 40 percent of expatriating Angelenos are returning to states of their birth. As is typical of other exurban shifts, the migrants are the better-educated, white and black members of the middle class.

Cracks are also beginning to appear in the business community. In recent years, many defense, aerospace, and general manufacturing activities have left Southern California for other parts of the country, for lower wages, looser environmental regulations, and friendlier commutes. Lockheed Corporation, for instance, is moving almost all of its aircraft production in Los Angeles County to Georgia. David Hensley, an economic forecaster at UCLA, says that, by the year 2000, the departure of companies and workers could be a flood. If this is true, the flood could spell "trouble in paradise."

A Short-Lived Urban Renaissance

Starting in the early 1960s, New York, Los Angeles, and many other metropolitan areas began to show new vitality. Mayors, nervous about the rising competitiveness of the suburbs, embarked on major redevelopment programs to reinvigorate the downtown and waterfront areas. Business leaders, for their part, supported city hall. Indeed, sparkling skyscrapers, convention centers, malls, and sports complexes typified the urban renaissance. Boston, Baltimore, and Philadelphia led the way on the Eastern Seaboard; San Francisco and Seattle, in the West. "City officials learned from their early mistakes with urban renewal, replaced shrinking federal aid, and acquired the entrepreneurial skills to cut deals with developers," says MIT professor Bernard Frieden. "Corporate leaders reportedly incapable of looking beyond a short-term bottom line not only bucked the prevailing suburban trend but put time and money into a campaign for downtown that lasted 30 years."

However, not all the hustle and bustle promoted long-term urban health. In the case of New York City, "the visible manifestation of economic growth became more important than the quality of life, particularly after the fiscal crisis of 1973," laments Carole Rifkind, an author and urban critic living in Manhattan. Mindless overdevelopment, particularly of skyscrapers, led to the gentrification of once-interesting neighborhoods.

By the mid-eighties, the so-called great urban revival had stalled. With some exceptions (Pittsburgh, Baltimore, and Minneapolis), U.S. cities could not sustain the private-public sector commitment needed to compete with the suburbs and penturbs. In this regard, the urban boom was probably misrepresented. The supposed recovery, Peter Drucker claims, "was not a sign of health, [but] a signal of the beginning of the end of the central city."

The decline has been delayed by the recent influx of overseas investors. Approximately 20 percent of the first-class commercial office space in Manhattan is now in foreign hands—Canadians, Japanese, British, and Dutch, in that order. Three-fourths of the large downtown office buildings in Los Angeles are foreign-owned or foreign-controlled, up from 25 percent in 1980. Whether it is Mitsubishi Estate's $846-million purchase of New York's Rockefeller Center or Showa Corporation's acquisition of the Arco Plaza in Los Angeles, few heads turn at the news of another foreign takeover of urban real estate.

"Thank heavens for the Japanese!" exclaims George Rossi, general manager for sales and leasing at the World Trade Center in Manhattan. For a landlord who has seen occupancy fall from 98 to 93 percent, the increased Japanese presence is a blessing. By the end of 1990, close to 10 percent of the center's occupants were Japanese. But the figure is considerably higher when other Asian and European companies are included.

Laurence Simmons, a vice president at Prudential Long Island Realty in New York, contends that the infusion of foreign capital was badly needed because domestic companies such as J. C. Penney and Exxon had fled the city. Overseas investment "certainly calmed down the possibility of having a real downturn," he says. If there was a silver lining in troubled urban America, it was stitched largely by non-American hands.

Limited by their dwindling treasuries, city officials have resorted to cosmetic attempts to boost public confidence. New York, Los Angeles, Boston, and Miami, for instance, are telling their taxicab drivers: "Be nice!" The Big Apple, in particular, has a long way to go to reverse the legendary brusqueness of its crabby cabbies. Will dollops of civility training obliterate years of bad manners? Most locals think not. "It's a way of life to be rude here," said a bellhop at the Marriott Marquis Hotel in Manhattan when asked about the program.

Americans remain cynical that cities can put on a kinder, gentler face. They know that the quality of urban life is in serious disarray and has been for some time. As we shall see, the transition of the United States from an industrial- to a knowledge-oriented economy further obliterated any serious prospect of an urban renaissance.

Two Worlds, Moving Apart

Cities once served a vast cornucopia of humankind. They blended rich and poor, privileged and deprived, for the better part of the twentieth century. Downtown areas were important value-added centers during this era of urban ascendancy. Manufacturing dominated the inner city, and industrial work offered opportunity and advancement to Americans of every color and class.

However, with the emergence of the postindustrial society, manufacturing employment steadily shifted from the inner cities to Sunbelt states and foreign countries. New York City jobs in manufacturing dropped from 22 percent in 1969 to 11 percent today. Since 1989, the Big Apple has lost 21,000 manufacturing jobs; since 1979, a whopping 326,000. In Los Angeles County, the number of manufacturing jobs slipped to 866,000 in 1990, from a decade high in 1987 of 914,000. Professor Saskia Sassen of Columbia University believes that many urban problems today are the result of cities being transformed from manufacturing and industrial economies to those based on service- and knowledge-oriented work.

Without a strong manufacturing base, a metropolitan area loses its cushion of economic and social diversity. The weakening of a city's industrial muscle makes it difficult to weather a downturn in its other mainstream businesses. Witness, for instance, New York's recent problems caused by the slowdown of its financial services sector. Equally important, a stockpile of blue-collar jobs in industry provides the first step on the upward-mobility ladder. The service sector, on the other hand, has not afforded the same career opportunities for the poor, especially recent immigrants.

Certainly, the demise of urban-based industry exacerbated the social disintegration in many big cities. Neighborhoods were decimated as millions of skilled middle-income workers and their families fled to the suburbs for comparable jobs, decent schools, and affordable housing. "The mass of [the] middle class—the great proportion of people that had sustained the cities—had simply gone, as had the factories that saved generations of poor from despondency and despair," says John Herbers. In the wake of this exodus, the central city found itself without the human skills needed to master the demands of a knowledge-oriented society.

Between Scylla and Charybdis

The loss of manufacturing and industry polarized the urban landscape. In short order, our big cities became "hypersegregated," a term demographers Douglas Massey and Nancy Denton use to describe the widening disparity between the rich and poor in New York, Los Angeles, Chicago, and other big cities. For example, in 1960, families in New York City had 93 percent of the median income of families in the suburbs. By the mid-1980s, that figure had fallen to 55 percent, a trend that was observed in many other metropolitan areas.

Of course, affluence and poverty always coexisted in the metropolis, but never more visibly than today. The downtown skyscraper symbolizes the stark contrasts of urban society today. "Lives of the upper executive classes are lived on one level," says David C. Walters of the *Christian Science Monitor*. "The poor in the slums live on another."

Urban apartheid is destroying America's big cities. More than a third of urban blacks and a quarter of Hispanics live below the official poverty line (about $6000 in annual income for a single person). Almost half of the low-income households that rent their homes spend 70 percent or more of their paychecks on apartments and utilities. And yet one in four urbanites resides in housing that is officially classified as inadequate. City children suffer disproportionately; more than a quarter of them fall into the "poor" category.

The plight of the impoverished contrasts sharply with the prosperity of upper-income families living in the metropolis. In New York, the 10,000 most affluent households pay almost 25 percent of the city's personal income taxes. Among the daily reminders of inequality: private schools, nannies, limousines, second homes in the country. Thus, a major dilemma of the big city: how to deal with the reality of a permanent underclass living amid general prosperity.

Aggravating the apartheid problem are the large number of middle- and upper-class Americans who elect to live in the suburbs and work in the city. For many of them, urban poverty and inequality might just as well be happening on another planet. Many metropolitan areas are becoming what UCLA's Allen Scott calls "biogeneous" societies, two polarized levels increasingly abandoning—and abandoned by—the middle class. A central reason older cities cannot solve their many problems is that their destinies are affected by disinterested people living beyond the urban fringe. Our downtowns, more and more, remain cut off from the suburbs—and the talent that suburban residents might lend to education, housing, transportation, and other community and social services.

Firms headquartered in the central business district find it increasingly difficult to deal with the dualities of urban living. Formerly, middle-income white and black professionals buffered them from relatively contained pockets of poverty and despair. However, with the flight of the middle class to the suburbs and beyond, those in the executive suite now find themselves in direct and often hostile contact with the underclass. Walk along the once-fashionable boulevards of New York, Philadelphia, Chicago, or Detroit. The clash of cultures cries out. There is nowhere to hide, nowhere to escape the harsh realities of the disparity between the haves and have-nots—as well as the dangerous consequences that disparity breeds.

In simpler times, corporate bigwigs could also delegate the administration of city hall to a relatively efficient class of civil servants, with generally satisfactory results. This enabled CEOs to work in the city and live in secluded sanctums called Greenwich, Wellesley, and Hillsborough. However, the recent series of financial crises, each seemingly more severe than the last, called into question the ability, if not the integrity, of urban officials. Every major corporation is forced to decide: Do we want to participate actively in a long-term process of urban reform, or should we simply abandon these wretched problems for a new homesite?

Bright Lights, Big Exodus

The choice for more and more companies has been to move. For some time now, big business has rejected older, traditional cities for newer, more accommodating metropolitan and suburban areas. The Northeast's drawing power as the location for the headquarters of America's largest industrial companies has weakened steadily during the past 3 decades. The biggest loser: New York City. As the accompanying table indicates, 27 percent of the *Fortune* 500 industrial concerns called the Big Apple home in 1960, 23 percent in 1970, 16 percent in 1980, and just 9

Number of *Fortune* 500 Headquarters by City, 1960–1990

1960		1970		1980		1990	
New York	130	New York	117	New York	81	New York	43
Chicago	43	Chicago	39	Chicago	25	Chicago	22
Pittsburgh	22	Cleveland	15	Pittsburgh	16	Dallas	15
Cleveland	17	Pittsburgh	15	Stamford (Conn.)	15	Houston	14
Detroit	13	Los Angeles	13	Houston	12	Cleveland	13
St. Louis	13	Philadelphia	11	Los Angeles	12	Pittsburgh	12
Philadelphia	13	Milwaukee	9	Dallas	11	Atlanta	9
San Francisco	11	St. Louis	9	St. Louis	11	Los Angeles	9
Los Angeles	11	Detroit	8	Cleveland	9	St. Louis	9
Toledo	6	Minneapolis	8	Minneapolis	8	Minneapolis	7
Dallas	6						

percent in 1990. Indeed, New York's defections read like a *Who's Who of Corporate America:* Exxon, Mobil, J. C. Penney, Kimberly-Clark, American Airlines—and more.

Gotham did not suffer alone. Chicago, Pittsburgh, Detroit, and Philadelphia also fared badly, losing about half their major hometown companies. The victors? Principally the Sunbelt cities Dallas, Houston, and Atlanta.

Nevertheless, it would be inaccurate as well as naive to describe this passing of corporate power as a battle of city against city. For some time now, the suburbs have been the biggest winners in the corporate migration war. The first major company to flee New York City was General Foods Corporation, when it relocated to White Plains, New York, in 1954. Ten years later, IBM moved out—to Armonk, New York. Since then, the floodgates opened to a variety of surrounding townships in New York, New Jersey, and Connecticut.

The exurban movement extends beyond the Big Apple. Almost half of greater Chicago's 44 *Fortune* 500 companies are based in its suburban corridor. The Windy City's most recent defection: Sears, Roebuck & Company, which is shifting its 6000-employee merchandising group to Hoffman Estates, Illinois (pop. 44,761). Similarly, the Big Three automakers are moving more and more of their strategic functions to the leafy likes of Troy, Warren, and Auburn Hills, Michigan. Furthermore, most of Dallas's alleged victories have been won by suburban Plano, Richardson, and Irving.

The inclination of U.S. firms to shift their command centers from older, bigger cities to increasingly newer, smaller ones is contrary to conventional thinking. The traditional theory of corporate evolution suggests that, in their embryonic years, firms often put down their roots in the hinterlands. Eventually, they are forced to flock to the metropolis for its sophisticated banking and support services. As William H. Whyte, author of *City: Rediscovering the Center,* put it in 1989: "Small companies need access to a wide range of specialized services and people. They cannot have this in house. They are not big enough. They cannot have this in some isolated location. They need to be in the center—or as close to it as rents and space permit."

This formula no longer applies. State-of-the-art technology makes relocation to remote locations possible. "If you have a good fax machine and a decent airport, it doesn't matter where you are," argues L. Clinton Hoch, president of the New York–based Metropolitan Consulting Group. "With the latest advances in telecommunications, a CEO can run his company from the moon—or Minnesota," adds *Fortune's* Alan Farnham.

In addition, the phenomenal out-migration of U.S. industry during the past 30 years dispels the former image of the head office as an immobile monolith. "Other than the utility companies and perhaps place-specific media companies like newspapers and television stations, virtually all companies today are actually or potentially footloose," says Louis H. Masotti, a professor of real estate at Northwestern University. "Such is the nature of corporate dynamics today." Besides, as U.S. firms continue to scale back the size of their headquarters, their mobility increases dramatically. This spells more bad news for big cities.

Cities Redefined

With the aid of modern technology, new locations are robbing traditional cities of their economic dominance. Even urban America's hammerlock on banking and commerce is weakening.

For years, big cities enjoyed special advantages as domestic and international financial centers. By *financial center*, we mean a money and capital market location whose participants (especially the financial intermediaries) have significant commercial relationships. It is an institutional hub that performs a wide range of services, including simple depository facilities, trade financing, currency exchange, and arbitrage. All such centers possess an adequate financial infrastructure, a favorable regulatory environment, freedom from confiscatory measures, and a strong historical role in trade and commerce.

New York City is especially blessed as a world financial hub, or so it would seem. Home of the New York and American Stock Exchanges, Gotham is the domicile for most of the money-center banks, large securities firms, insurance companies, and the U.S. head offices of foreign financial institutions. In fact, 60 of the 500 largest U.S. service corporations have their command posts there. In the financial world, "the center of the pork chop is still New York City," says George Sternlieb, professor of urban planning at Rutgers University.

Nevertheless, the Big Apple can hardly afford to rest on its laurels. Technology leader Citicorp has found that it can handle its credit card operations as effectively in Sioux Falls, South Dakota. New York Life Insurance Company is relocating a portion of its back office operations to Ireland. Merrill Lynch & Company has shifted almost 3000 financial jobs to three different New Jersey locations. Various divisions of Bankers Trust N.Y. Corporation, Paine-Webber Group Inc., and Donaldson, Lufkin & Jenrette Inc. have also left Manhattan during the past 3 years.

The real shocker, though, was the 1987 defection of Deloitte, Haskins & Sells to Wilton, Connecticut. The migration of one of America's largest accounting firms represented the first time a top financial services firm moved its headquarters out of an urban metropolis. In explaining Deloitte's reasoning, Vice Chairman Jerry Kolb said at the time that its employees would be "more creative and productive in a suburban setting."

In December 1990, Morgan Stanley & Company took an option to buy a piece of property in Stamford, Connecticut, that could be the site of its future headquarters. The investment bank began to seek zoning approvals that would permit such a move, while continuing to negotiate with New York City officials for special incentives. Morgan's tactics came on the heels of similar discussions that induced leaders of New York's commodity exchanges to spurn an attractive offer to cross the Hudson River to New Jersey.

Despite having fended off these defections, Gotham faces a serious challenge as the world's financial hub. "New York is no longer the single dominant international center it was in times past," says Renato Ruggieo, Italy's Minister of Foreign Trade. Several other cities in Europe and the Far East, he argues, are gaining in importance. Again, technology is the great equalizer. It makes it possible for financial-services businesses to be dispersed freely around the world.

"The whole notion of dominant financial centers became antiquated with the telecommunications satellite," contends John G. Heimann, vice chairman of Merrill Lynch and Company, Inc. Global communications enable securities concerns to spread their operations around the world, in order to find the lowest business costs, the most talented professionals, and the least hostile regulatory environment. Look for other cities—London, Tokyo, Singapore, and Hong Kong—to challenge New York's leadership in high finance.

Other U.S. cities have also seen their grip on a lifeblood industry wither away. Detroit, for instance, is no longer the stronghold of the automobile business. In 1941, the Motor City made 90 percent of the cars in the world. Only 25 years ago, it produced more than one-half the global supply. Today, "Motown" accounts for only about 17 percent of world production. Similarly, filmmaking and Los Angeles were closely linked for many years. At one time, Hollywood made 85 percent of the country's movies; today, 60 percent. The main beneficiaries of this "runaway production" are states like New York, Florida, North Carolina, Texas, and Illinois—that, ironically, advertise in the entertainment newspapers in L.A. and on the billboards hovering over Sunset Strip. Other municipalities that have been forced to shed—or share—their trademark industries: Hartford in insurance; Akron in tire manufacturing; and Pittsburgh in steelmaking. Such are the competitive realities of a postindustrial economy that pits nation against nation, state against state, and city against city.

The Shape of Things to Come

Throughout history, the average lifetime of our cities has been limited. Just recall the cases of the once great trading centers—the Hellenic city-states, the prosperous communities of Asia Minor, and in more recent times, Alexandria, Venice, and Genoa. To avoid becoming an endangered species, contemporary cities must begin to assume a different shape. But how?

For starters, the modern metropolis must take on functions quite different from those it once fulfilled. "In its present form," Peter Drucker argues, "the city has already outlived its usefulness." He predicts that center city may become "an information center—the place from which information (news, data, music) radiates." *The New York Times* urban watcher John Herbers also believes that metropolitan areas must concentrate on a much narrower range of activities: finance, communications, entertainment, and tourism. Today's cities are "specialized subordinate nodes in their overall metropolitan areas," says Herbers. Similarly, William H. Whyte foresees a redefinition of the city's historic role as a meeting place. "While the city has been losing functions (manufacturing, computer operations, and the like)," he says, "it has been reasserting its most ancient one: a place where people come together, face-to-face." But one wonders: Will the apartheid of urban America compromise its potential as a great meeting place?

The implications for government planners and business executives may be well worth considering. For traditional cities to survive, a broad base of community support must be present. The golden ghettos of the posh suburbs which adjoin New York, Chicago, and Detroit not only reflect business's inattention to the problems of inner cities but also offer highly visible targets to dissidents. Disaffected segments of any urban society simply will not allow corporate America, already the subject of intensive scrutiny, to promote such dual economies. For CEOs, too, unbalanced growth is bad business, for it detracts from the fundamentally positive effects of private enterprise.

In earlier times, a former era of a few farsighted executives took the lead in demonstrating the contributions that world-class corporations can make to urban development. David Rockefeller, Walter Wriston, and Henry Ford II, in particular, supported the construction of whole new urban environments in New York and Detroit. A similar breed of CEOs in Minneapolis, Pittsburgh, and Chicago also have made major commitments to rebuild their center cities. But they are the exceptions.

To poet Joel Oppenheimer, it is the indispensability of today's cities that reduces their human despair:

we here are always alone
every city alone in this country
which has never learned to accept its cities
every city on its own alone and doomed
born to lose written on its walls
yet here we stay in it and keep coming to it
we keep pouring ourselves in and out.

Still, indispensability alone is not enough. Cities must compete with a growing array of alternative habitats. "The advance of technology, the change from a manufacturing to a service- and information-based economy, and the accumulation of private wealth have made it possible for people and commerce to settle pretty much where they please," says author Jon Bowermaster. And make no mistake: we are highly mobile. The average American moves 11 times in a lifetime; nearly one-fifth of the population relocates each year. Accordingly, U.S. cities must respond to these trends or run the risk of committing financial suicide.

A Final Note

In describing Oakland, Gertrude Stein once offered words that remain a classic urban put-down: "There is no *there* there." A century later, Americans are applying the writer's comments to other big cities. They believe that establishing a "there there," or making a difference, remains elusive for most metropolitan areas.

What bothers Americans most is not so much the crime, pollution, and decay of the metropolis but their own inability—individually and collectively—to effect change. People want to reside in communities they can influence. For this reason, they are expressing their frustrations with their feet—moving farther and farther away from the traditional urban center.

3
From Suburbia to Penturbia

America's suburbs first bloomed outside New York, Boston, and Philadelphia in the early decades of the nineteenth century. However, bedroom commuting as we know it did not come into vogue until some time after 1900. Slowly, people began to flee the central cities—by horsecar, steam railroad, electric streetcar, and, more important, automobile. By 1929, such suburbs as Cleveland's Shaker Heights and Detroit's Grosse Pointe were 10 times as big as they had been a decade earlier, and Americans owned 27 million motor vehicles. The automobile society had arrived. "No other invention altered urban form more than the internal-combustion engine," said Columbia historian Kenneth T. Jackson.

The Great Depression and World War II temporarily stalled the outmigration of mobile Americans. By the mid-1940s, there was an enormous pent-up demand for housing. A generation of newly wed veterans, propelled by cars on federally subsidized highways and roads and financed with mortgages from the Federal Housing Administration and the Veterans Administration, migrated to the leafy borders of the city. "A frontier mentality prevailed," says Roberta Brandes Gratz, author of *The Living City*.

Were Americans racing *to* the suburbs or escaping *from* the cities? Urbanologists continue to debate this point. No doubt, the post-World War II exodus to the suburbs was driven, originally at least, by older cities' inability to cope with their growth and diversity. Urbanites were fed up with crime, overcrowding, dirt, high taxes, poor schools, and the like. The idyllic glades that dotted the outskirts of the big city bore few of these inhospitable conditions; they seemed a welcome refuge. Nevertheless, an equally powerful attraction was the distinctively American urge to own one's own home that suburbia represented. President Franklin D. Roosevelt sensed this when he remarked: "A nation of homeowners, of people who own a real sense of their own land, is unconquerable." In our opinion, the democratic ideal of securing an affordable home probably outweighed Americans' desires to avoid the hassles of urban living.

Thanks to Washington, low-density housing came within reach of the middle class. Private, detached homes were a good deal, and no one was better at proffering them than the famous real estate development firm of Levitt & Sons. These Pied Pipers of the Suburbs showed the way to the new life. For as little as $7900, John and Jane Doe could own an 800-square-foot box house in the greenbelt—an area once the exclusive domain of the upper-income and upper-middle-income class. Quickly, clones of Levittown, New York, and Pennsylvania, sprang up across the countryside. Shortly thereafter came the boom in road construction, automobiles, and shopping malls.

Little Kings and Queens

New shoots of suburban growth began to green economic fields throughout the United States. Most of the sprouts bloomed next to traditional urban centers of finance and industry. "Suburbia was the region of opportunity during the first half of the twentieth century, when millions of people presided as little kings and queens over their one-sixth acre domains," says Jack Lessinger. Their kingdoms, in fact, grew well past the century's midpoint. Between 1950 and 1970, American cities grew by 10 million people, while their outlying townships exploded eightfold. By 1970, the percentage of Americans living in the suburbs was almost exactly double what it had been in 1940, and more Americans lived in suburban areas (37.2 percent) than in cities (31.4 percent) or in rural areas (31.0 percent). By the end of the 1980s, suburbia's share of U.S. population had increased to 44.3 percent, compared with 31.5 percent for the city and 23.3 percent for rural areas.

Initially, these cozy enclaves were too regal, too exclusive, insulating their "little kings and queens" from the egalitarian values that most Americans had fought hard to attain. Minorities and low-income groups found it virtually impossible to cross the treacherous moat that separated the suburbs from the inner city. But slowly this changed. Black suburbanization became a major phenomenon in the 1970s as more minorities entered the middle class. By 1988, the proportion of suburban blacks to all blacks reached 25 percent. "Today, the suburbs are literally picking off the more successful blacks, and those who move are denying [the cities] their presence—and their taxes," laments political scientist Wilbur C. Rich of Detroit's Wayne State University.

With its newly acquired populist face, suburban America found it more and more difficult to accommodate the inflow of newcomers. Soon, land became too expensive to permit building the kind of housing that most middle-income people could afford. The only course of action was to widen the franchise fringe of the suburbs.

Across the nation, smaller cities and towns sprung up on urban perimeters. Rings of "urban suburbs" grew in concentric circles, forming a kind of Republican doughnut around the traditionally strong Democratic center city. This ringing, or widening, of the suburbs is sometimes called "exurbia," a term that refers to the scattered residential and commercial growth on the fringes of a city. In many instances, the outer rings remain closely linked to the urban core. Job allegiance is primarily to the big city, with residents trading off inexpensive housing for longer commutes to the metropolis.

Twenty-five years ago, New York City's commuter fringe cut across points of Long Island, Connecticut, and New Jersey at a radius of about 30 miles from the Big Apple. Later, the perimeter of the circle stretched to about 60 miles from Manhattan. Today, another ring—including Pennsylvania's northeastern border—about 80 miles from Times Square is on the fringe of New York's expanding metropolitan region. Lured by lower housing prices, growing numbers of New York and New Jersey residents are settling in dozens of small Pennsylvania communities stretching from the old mill town of Easton to the heart of honeymoon land in the Pocano Mountains. These hearty souls brave 2-hour trips into Manhattan each day.

The exurban movement is visible everywhere. In northern California, migrants are rushing inland to Solano County, northeast of San Francisco. "The pattern is a diffusion outward," says Elizabeth Hoag, city population expert for the state of California. The surrounding townships of Vacaville, Fairfield, Benicia, and Dixon represent the last affordable region in the Bay Area. Again, there is a heavy price to pay—namely, a murderous 50- to 70-mile commute to San Francisco. Similarly, the Lake Elsinore region southeast of Los Angeles is the fastest-growing part of the fastest-growing county in California, the so-called Inland Empire. Its primary draw: tract houses priced between $100,000 and $250,000. However, here too, residents must endure "supercommutes," 2-hour-plus drives to work in Los Angeles, Orange County, and San Diego.

Given these distances, most Americans living on the urban fringe naturally prefer to work closer to home. People lead, companies follow. That is the present direction of the exurban flow. "The trend now is for businesses to move where their employees are," says Sean Quinn, a city planner overseeing economic development for Fairfield, California, a growing city of 70,000 located 45 miles east of San Francisco. For instance, Anderson-Barrows Metal Corporation, which manufactures brass fittings for the plumbing industry, recently put up a major facility in Palmdale, California, on the edge of the Mojave Desert. "Many of my employees had already moved to the area [from greater Los Angeles]," says Chairman Dave Anderson. When the company opened its doors in Palmdale, there were 10 positions open; 1300 people applied. Therefore, one thing is clear: It is John and Jane Doe, not General Motors and General Foods, who cause the suburban envelope to be stretched.

Footloose home buyers are usually one or two steps—or rings—ahead of most employers. By the time a critical mass of companies has invaded a suburb, property prices are beyond the reach of the middle class. Prospective home buyers must then pick up and move to the next ring to find moderately priced real estate, despite a more difficult commute back toward the inner suburbs or the central city. Eventually, working folks rise up in anguish, clamoring for a stronger base of local employment. People who go to the fringes cause job creation; job creation causes more people to go there, says economist Michael Greenwood. Their demands, in turn, are forcing bedroom communities to become economically more self-sufficient.

For some time now, suburban officials have sought to secure their own store of *Fortune* 500 companies, beef up their cultural amenities, and build an infrastructure not unlike that of the metropolis. This process of "infilling" has led to the thickening of present-day suburbia. Actually, the malling of America began in the sixties, when town planners attempted to surpass the central city as a shopping mecca. And their efforts paid off. By the end of the decade, suburban malls had vanquished downtown department stores as the nation's retailing hubs. In addition, the evolution of sophisticated shopping centers conferred geographical cachet on the borderlands, says geographer Peter O. Muller of the University of Miami. "Suddenly, sleepy backwoods areas became fashionable."

Megamalls anchor today's multiringed suburb. Some 32,560 shopping centers, employing 9.4 million people, cater to what novelist Tom Wolfe calls America's "splurge generation." These self-contained monoliths include everything from K-mart department stores to full-blown amusement parks. "The trend toward regional mall proliferation—whether on empty cornfields or as replacements for downtown Main Street—is altering the American countryside and restructuring the national retail economy as significantly as mergers and acquisitions are altering the corporate landscape," says Roberta Brandes Gratz.

During this go-go period, big business began taking the suburbs seriously. Once the federal highway system was completed, companies had no incentive to remain in the inner city. "Any location on the expressway was just as accessible as anywhere else," claims Professor Muller. Initially, firms established smallish branch offices, data processing centers, and research laboratories on the borders of the big city. Shortly thereafter, the first major industrial and office parks appeared. By the 1970s, prestigious regional and national headquarters were also shifting to the suburbs, lessening the perimeter's economic dependency on the traditional urban core. Today, almost 60 percent of all new first-class commercial office space is being built in the suburbs.

With the influx of blue-chip companies, the urban fringe developed its own persona. It became part of a "complex 'outer city,' which now included jobs as well as residences," says Rutgers historian Robert Fishman. "Increasingly, independent of the urban core, the suburb . . . lost its traditional meaning and function as a satellite of the central city." Some suburbs even snipped away at the longstanding dominance of New York and other big cities as international business centers.

The Global Suburb

Consider the case of Coral Gables. Once a sleepy bedroom community in southern Florida, "the Gables" has become the "Gateway City to Latin America." Today, it houses the Latin American regional offices of over 75 multinational corporations, including Texaco, IBM, Dow Chemical, Rockwell International, and ITT/Sheraton, as well as the world headquarters of such diverse businesses as dance studios (Arthur Murray, Inc.), security systems (Wackenhut Corporation), and ocean cruises (Carnival Cruises and Norwegian American Lines). Add to the list the 71 foreign trade and consular corps offices, the 99 foreign banks, and 17 binational chambers of commerce in the Coral Gables vicinity. (The overseas banks include 32 Edge Act facilities, the largest collection found in any U.S. city, including New York.)

The story of Coral Gables began in the early 1960s with its city officials' concern about the serious decline in their major industry, retailing. In an effort to broaden the city's tax base, the Office of Community Development investigated several possible nonpolluting, service-oriented industries. But the model for the future lay right under their noses. In their search, the city planners stumbled across Jersey Standard's Latin American headquarters, which had moved from Montreal to the Gables in 1951. That one move appeared to offer a precedent for other multinationals, and a group of top business and civic leaders formed a committee to assist the Office of Community Development in marketing Coral Gables to other companies with significant Latin American interests.

The effort was successful. By 1967, Dow Chemical, Gulf Oil, and Coca Cola had joined Exxon. Since then, the most enthusiastic marketers of the city have been transplanted executives from companies that have moved there. Today, Coral Gables is actively seeking the Latin American headquarters of Asian and European multinationals. To date, the Bank of Tokyo, Hyundai, Panasonic, L. M. Ericsson, and Swedish Match oversee their South American operations from the Gables. This innovative suburb is also playing another variation on the theme by wooing the North American regional offices of Latin-owned corporations.

"We've barely scratched the surface of what we can do," says Catherine B. Swanson, the town's development director. Her office is currently working with 20 firms considering plunking down a regional headquarters in the Gables. In the years to come, an increasingly varied group of worldwide organizations are likely to be domiciled in this pleasant subtropical setting.

Why Coral Gables? Why not Miami? "There's only one reason," recalls J. William Cochran, former senior executive-in-residence for ICI United States, Inc. "Coral Gables went after the business." Ironically, the top officials in its Office of Community Development began their careers in Miami, where many of the initial concepts of building a headquarters city were developed. But Miami was unable to secure the necessary support for regionalism. Frustrated, its best urban planners moved to Coral Gables and won the support of this smaller, more cohesive community of 41,000. Once a nucleus of regional offices was established, Coral Gables never looked back.

To be sure, the ability of suburbs to make timely commitments to multinational corporations in an environment relatively free of the urban problems of budget deficits, decay, and crime gives them special advantages over traditional cities. However, efficient air transportation and communications links with the rest of the world are crucial for headquarters sites. Without an easy 10-minute drive to the Miami International Airport, Coral Gables would not have achieved its current level of success.

Seeds of Self-Destruction

Coral Gables continues to prosper, but business growth in suburbs nationwide began to level off in the 1980s. The more typical exurban experience has been one of false hopes and promises. The American dream of living in the borderlands slowly turned into the American nightmare of traffic-clogged commutes, unaffordable housing, rising crime rates, and marginal public schools. The blight is most visible in the inner rings of the multitiered suburb. There, many towns are encountering fiscal, educational, racial, and housing crises as severe as those that troubled major cities in the 1960s and 1970s.

Take poverty, for instance. Twenty years ago, a 4 to 1 income ratio separated the richest and poorest U.S. suburbs. Today, the ratio exceeds 12 to 1. More than 9.5 million suburbanites live in poverty, compared to 13.9 million in the cities. (Nationwide, approximately 32 million Americans are classified as "poor.") "Poor suburbs range from old bedroom towns in the East to the new barrios in the West," says Pierre deVise, an urbanologist at Chicago's Roosevelt University. Ford Heights, Illinois; Cudahy, California; Florida City, Florida; and Camden, New Jersey, are a few of the most destitute.

"Major twentieth-century problems can now be seen to have an important suburban dimension," writes Columbia's Kenneth T. Jackson, author of *Crabgrass Frontier*. The familiar process of ringing-infilling-ringing so urbanized many traditional suburbs that it afflicted them with the metropolitan malaise. More and more outlying areas acquired overbuilt downtowns of their own. White Plains, New York, "out-Manhattans" Manhattan; the Dallas–Fort Worth "multiplex" includes high-rise centers sprawling over 11 counties; 20 miles north of Atlanta, the once-rural communities of Marrietta and Rosewell are developing their own high-density skylines. In Southern California, Newport Beach, Irvine, and Anaheim have towering office buildings, sky-high rents, and traffic jams that rival anything in Los Angeles.

But the metropolitanization of the suburbs is probably the messiest outside Washington, D.C. Gridlock on the Capital Beltway resembles that on the highways around Los Angeles; rush-hour traffic jams are among the nation's worst. Fairfax County, Virginia, suffers especially badly. Its population surged from 174,000 in 1980 to 771,000 in 1989. In its midst sits Tysons Corner, which a short time ago was a country crossroads set in apple orchards. Today, it is the largest and sloppiest of Washington's suburbs, located 11 miles west of the central city.

Tysons Corner has evolved into a gigantic blob of jobs, stores, hotels, and housing. Its anchor is the sprawling, enclosed Tysons Corner Center, possibly the most successful large-scale shopping mall in America. The 1.9-million-square-foot facility lures shoppers into five department stores, 237 specialty shops, 21 restaurants, and two movie theaters—all plopped down on 90 acres of once-pristine Virginia countryside. The center's monumental success (its gross sales rank within the top 1 percent of the nation's malls) has led to another megaproject right across the road: the Galleria at Tysons II. Also, within 10 minutes' driving distance is 13 million square feet of commercial office space—more than Miami, New Orleans, or Boston can offer.

However, the most frantic activity in Fairfax County is farther out, in small towns like Herndon, Virginia. Once the heart of the hunt country, this ville of 15,000 people sits directly in the path of nonstop development. Like many other rural communities, it was blinded by the promises of go-go developers and entrepreneurs, who insisted that bigger was better. Local officials aggressively recruited several corporate headquarters, including Computer Sciences Corporation; the Airline Pilots Association; C3 Inc., a custom designer of computer services; and CH2M Hill, Inc., a technical services firm. To accommodate this growth, the town, which occupies just 4.25 square miles, added 4.25 million square feet of office space, with an additional 1.6 million square feet under construction or proposed. Today, Herndon is virtually out of space for additional growth.

Overdevelopment is poisoning Fairfax County's rural character. The main highways are clogged with traffic jams. The price of housing is now beyond the reach of many young couples. There are no longer enough workers to fill jobs, blue and white collar. Despite the corporate influx, taxes increase often, to pay for schools, hospitals, jails, courts, and other public services. Worried folks in bordering communities warn their public officials: "Don't Fairfax our little town!"

Curbing Suburban Growth

Understandably, residents of Fairfax County and suburbs across the country are shifting from pro development to pro environment. Many question whether their municipality can balance economic growth with the precious rural character it once enjoyed. One such critic is Benjamin Weiner, president of Stamford, Connecticut-based Probe International Inc., which advises multinational corporations on political risks. Writing in *The New York Times*, he decried the "corporate curse of southern Connecticut," the invasion of unchecked economic growth. "The sad reality is that the quality of life in this area has diminished perceptibly. . . . It's no suburban paradise. In fact, southern Connecticut is beginning to look a lot like New Jersey: traffic jams and street peddlers in Greenwich; overbuilding in New Canaan."

What suburban dwellers like Ben Weiner want most to avoid is the "Manhattanization" or "Los Angelization" of their communities. "There's a new political power base out there in suburbia that's hard to put your finger on, [but] seeds are being planted that will sweep the nation," says Mark Baldassare, a professor of social ecology at the University of California at Irvine. That force is the much-publicized "Nimby" (for "not in my backyard") movement.

Leading the naysayers' charge are the most recent migrants to the burbs. "Everyone who comes into Somers [New York] wants to be the last one here," says Robert L. Stuart, 38, who runs his family's farm in this peaceful burg in northern Westchester County. People who have just moved from the dirt and decay of the big city want in the worst way to fulfill their rural fantasies and legitimize the reason for their move. But when they discover that their idealized vision of suburbia bears little resemblance to the overbuilt maze of high-rise buildings, shopping malls, and expressways, they rapidly become disenchanted.

Long-term residents, on the other hand, tend to be split over the growth issue. Farmers hoping to unload unproductive land at inflated values favor development. So do other old-timers, who look to the immigrating companies and their employees to keep the public schools, libraries, transportation, and other services going. But over time, most people usually swing over to the Nimby camp.

The same public officials who once swooned over *Fortune* 500 companies are adopting a decidedly more hostile attitude toward big business. In 1990, overbuilt Fairfax County passed strict "downzoning" measures that restrict the amount of development on land zoned for commercial purposes. Local officials canceled national ads inviting high-tech firms to "the next Silicon Valley." Nowadays, "we do not advertise for outside expansion," says John E. Lynch, vice chairman of the Fairfax County Economic Development Authority. "We're taking care of our own."

Growth-control measures appeal to a wide range of local supporters, including liberals and conservatives, environmentalists, and urban reformers. Population-Environment Balance, Inc., a Washington-based environmental group, surveyed 1650 local communities across the country. One in five had instituted various land-use controls, and many said that they planned to blend in growth-management strategies soon, says Robert Gray, who conducted the study.

State governments are actively supporting these neighborhood naysayers. Whereas billboards in New Hampshire once welcomed newcomers, the popular sentiment today is: "Welcome to New Hampshire— Now Go Home." People in the Granite State, the sixth-fastest-growing state in the country, are now eager to preserve breathing space—absorb past growth and prepare for the future. State and local governments throughout the nation are getting a clear message: curb suburban sprawl.

Some states are responding. Florida has the strongest growth-management program in the country. Until recently, the Sunshine State had operated as a kind of free spirit where almost anything a suburban developer proposed was acceptable. When it came to planning and zoning, "we were the cow's tail of the nation," recalls John M. DeGrove, director of the Florida Atlantic University–Florida International University Joint Center for Environmental and Urban Problems. However, in 1985 the legislature passed the state's growth-management act, which requires cities and counties to file comprehensive development plans including standards for water, drainage, schools, police, roads, and other needs. The plans are then reviewed by the State Department of Community Affairs, which sends them back for revision if they are deemed inadequate. State funds for infrastructure can be withheld if the plans are not approved. Also under review is additional legislation to establish an urban-growth boundary around every metropolitan area in Florida—in essence, a dividing line between city and countryside that developers cannot cross.

The notion of limits has also reached California, where two of every three residents favored curbs on "the spread of urbanization into underdeveloped areas of my county," in a recent survey. State and local officials responded by enacting tough controls on a number of large projects, including Irvine and Rancho Santa Margarita in Orange County. New Jersey, Vermont, Rhode Island, Oregon, and Georgia also have passed far-reaching, growth-management restrictions on suburban expansion.

Many special-interest groups actively support the Nimby movement. Most prominent are the nonprofit, "friends" organizations that seek to balance conservation and development in their states. The first of these groups was launched in Oregon in 1975; similar units have formed or are forming in 14 other states. Another subset of Nimbys wants to protect American pastureland from encroaching suburban developers. There is legitimate cause for concern, since two-thirds of American farmland is on the fringes of metropolitan areas. In fact, the country lost 2.3 percent of its agricultural land from 1982 to 1987, continuing a steady decline that began in 1950. Over a year's time, this represents 1.5 million acres lost to development.

Belatedly, perhaps, the barricades are going up. Forty-six states have some kind of right-to-farm law, which protects the farmer from most legal action brought by expansion-minded neighborhoods. In 22 of these states, local governments can apply special provisions to restrict growth on agricultural land. More recent legislation in several states goes a step further, allowing state and local governments to pay farmers for not commercially developing agriculturally productive farmland.

Nimby groups as well as state and local governments often insist that they do not wish to stop suburban development but, rather, modify it. "Selective" or "productive" are their preferred adjectives for "growth." Nevertheless, the message is clear: The welcome mat for big business in the suburbs is slowly being withdrawn. "We're headed into an era where a lot of these major suburban growth areas will simply not grow any more," says Robert H. Gidel, managing director of Alex. Brown Kleinwort Benson Realty Advisors of Baltimore.

Today's congested suburbs are rapidly running out of rings, or space. The spread of expensive housing in many American fringe areas currently prevents middle-income people from finding affordable homes within an acceptable commuting range of their jobs. The alternative eventually becomes obvious. "When commuting becomes intolerable, the employee relocates his job or the employer relocates the company," says Regina B. Armstrong, a consultant at the Regional Planning Association, an independent research organization. The shortage of accessible, affordable housing is one of the great brakes on how much economic development can occur in a region, she adds.

Battering the Bottom Line

Limited space for expansion, overdevelopment, high taxes, and tight labor conditions are causing the vacancy rates of commercial property in the suburbs to exceed those in the downtown area. According to a national survey by Cushman & Wakefield, a real estate brokerage firm, suburban markets are posting vacancy rates that are 5 to 10 percentage points higher than in city markets. However, this has not made doing business in the borderlands any cheaper. As noted in Chapter 1, the Metropolitan Consulting Group found the differential between costs in the downtown city and those in the suburbs to be less than 10 percent—and the gap is narrowing.

In some cities, it may have completely closed. A recent study commissioned for *The New York Times* by Runzheimer International, a leading management consulting firm in Rochester, Wisconsin, showed that it actually may be somewhat less expensive to live in New York City than in the surrounding area. The firm drew similar conclusions for Washington, San Francisco, and Los Angeles. Rising labor costs are especially worrisome. More and more suburban-based businesses report severe difficulties hanging on to their good people. Employers argue that younger managers, stationed in the field, are increasingly reluctant to accept promotions to the head office, as living costs soar. Rather than engage in a dogfight to attract or retain workers, many firms find that moving out of the suburbs is the only feasible solution. Eleven percent of 190 companies in the Boston–Washington corridor or on the West Coast said that they were forced to relocate operations to meet their labor needs, according to a survey by PHH Fantus, the nation's largest relocation firm. Another 14 percent of the firms surveyed said that they consider relocation to be the best response to the tight labor market.

For example, specialty toolmaker Adamus Carbide Corporation moved from suburban Kenilworth, New Jersey, its home for 36 years, to Oak Ridge, Tennessee. There it was able to find a plentiful supply of skilled workers and professional staff. Other firms are adopting a similar strategy. "The brain drain to nice areas will begin to dominate decisions about where to grow," says David Birch of Cognetics Inc.

What, then, is the future of the modern-day suburb as a headquarters center? It is not rosy—unless these multiringed communities can find a cure to the most insidious strains of "the urban disease." That is unlikely, given the problems of Fairfax County, Orange County (California), and other fringe areas. "The basic concept of the suburb as a privileged zone between city and country no longer fits a posturban era in which high-technology research centers sit in the midst of farmland and grass grows on abandoned factory sites in the core," argues urbanologist Robert Fishman. "The history of suburbia has come to an end."

Even William J. Levitt, the octogenarian who practically invented the modern suburb, concedes that the days of living on the urban fringe are over. In the late 1960s the famous builder began hyping the need for "primary employment towns" in remote areas. As he envisioned them then, these penturban villages would not be bedroom communities but complete economic entities where people would have a wide range of jobs. "The key is employment," Levitt said. "I think at first they should be planned for populations of 50,000, though, of course, they would grow to different sizes." These new towns would be sponsored by private industry in conjunction with government. The concept "was valid then," he contends, "and it's even more valid now."

Levitt's futurist vision is taking shape today, albeit in somewhat different form. People looking for affordable homes, clean air, less crime, garden plots, play space for the kids—all with commuting distance of their jobs—have but one choice: penturbia.

Blighted Suburbs, Booming Penturbs

Cities and towns along the new frontier are converting more and more people to their way of life. In numerous opinion polls, Americans have confirmed their love of rural and semirural spaces and the small-town values exemplified in Norman Rockwell's canvases. In 1986, for instance, Gallup pollsters asked people where they preferred to live. "Given the opportunity," George Gallup, Jr., concluded, "almost half of the American adults would move to towns with fewer than 10,000 inhabitants or to rural areas." In 1990, the Gallup organization discovered similar opinions. Small towns were the preferred homesite of 34 percent of those interviewed; 24 percent chose a suburb; 22 percent picked a farm; and 19 percent favored a city. Four of five respondents lived in a metropolitan area. The polls' message remains unmistakable: A vast majority of Americans simply do not like large cities. Nor are they especially fond of large suburbs.

If we look at the demographics, population growth is largely in states with low-density development. According to preliminary projections published by the U.S. Census Bureau, the fastest-growing states in the 1980s were Nevada: 50 percent; Alaska: 35 percent; Arizona: 33 percent; Florida: 31 percent; and California: 24 percent. For the 1990s, the prediction is Arizona: 23 percent; Nevada: 21 percent; New Mexico: 21 percent; Florida: 20 percent; and Georgia: 19 percent. Fastest growth does not mean the most growth, however. Almost half the total U.S. increase for the rest of the century will occur in just three states—Texas, Florida, and California—which are expected to gain 9.5 million people. Of the 18.9 million new jobs expected to be created by the end of the century, 3.4 million will be in California. The country's Sunbelt bookends, Florida and California, are projected to add more than a million new jobs each.

Warm weather, wide open spaces, and good jobs—an unbeatable combination. It is why Americans continue to follow the sun. Four states—California, Arizona, Texas, and Florida—accounted for 63 percent of the country's population growth over the last decade. Indeed, Felicity Barringer of *The New York Times* reports that "at least 55 percent of Americans now live in the South and the West, up from 52 percent in 1980, and 48 percent in 1970. By contrast, only 20 percent of Americans live in the Northeast, down from 21.7 percent a decade ago, and 24 percent live in the Middle West, down from nearly 26 percent in 1980."

This also explains the viability of an elite group of midtier cities in the Sunbelt—among them, San Jose and Sacramento, California; San Antonio and Austin, Texas; Tucson, Arizona; Jacksonville and Tampa, Florida; and Charlotte, North Carolina. The U.S.'s fastest-growing city during the 1980s was Fresno, California, a farm town turned high-tech. It grew by 61 percent and has more than 350,000 residents. Despite their size and urban features, Fresno and other smaller Sunbelt cities still have streets that are remarkably residential, possessing a quiet, comfortable ambience. Places like these produce a better quality of life—less congestion, less pollution, less frustration. By contrast, almost every big city in the Northeast and Midwest lost people during the past decade; the only exceptions were Indianapolis, Indiana, Columbus, Ohio, and, because of the influx of immigrants, New York.

The real winners of the recent census were the Sunbelt and penturbia.

An interesting subset of population gainers were state capitals and university towns. About two-thirds of all centers of state governments, especially those in the Sunbelt, reported gains, as did educational hubs. Capitals that were both the seat of government and a state university— Madison, Wisconsin, Columbus, Ohio, and Austin, Texas, for example— far outstripped their states' growth. They beat out most traditional urban areas in population growth, as people were lured by everything from lower housing prices to sophisticated amenities. Let us consider in greater detail the ground swell of popular support for the penturban lifestyle.

Penturban Chic

Heartland values are definitely in vogue. *Business Week* recently declared Peoria "in" (along with babies and social commitment); New York (along with singles and materialism) was pronounced "out."

"These days the word 'country' means big business in American towns and cities," writes Elaine Greene of *The New York Times.* "Country sells clothing and fabrics, groceries and restaurants, house plans and home furnishings that range alphabetically from afghans to zinc-leaded dry sinks." Restaurant menus are rejecting nouvelle cuisine for Cajun cooking, Tex-Mex dishes, even meat loaf. Haute couture is also "penturban chic," highlighting bulky sweaters from Lands' End, the Dodgeville, Wisconsin, mail-order house, and children's overalls from Oshkosh B'Gosh of Oshkosh, Wisconsin.

Contemporary architects, too, are reshaping the American home to feature elements long associated with small town: welcoming foyers; generous communal kitchens; spacious living rooms centered around a fireplace; roomy attics; storm cellars; and perhaps a stone fireplace. In place of picture windows, sliding glass doors, and vinyl or aluminum siding are wood shingles, clapboards, and deep front porches like those that graced the quaint old homes of rural America. Unpretentious interiors accent warm woods, wicker, cane, and burnished metal pieces. Cozy rooms filled with flowery chintz and American folk art reinforce the contemporary country look.

Our reading habits also epitomize the national mood to re-create rural life. Hearst's *Country Living* magazine currently enjoys the most rapid circulation growth of any major American periodical. The word "country" appeared in the title of 10 different home magazines recently displayed at a large newsstand in the Pan Am Building in Manhattan. "Country was the hot category of the 1980s," said Scott Donaton, who covers magazines for *Advertising Age.* "Almost everyone we've talked to has said country would stay hot through the 90s." The success of country magazines, claim publishers and editors, is due to their ability to craft themselves as a nostalgic nostrum in an ever-cynical modern world.

Best-seller lists are another barometer of country's new magnetism. The commonsense genre of Reverend Robert L. Fulghum, Garrison Keilor, and Baxter Black reaffirms the sanctity of an ordinary, simpler lifestyle. What is sentimental drivel to some is a spiritually uplifting parable to others. The literary terrain of columnist Lewis Grizzard is also the commonplace, the small towns that remind us of the America of Fourth of July celebrations and the village green. To a growing segment of heartland readers, he is what Jimmy Breslin is to New York and Mike Royko to Chicago. Add to the list of small-town realists important writers such as Pat Conroy, Mary McGarry Morris, Carolyn Chute, Rick Bass, Bobbie Ann Mason, Richard Russo, and Larry McMurtry. Their message: The older values and symbols of small town, U.S.A., need not conflict with the faster rhythms of a postindustrial society.

The mood swing toward a penturban lifestyle suggests that many people in this country have a sense of the countryside that is comfortable and replete with solid family values. People are more prone than ever before to explore the prospects of living and working on the new corporate frontier.

Frontier Boomtowns

Beyond the outskirts of many U.S. cities, a cluster of penturban communities are on a rocket ride. In some instances, they were semiagricultural villages only a decade ago; in others, they are older towns, once the victims of hard times, that are making a comeback. To cite just 10 rising stars:

1. Naples, Florida. Completion of the I-75 freeway opened Naples (pop. 152,099) and surrounding communities on the west coast of Florida to an influx of Midwestern retirees. It was the nation's highest growth area in the 1980s. Located between Tampa and Miami, Naples has many attractions, including beaches, not-so-touristy towns, farmlands, and, believe it or not, the Everglades swamp. "We're getting a lot of people who are looking to escape the dense, overcrowded conditions on Florida's east coast," says Stanley Litsinger, Collier County's growth-management director.

2. Olympia, Washington. The state capital will be the fastest-growing metropolitan area of the 1990s, predicts NPA Data Services, a Washington, D.C., marketing firm. Quality of life is the major attraction of this high-flying community of 150,000. Olympia proudly boasts stunning landscapes, recreational bonanzas, clean air, and elements of bright lights, big city. These attributes helped place the city in the top 10 percent of *Money* magazine's "best places to live" list.

3. Princeton, New Jersey. Once a halfway house for commuters bound for New York and Philadelphia, this famous university town of 90,000 has forged its own identity. Princeton Park, Princeton South, and Princeton Pike form part of the infrastructure that has attracted a slew of major corporations. Superior schools, reasonable land, and the cultural benefits of neighboring Princeton University place this New Jersey township on many firms' most-favored list.

4. Portland, Maine. Located on the southeastern coast of Maine, this once-bustling shipbuilding center has become a regional tourism and financial center. With Bean Town only 100 miles away, Portland benefits from the "Boston ripple"—pulling in young professionals with its lower real estate and living costs. Pleasant streets lined with old brick and clapboard buildings, diverse restaurants and trendy shops within blocks of the harbor, and first-rate entertainment facilities attract people who value lifestyle over fat incomes. "We're crammed with doctors and lawyers who didn't want to grind it out in New York," says Pamela Plumb, a former city official of the 65,000-person community.

5. Manchester, New Hampshire. Until recently, the ancient redbrick textile mills lay dormant, covering this New England town with a shroud of despair. Today, these buildings house a cluster of high-tech companies, malls, and financial-services firms. The local airport, which was built in 1983 to accommodate 50,000 passengers a year, now handles 300,000. "We generate new small businesses better than anyone," boasts Jay Taylor, executive vice president of the Greater Manchester Development Corporation. Forty percent of the newcomers to this revitalized community of 115,000 are from neighboring "Taxachusetts"—the Granite State has no sales or income tax. (*Money* magazine recently ranked New Hampshire as the best "tax haven," followed by Florida, Alaska, Texas, and Nevada.)

6. Des Moines, Iowa. The capital city of the Hawkeye State claims to have the greatest concentration of employees in finance, insurance, and real estate outside New York City. This hub of regional banking includes financial institutions that account for assets of about $12 billion; 66 insurance companies are also situated there. "What we sell is a reasonably priced, well-educated labor force, and a pleasant lifestyle," says Donald

Doudna, the state's director of insurance development. To make relocation even more appealing, the Iowa legislature repealed the state's tax
on annuity premiums. But there is more to Des Moines than tax breaks.
Its famous civic center welcomes touring companies in all the arts and
well-known performers, including Mikhail Baryshnikov, Rudolf Nure-
yev, Itzak Perlman, and Iowa native Simon Estes.

7. Scranton/Wilkes-Barre, Pennsylvania. Located 20 miles apart,
these two cities are rapidly becoming the home of many large data processing shops—those of Prudential Asset Management, J. C. Penney,
and Nabisco, for example. Northeastern Pennsylvania has an ample supply of inexpensive housing, plus one of the nation's lowest crime rates.
With unemployment more than 6 percent, major employers also are un-
covering a large pool of highly qualified workers. Turnover among workers in the region is virtually nil.

8. Wilmington, Delaware. Farther south, this Delaware township
began to broaden its economic base a decade ago. Its target: the back-
office operations of New York's financial institutions. In 1981, the state
abolished the usury ceiling on credit card interest and fees and reduced
the tax rate on the net income of large banks from 8.7 percent to 2.7 percent. By 1989, 41 out-of-state banks—among them Chase Manhattan,
Citicorp, and Marine Midland—had relocated their credit card and
back-office activities to Wilmington. In May 1990, Delaware Governor
Michael N. Castle signed a law allowing banks to underwrite insurance
and sell it by mail across the country. Immediately, several banks announced their intention to open insurance operations in Wilmington.
    In the past decade, 12,000 new jobs were created for area residents.
"We had a mass exodus of many young people in the late 1960s and
1970s," recalls William Wyer, former president of the Wilmington
Chamber of Commerce. "Now, they're staying."

9. Fort Collins, Colorado. This Rocky Mountain magnet, nestled in
the eastern foothills of northern Colorado, is expected to nudge 95,000
in population by 1992. Established in 1864 as a military post to protect
incoming settlers from the mostly peaceful Cheyenne and Arapaho
tribes, Fort Collins is home for more and more companies. Kodak,
Teledyne/Waterpik, and NCR have set up shop in the area, along with
up-and-coming Vipont Pharmaceutical, makers of Viadent antiplaque
toothpaste, which has its headquarters in Fort Collins.
    The 35-square-mile penturb, averaging only 69 cloudy days a year, is
an outdoor paradise. The Horsetooth Reservoir, situated in the Rocky
Mountains' Front Range, is where Fort Collinsites go to water ski, fish,
and swim. Indoor types hover around Colorado State University and the

new downtown performing arts center, where a broad spectrum of cultural and entertainment activities is available. This miniboomtown, says John Herbers, is "tailor-made for the young people who have been entering the work force in recent years—the 'baby-boomers,' the 'yuppies,' those moved by Ronald Reagan's appeal to patriotism and optimism, those ready to abandon some of the philosophy and standards of older generations who would remember what life was like in the teeming cities and the Great Depression."

10. Peoria, Illinois. Jim Maloof, mayor of this oldest settlement in Illinois, gives visitors a mug painted with the names of the great cities of the world: "London, Rome, Paris, Peoria." "We can offer anything in Peoria that the big cities can offer," he says emphatically. "Besides, we have no rush hours."

Over the years, this community has changed its spots several times— from a hell-raising den of iniquity at the turn of the century to a Caterpillar-dominated town for 5 decades to a diversified, vibrant economy today. New industries focus on medicine, aerospace, the automotive parts market, and agricultural research. The Peoria Agricultural Research and Development Corporation has joined with the USDA Federal Laboratory and six private companies to help develop the community of 113,504 into a major biotechnology research center.

This once-dreary agricultural ville on the bluffs of the Illinois River has been rejuvenated. One of the town's proudest achievements is the $64 million downtown civic center which has an 11,000-seat arena and a 2200-seat theater. The city also boasts its own symphony orchestra (the tenth-oldest in the United States), ballet, opera, theaters, and minor league franchises in hockey and baseball. When asked: "Will it play in Peoria?" most observers agree that what is now playing in Peoria is prosperity.

Many other examples of the frontier renaissance could be cited. Hubs without the hubbub, communities that combine big-city amenities with small-town charm and friendliness, are winning friends in many corporate boardrooms.

Neotraditional Thinking

The pattern of penturban development is decidedly different from that of the traditional suburb. Rather than obliterating the small towns and villages in their path, these townships are preserving old landmarks and the essential character of their communities. One important catalyst: the Main Street revitalization program, launched 11 years ago by the National Trust for Historic Preservation. It encourages the renovation of old downtown areas across the nation. Aided by tax incentives, about 500 communities in the United States, with populations ranging from 5000 to 50,000, have spiffed up historic buildings, rekindled economic vitality, and invigorated their downtowns with a sense of vibrancy and fun. By doing so, many small towns have begun to entice businesses back to their Main Streets.

Nowadays, infrastructure concerns dictate where a lot of companies go. If moderately sized communities cannot serve moderate- to large-sized companies, they really don't have much of a chance of attracting corporate headquarters. Therefore, many penturbs, besides restoring their "old towns," are taking the lead in developing new business parks, highly flexible and packed with a multitude of amenities—day-care centers, lodging and entertainment facilities, jogging trails, lakes and lush landscaping—missing from postwar suburbia. These self-contained communities, or "minicities," foster a lively, people-oriented atmosphere. They are being "developed as a complete working environment, with entertainment, hotel services and physical fitness facilities that are carefully planned and aesthetically sensitive to their environment and natural surroundings," says George D. Hack, a senior consultant at Peckham Guyton Alberts & Viets. In addition, these minicities offer firms state-of-the-art technology ranging from digital switching and fiber optics to voice and data networks. Local planners know that sophisticated telecommunications centers are vital to attracting high-volume users in banking and financial services, data processing, research and development, government, and education.

Furthermore, the new frontier movement is stimulating a new breed of neotraditionalist architects. Their goal: to re-create the beloved American small town of the past in new communities that provide working families with services such as day care and communal dining. In doing so, the neotraditionalists seek to dispel the emptiness in American life and fill the void through community design. Some of the more prominent examples of their work are Mashpee Commons in Mashpee, Massachusetts; Seaside on the Florida Panhandle; Laguna West, 12 miles south of Sacramento, California; and Gaithersburg, Maryland, about 45 minutes outside Washington, D.C.

Unlike traditional planners, these bold thinkers are shaping the penturbs for people, not cars. Suburban parents, for instance, are often forced to log more miles on their cars than Mario Andretti does—chauffeuring their children from home to school to extracurricular events and back home. Such tasks disappear in these "enclave developments," where virtually everything—post office, banks, library, churches, and schools—is within a "pedestrian pocket," or convenient walking distance of the town center. As a result, these new towns are decidedly less sexist than the older suburbs that "restricted married women with children to a life of neighborhood-oriented domesticity," says Rutgers' Robert Fishman.

Through their architecture, the neotraditionals also seek to attract single or divorced people, single parents, young childless couples, and older "empty nesters," widows and widowers—groups long neglected by the sprawling suburb. The penturban township of the future offers a measure of community and security frequently lacking in urban and suburban living. Certainly, the communal instincts of these idealistic planners represents a major departure from traditional suburban living. "The neotraditionals are taking a giant step backward in order to move forward," says Todd Zimmerman, a Clinton, New Jersey, housing consultant. "They are going against every conceivable housing trend since the end of World War II."

By blending the old and the new, penturban towns—in either traditional or neotraditional form—are far more livable than the big city or suburbs. They offer access to nature and open space as well as many of the choices and amenities of the metropolis. Hence, their development strikes directly at urban and suburban areas, where the lifestyle is more frantic and the costs are higher. This explains people's growing preference for the new corporate frontier. But what does a community gain from attracting business headquarters?

Tangible and Intangible Benefits

No doubt, each township has its own reasons for stalking America's postindustrial giants. For some communities, economic incentives— more jobs, additional tax revenues, and greater industrial balance—are the primary spurs. For others, noneconomic considerations, such as cultural enrichment, social diversity, and intellectual stimulation, are more important considerations. However, among the more obvious benefits of winning corporate headquarters are the following.

1. Tax Revenues. Depending on size and composition of a company, the taxable wage bill of its headquarters staff may benefit a community anywhere from several million to a hundred million dollars. Somewhat less important are commercial property taxes. Of least consequence is the potential from corporate income taxes, since the profits of the typical corporation are earned either in its base of legal incorporation or by its operating companies, with relatively little income allocated to head-quarters. When all sources are considered, however, cities and towns realize a sizable net gain in tax revenues from their resident companies.

2. Expenditure Effects.   Usually, considerable after-tax dollars of local firms and their employees will be spent in the community. Every payroll turns itself over seven or eight times, so the attraction of a company paying out $100 million a year in wages could benefit a city or town as much as $800 million annually, excluding the gains to the firm's suppliers, distributors, and other groups. So whether reducing unused office space or lining the pockets of local entrepreneurs is the result, the primary and secondary effects of head office spending are significant. Conversely, the downside of any serious defections of corporate headquarters is staggering.

3. Employment Opportunities.   Head offices are not labor-intensive. Most corporate command posts hover between 50 and 500 people. Since local hiring is initially confined to unskilled and clerical employees, with top managerial slots reserved for incumbents, these units do not immediately add significantly to local employment. Over time, however, the job base at the center often absorbs other organizational units—research and development laboratories, management training facilities, and, in some instances, operating companies. Taken together, the employment effects can be profound. Greater Dallas, for instance, witnessed a net gain of almost 16,000 positions with the arrival of American Airlines, J. C. Penney, and GTE Telephone.

Also, there are important spillover effects. Accounting firms, banks, advertising agencies, and the like, which sell supporting services to major corporations, enjoy expanded career opportunities. Thus, while attracting the headquarters of companies will not immediately correct a town's unemployment problems, impressive job prospects often follow.

4. Cachet.   The advantages of increased tax revenues, local expenditures, and employment, though substantial, are frequently overshadowed by an intangible benefit: call it prestige. What better way to diversify a community's economic base than through these nonpolluting, knowledge-oriented command posts? "Blue chips? No, they're gold chips!" the former mayor of one penturb told me.

Community enrichment occurs on many fronts. Often accompanying the arrival of major corporate tenants is an overall upgrading of the business environment. Professionalism tends to rise, bank tellers learn courtesy and efficiency, apathetic public officials become more responsive. Behind the scenes, however, a more fundamental change shapes the future image of the community. A "gold chip" corporation brings with it a group of executives who are prime movers in their adopted hometown. Through their strategic positions in business, they give the city or town a unique insight into the social, political, and economic conditions of the global economy.

"Home offices *make* this city," beams Curtis L. Carlson, the 76-year-old founder and sole owner of Carlson Companies, a $6-billion Minneapolis conglomerate that includes the Radisson Hotels International chain. His pride reflects the positive impact that big business can have on a community. With a critical mass of corporate headquarters comes a knowledge base that is the envy of many other cities. It tells the world: "We have arrived. We are a major player in commercial affairs." This stock of world-class know-how can best ensure the economic well-being of any community, large or small.

Given the benefits, local planners must understand the unique advantages that their small city or town offers big business. The next chapter examines the special drawing power of the new corporate frontier.

4

The Case for the New Corporate Frontier

The choice of small-town America has plenty of historical precedent. Some of the nation's most hallowed corporations, including those cited in the accompanying table, are still situated in the remote locales they call home. In some cases, the location was determined by proximity to raw materials.

Feisty Frank Phillips located Phillips Petroleum in Bartlesville, Oklahoma. It was then a one-horse town 50 miles north of Tulsa, and it was the site of the company's first gushers. Elsewhere, Tabasco (from the Spanish, for "damp earth") has been growing in Louisiana since an unknown Confederate soldier brought back some dried peppers and gave them to Edmund McIlhenny, who planted the seeds in his wife's garden on Avery Island. Now in its 126th year, the McIlhenny Company sells over 60 million skinny bottles of its fiery, red pepper sauce from its historic home, which rises above the swamps and bayous of southwestern Louisiana 120 miles west of New Orleans.

In other cases, it was proximity to ready capital. Clessie Cummins was chauffeur to the leading banker in Columbus, Indiana, when he persuaded his employer to finance a new diesel engine. The venture became Cummins Engine. Sam Walton believed that the thrifty nature of Bentonville, Arkansas, was an appropriate venue from which to introduce Wal-Mart discount stores to other Southern towns with populations of 25,000 or less. Around the turn of the century, William E. Sullivan, a mechanical engineer, reckoned that the prosperous central

Partial Listing of Frontier Companies

Company	Primary business	Location	Population
Albertson's	Supermarkets	Boise, Idaho	125,738
Bandag	Tire retreading	Muscatine, Iowa	22,881
Bassett Furniture Industries	Furniture	Basset, Virginia	2,950
L. L. Bean	Mail order	Freeport, Maine	6,905
Ben & Jerry's Homemade	Ice cream	Waterbury, Vermont	1,702
Boise Cascade	Diversified industrial	Boise, Idaho	125,738
Caterpillar	Earthmoving equipment	Peoria, Illinois	113,504
Corning Glass Works	Glassware	Corning, New York	11,938
Cummins Engine	Diesel engines	Columbus, Indiana	31,802
Deere	Farm equipment	Moline, Illinois	43,202
Dow Chemical	Industrial chemicals	Midland, Michigan	38,053
Fort Howard	Paper products	Green Bay, Wisconsin	96,466
Gerber Products	Processed food	Fremont, Michigan	3,875
Herman Miller	Furniture	Zeeland, Michigan	5,417
Hershey Foods	Foods, confectioneries	Hershey, Pennsylvania	13,249
Geo. H. Hormel	Processed foods	Austin, Minnesota	21,907
Kellogg	Cereals	Battle Creek, Michigan	53,540
Lands' End	Mail order	Dodgeville, Wisconsin	3,882
McIlhenny	Hot sauces	Avery Island, Louisiana	575
Masco	House fixtures	Taylor, Michigan	70,811
Maytag	Household appliances	Newton, Iowa	14,789
Mrs. Fields Cookies	Cookies, confectioneries	Park City, Utah	4,468
Perdue Farms	Processed chicken	Salisbury, Maryland	20,592
Phillips Petroleum	Petroleum	Bartlesville, Oklahoma	34,256
J. M. Smucker	Jams and jellies	Orrville, Ohio	7,712
O. M. Scott & Sons	Lawn-care products	Marysville, Ohio	9,656
Tecumseh Products	Engines and compressors	Tecumseh, Michigan	7,462
Wal-Mart Stores	Retail stores	Bentonville, Arkansas	11,257
Westpoint-Pepperell	Textiles	West Point, Georgia	3,571
Whirlpool	Household appliances	Benton Harbor, Michigan	12,818

Illinois farming community of Jacksonville was the best location from which to launch his fascinating new contraption: the Ferris wheel.

Other entrepreneurs stumbled into the boondocks by accident—or sheer fright. When Milton Hershey was trying his hand at taffy making, a Philadelphia trolley car destroyed his pushcart. This catastrophe—plus a string of bankruptcies and a meddling father—propelled him westward, to Pennsylvania dairy country. Success soon followed: Milton bought 2000 acres of farmland, built a factory, and began turning out his world-famous chocolates.

Many of the United States' most recent tycoons are equally bullish on small towns. They include Debbi and Randall Fields, cofounders of Mrs. Fields Cookies, the 520-unit-plus cookie and confectionery company; Mo Siegel and John Hay, whose Celestial Seasonings became the nation's fourth-largest tea processor; and computer chip maker Joseph L. Parkinson, who launched Micron Technology in 1978 with his twin brother, Ward, from the basement of a dentist's office. In each instance, their headquarters are in seemingly unlikely spots: Park City, Utah; Boulder, Colorado; and Boise, Idaho—respectively.

The newest entrepreneurs in the United States, like the visionary eccentrics before them, are convinced that fledgling businesses can be run effectively from beyond the urban fringe. But how? Executives cite three important advantages: lower operating costs, superior lifestyles leading to higher productivity, and better integration of modern technology.

Bountiful Bargains

Small-town living does wonders to the bottom line: cheaper labor, reduced occupancy costs, favorable tax rates, and more. A "bargain" is how Dow Chemical's chief executive Frank P. Popoff describes Midland (Michigan) living. "You get a lot more bang for your buck for housing, transportation, recreation, parking, meals—the whole shebang." Or consider Boise, Idaho, the home of nine major corporations. Its cost of living index of 96.8 (versus the national average of 100) has dropped steadily since 1978 and now is one of the lowest in the West.

Frontier locations offer significant savings in head office costs. Within the same region, these expenses can be 20 to 50 percent lower than they are in the city or suburbs. Naturally, cost-conscious companies want to pinch every penny. Target number one is the posh downtown corporate office. "What's an industrial headquarters besides a lot of overhead and some top executives?" asks Philip D. Restifo, managing director of Galbreath Company, Manhattan-based relocation advisers. "The few who need to see bankers or lawyers or rub elbows with other executives at 'Twenty One' can keep an apartment in the city. No company is going to pay $50 a square foot so a bunch of accountants can go to the Metropolitan Museum on their lunch break." Cost pressures are forcing firms either to prune or to eliminate their metropolitan headquarters—or to move elsewhere.

The virtues of a dedicated work force further enhance small-town America's cost advantage. "We are a town of somewhat nerdy, hardworking ants, taking pride in our labors," says Cummins Engine director William I. Miller of Columbus, Indiana. Similar attitudes prevail in other penturban communities. "Our employees are really hardworking people with a really solid work ethic," says Al Egbert, manager of McDonnell Douglas's plant, which subassembles MD-80 commercial aircraft on the fringe of the Salt Lake City Airport. "It's the main reason we upped our game plan from 350 to 1000 people. They're really interested in doing a good job, and that shows in the kind of productivity gains we've received."

Not only is productivity higher, but turnover is lower. Boise Cascade's top 250 managers average about 20 years of service with a company that just recently celebrated its thirty-third birthday. Typically, there are more quarter- and half-century club members in penturban businesses than in their big-city peers. Loyalty is still in style in frontierland.

Lifestyle Advantages

The appeal of pastoral living goes beyond cheap rents and a superior work force, though. "Cost factors are often of less importance than quality of life," says David Birch of Cognetics Inc. "A region's livability and aesthetic appeal, as well as the quality of services being provided, are a community's most important assets." Qualitative factors are becoming increasingly influential. Thirty years ago, reports *Site Selection* magazine, lifestyle issues did not crack the top nine locational factors. However, they have ranked first for each year since 1988.

"These days, quality of life is increasingly important; in some cases, more so than money," says Finn M. W. Caspersen, chairman and CEO of Beneficial Corporation. Six years after taking control of Beneficial, the nation's 34th-largest financial institution, he moved the company from suburban Morristown to rural Peapack, New Jersey. Caspersen acquired large tracks of New Jersey farmland so that Beneficial employees could benefit from the pristine qualities of penturbia. The move, he claims "was a personal and corporate goal to attract the most qualified people to the company."

"Crime-free, clutter-free, and hassle-free" is the pitch of semirural

communities like Peapack. In an increasingly paved-over America, any
locale that promises clean air, affordable housing, and a bit of greenery
is likely to win friends. These benefits are exactly what today's baby-
boomers want. U.S. provinces, where local rates of serious crime frequently are far below the national norm, are havens in a seemingly violent society. For instance, Iowa's violent crime rate is 62 percent lower
than the national average. People still enjoy strolls through tree-shaded
neighborhoods, even at night.

The prospect of better schooling is another penturban plus. According to Robert Ady, president of Chicago-based PHH Fantus, coping with
the shortage of skilled labor is the most critical factor in site selection.
More than 65 percent of U.S. companies report serious problems in ob-
taining qualified workers. This scarcity of trained labor is driving American business to communities blessed with industrious, well-educated
workers.

Generally speaking, the new corporate frontier ranks high in its ability
to deliver the talent needed to compete in the information age. "We
don't have a problem getting capable people in our business," says Allen
Jacobson, chief executive officer of 3M Corporation. "We operate
largely in the Middle West, largely in small towns. We get good people
[who] are well-educated. We're not spending a lot of money on reme-
dial education or illiteracy or any of those things." Similarly, executives
of Iowa's blue-chip companies—Amana, Bandag, Deere, Hon Industries, and Maytag—beam with pride when the subject comes to education. "You can't build Maytag-type quality just anywhere," boasts Chairman and CEO Daniel J. Krumm. "You need the talented, well-educated,
productive people Iowa has provided to Maytag since 1892."

Krumm has good cause to beat his chest. Iowans are the most literate
Americans. They have ranked first and second nationally in SAT and
ACT college entrance scores since 1985. The state also graduates 23 percent more students than the national average, and its residents have
earned more undergraduate degrees per hundred thousand than any
other state. Outside studies confirm that, on average, public school students from the Hawkeye State are a year and a half ahead of their peers
across the country. This talent base is a major plus not only for Iowa's
home-grown corporations but for out-of-staters as well.

Professionally minded parents want to build their careers in areas with
a strong commitment to public education. "We decided some years ago
that we didn't want to raise a family in the San Francisco Bay area," says
cookie maker Debbi Fields. "Schooling was a major reason," adds hus-
band Randy. "We wanted our kids to go to public schools, and, in Park
City, the public schools are super." Statewide statistics bear this out: Utah
devotes a higher percentage of its budget to education than any other

state; 90 percent of its high school graduates go on to college; it has the country's highest literacy rate; its SAT scores are 15 percent above the national average; and it is rated number one in the United States for advanced placement.

With its heavy emphasis on education, Utah offers not only a highly skilled work force but also a research and development environment that has spawned some of the nation's most successful companies. One home-grown star is WordPerfect Corporation, the world's best-seller of word processing software. In 1979, two entrepreneurs launched the business in their basement. Today, it occupies 180,000 square feet of space in Orem, and 1990 sales were $178 million. WordPerfect's phenomenal success is typical of a state nationally recognized for its leadership in energy, aerospace, biomedicine, and high-tech start-ups. Without question, Utah's achievements stem from its deep-seated commitment to public education.

Active involvement on school boards, parent-teacher associations, and even in classrooms typifies the pride big companies display in their small-town public schools. In Oklahoma, only the university towns of Norman and Stillwater have more residents with advanced degrees than Bartlesville, thanks to Phillips Petroleum. Bartlesville's 6500-student public school system sends most of its graduates to college, and it regularly produces an unusually big crop of finalists in the competition for National Merit Scholarships.

Penturban communities don't skimp on technical training either. Rockwell International's Avionics Group chose to expand its Cedar Rapids facility because of Iowa's Industrial New Jobs Training Program (INJTP). This nationally recognized effort offers comprehensive instruction in electronic communications, computer sciences, industrial electronics, energy technologies, and statistical process control. INJTP, operated through the state's 15 community colleges, provides funds for screening, testing, classroom instruction, and on-the-job training. Participating companies may receive reimbursement for up to 50 percent of new employees' wages and benefits for the first year; they may also be eligible for a new jobs tax credit of up to $600 for each new position created. As proof of its effectiveness, INJTP has helped more than 200 businesses create 19,000 jobs in small towns across the Hawkeye State.

The combination of superior education and comprehensive real-world training makes for a more productive work force. In Iowa's case, U.S. Department of Commerce data indicate that the state produces 49.6 hours of value for every 40-hour week. That is 24 percent higher than the U.S. average, putting Iowa third in the nation. In our discussions, many leading employers insist that their workers in Small Town, U.S.A., consistently outperform those in the big city.

Affordable housing is another major benefit of frontier living. "Good-bye city, hello country life" is a familiar refrain today. More and more people are discovering that they don't need to be an investment banker to buy a decent home in the outback. Cheap, abundant land translates to reasonably priced housing, and the cost of heartland homes generally is 25 to 50 percent below that of most homes in metropolitan areas. In 1990, a new three-bedroom, 1600-square-foot home in a typical pen-turban community sold for about $80,000 compared with $136,100 in Seattle, $182,300 in Boston, $211,500 in Los Angeles, or $243,600 in Orange County, California—or the national median of $95,900. These low prices are enabling first-time buyers to enjoy the benefits of home ownership in pleasant surroundings. Migrants from the big city are able to unload their houses at inflated values and buy in the country much more cheaply—and get away from the smog, traffic jams, gang violence, and other hassles of the center city.

Corporate America understands the ramifications. Unless its home base can provide an adequate number of affordable houses, a firm can expect wholesale defections of talented people. California-based businesses are experiencing this problem in spades. Last year, an estimated 462,000 Golden Staters fled for greener, less crowded pastures. Urban specialist Thomas J. Jablonsky of the University of Southern California calls this exodus unique because until now "people have never left this area because they were disgusted with it." Painfully high housing prices are largely responsible.

Marc and June Munger traded in their cramped home in Newberry Park in Southern California when they leaped at IBM's offer to transfer Marc, 47, to Boulder, Colorado. Although this move left June, 40, without a job, it meant buying their dream house—a two-story, five-bedroom house with an art studio. "It's been a better lifestyle for everybody," says Marc Munger.

California's historic out-migration is "part of the natural evolutionary process of urbanization," claims USC's Jablonsky.

Evidence abounds that more and more people today are downshifting in search of a simple life. These folks fancy a clean and healing escape from what Henry David Thoreau described as those who "lead lives of quiet desperation." Not all the emigrants are spiritual descendants of Thoreau, though. The simple life that is now unfolding is not just a need for "a rural homestead or a yen for L. L. Bean boots and trail mix," says David E. Shi, associate professor of history at Davidson College in North Carolina and author of *In Search of the Simpler Life: American Voices Past and Present.* "Simplicity is a state of mind. It's learning the difference between personal traps and personal trappings."

Lifestyle issues, including the choice of where to live, outweigh the lust for personal trappings that characterized the eighties. "It's happening more and more," says Douglas McCable, associate professor of industrial and labor relations at Georgetown University. "A lot of yuppies have realized that a very fast-paced lifestyle can't be kept up for a long time. They're turning back to family values . . . [and] moving to smaller cities and rural communities."

To many working families, the simpler life and more of it compensate nicely for Yankee Stadium or the Hollywood Bowl. According to *Time* magazine, when Equitable Life Assurance Society summoned Jim Crawford, 44, back to Manhattan from its Des Moines office, he simply could not relinquish his Iowa lifestyle. "We based that decision on the quality of the environment," he says. "People do work hard here, and there is a deep appreciation for family life." Crawford traded a higher salary and a 2-hour commute for better schools and more free time. "We wonder how we did it, how we went through the routine," he says of his former days in the Big Apple.

Americans today are looking for cleaner communities where they can walk down the street with a smile on their faces and the knowledge that people care. One such convert is Christopher Banus, founder and chairman of Granitech Corporation, a maker of specialized flooring and construction materials. Plagued by the housing costs, pollution, stress, and congestion of Boston, where he lived and ran a similar business for many years, he fled to Fairfield, Iowa. When Banus started Granitech in 1986, his neighbors offered forklifts and moving help for free. "If you want to go skiing, go skiing. If you want to buy $75 ties, go to New York," says this modern-day homesteader. "But if you want to live a stress-free life, move here."

Nationally syndicated newspaper columnist Mary McGrory gained a similar impression of the Hawkeye State when she covered the 1988 presidential caucuses. "Iowa is a state where kindness is rampant. I guess you could meet a churl in Iowa, but you would have to go out of your way. It's like getting a bad meal in Italy. The odds are against it."

McGrory's comments are not unusual, and they could be applied to many other semirural settings. The open, friendly people soon convert newcomers to their strong beliefs in the importance of traditional values such as home, family, and community. Frontier types still believe that their personal success is a matter of hard work and creative thinking and that people are limited only by their own ability, desire, and drive. These virtues help explain why the high-draw locations of the 1990s are not the metropolises of New York and Los Angeles but smaller, more habitable cities and towns.

Forest from the Trees

Several years ago, I visited Arthur C. Clarke, author of the space saga that began in *2001* and *2010* and continues in *2061: Odyssey Three*. "How can you create such futuristic visions from your home in Sri Lanka, an impoverished third world location in the Indian Ocean?" I asked. He told me that by separating himself from the mainstream, he was able, literally, to distance himself from the "contagious effects" of the current and near-term technology being crafted in Europe, North America, and Japan. Distance, Clarke claimed, gave him the clarity to project his thoughts beyond the next wave of change—a factor that gives his writings their special force. In a more practical vein, the world's leading writer of science fiction also pointed out that his home on the outskirts of Colombo was directly linked to his editors in London and New York by state-of-the-art satellite communications. So, in a professional sense, he never felt out of touch.

Arthur Clarke's message recurred frequently during the course of my research. Hamlet dwellers argue that by being somewhat removed from the mainstream, they are able to distinguish the forest from the trees. "Distance-induced objectivity," in part, triggered Hudson Institute's move 9 years ago to Indianapolis from Croton-on-Hudson, 45 miles upstream from New York City along the Hudson River. The famous think tank sold its 22-acre, seven-building estate to trade in, in its words, "ivory tower elitism" and "Eastern snobbery" for the down-to-earth ways of a midsize Midwestern city.

"It's that search for the common attitude—being close to common sense—that argued being away from the East Coast," says R. Mark Lubbers, Hudson's corporate vice president. "That's the intellectual force that moved us." Adds President Mitchell E. Daniels, Jr.: "We strongly believe that perspective is enhanced by distance." So far, the public policy research organization has found happiness in being removed from the power centers of New York and Washington. The move confirmed Hudson Institute's own prediction concerning "the end of geography"—the coming of an age in which ease and speed of travel and electronic communications are lessening the need to locate in the middle of the traditional urban hub.

Over the years, out-of-the-way towns have churned out their share of seers, especially in the financial community. Few investment philosophers have earned the reputation of John Marks Templeton, 78. At 56, the renowned dean of international investing crafted his second successful career, in Nassau, the Bahamas. The Tennessee-born Templeton, who is a British citizen and was knighted in 1987, lives on the grounds of the exclusive Lyford Cay Club, a half hour's drive from the crowded tourist haven of Nassau. Today, he advises 52 mutual funds and 100 institutional accounts with total assets of $15 billion.

How about the "Sage of Omaha"? The famed investor Warren Edward Buffett built a nearly $4-billion fortune by taking big stakes in select companies such as GEICO, Capital Cities/ABC, Coca-Cola, and the Washington Post Company, and holding on, more or less, forever. The stock of his $2.5-billion Berkshire Hathaway Corporation has multiplied thirtyfold over the past decade, and the company has grown like a beanstalk. The remote Nebraska cornfields, he contends, polished his Midas touch.

"I think it's a saner existence here," he says. "I used to feel, when I worked back in New York, that there were more stimuli hitting me all the time, and if you've got the normal amount of adrenalin, you start responding to them. It may lead to crazy behavior after a while. It's much easier to think here."

Antiseptic locations are home for a string of other talented, but less famous, financial advisers. They include:

- Steve DeCook, 47, one of the nation's best traders of agricultural commodities. From January 1975 to June 1988, he achieved an annual compound rate of return of 37.8 percent. DeCook trades not from the glass towers or trading pits of New York or Chicago; instead, he works out of a four-room office in Ankeny, Iowa, a bedroom community of 15,000 people—10 miles north of Des Moines.

- Robert J. Eggert, 76, a retired business economist (Ford, RCA), active breeder of quarter horses and hyperactive editor of *Blue Chip Economic Indicators*. He publishes monthly newsletters featuring articles by top economic forecasters around the country and also calculates consensus estimates that are now widely accepted as an industry benchmark. His home: the red rock canyon town of Sedona in north-central Arizona.

- Anthony Correra, 54, president of Sandia Asset Management, the widely regarded hedge firm. The former E. F. Hutton analyst moved west 11 years ago to toil high up in the Sandia Mountains of Albuquerque, New Mexico. "When things get bad," he says, "I walk through the mountains and eat chili."

U.S. advisers in the hinterlands unanimously reaffirm the message that being off the beaten path allows them to be more objective. Robert Prechter, the 41-year-old Elliott Wave theorist, claims: "Professionally, it's important to be away from the whirlwind that is the Wall Street crowd." His home on Lake Lanier in Gainesville, Georgia, is wired directly into Wall Street through a satellite TV dish, a sophisticated computer network, and banks of telephones. From a similarly equipped office overlooking Whitefish Lake in the Rocky Mountains of Montana, Jim Stack churns out his *Investech Mutual Fund Advisor* and *Investech Market Analyst*, both ranked among the nation's top 10 investment newsletters. One of a handful of pundits to predict the October 1987 stock market crash, Stack explains his success by saying: "Sometimes we see things a little clearer out here."

Larger companies, too, believe that remoteness can enhance objectivity. Herbert Dow and his son Willard insisted that the isolation of Midland, Michigan, strengthened Dow Chemical's deliberate and often stubborn policy of independent research and development. The family feared that if Dow moved closer to its competitors, it could become an imitator and not an innovator. By the same token, Gary Michael, vice chairman of Albertson's, the highly regarded supermarket chain headquartered in Boise, Idaho, says: "We like our remoteness. It allows us not to get caught up in nonproductive time where all companies follow each other closely. We're simply not influenced by surrounding companies."

Distance Redefined: The Impact of Technology

Sophisticated communications equipment ensures that these independent thinkers are not blinded by their isolation. Even the most remote businesspeople can be close to where the action is and still have access to home base. Today's executives are discovering that ever-smaller, ever-lighter, ever-more-capable high-tech gadgets are the next best thing to being there. Personal computers, cellular phones, fax machines, electronic pagers, and a constellation of other high-tech devices enable them to work anywhere. These miracle machines dramatically affect the way people live, think, communicate, and work—increasing productivity, streamlining communications, and providing immediate access to essential data. They are giving birth to the mobile executive, the mobile headquarters.

Thanks to Compliment Vans of Comanche, Iowa, those in the fast lane can drive the Executive Mobile Office. This black Vista van is equipped with every office amenity from a cellular fax and phone to a cherry wood desk and credenza. The Italian leather trifold sofa opens into a queen-sized bed. "We've got a tiger by the tail," says one Compliment Vans executive. "To date, we've had over 1000 inquiries."

Bolder still is the joint venture of Nissan Motor Company and Hitachi Ltd. to create a rolling office. The alliance, named Xanavi Information Corporation, will develop, produce, and sell mobile telephones, fax machines, TV sets, videocassette recorders, and navigation systems. Its projected sales are 20 billion yen ($151 million) by 1994 and 100 billion yen by 2000.

At a growing number of airports, stranded travelers can also spend their spare time in a well-equipped business center—an in-airport cluster of around-the-clock, seven-day-a-week offices and work stations equipped with telephones, typewriters, personal computers, copiers, and other standard office equipment. The Tele-Trip Company, a subsidiary of Mutual of Omaha, operates 22 of these facilities at various U.S. airports.

To liberate the business traveler further, the aviation industry is introducing the "smart seat." Trans Com, Airvision, and Matsushita Avionics are developing tiny TV screens placed in the back of seats that will allow passengers to access their home computers, catch up on electronic mail, and make last-minute hotel or car reservations from the air. "If airlines make it a work environment, flying won't be lost to time and business travelers will pay to stay productive," says Thomas R. Riedinger, a retired projects officer at Boeing Corporation.

Once futurist notions, mobile, flying, even floating offices are becoming a reality today. Then, there is the impact of video conferencing, which permits people to hold business meetings over long distances. In 1979, Boeing introduced this new technology, called the *interaction television system*, or ITV, to allow teams of engineers designing similar aircraft at different plants to talk to each other through closed-circuit cable television. "We've used ITV on every plane since then," says Mike Schelenberger, manager of switching and application implementation. Teleconferences are such an integral part of Boeing's design process "that the company would have an uprising on our hands if we stopped using them." IBM, Ford, Prime Computer, Hercules, and McDonnell Douglas are other major ITV users.

Obviously, advanced telecommunication is extending the new corporate frontier. It makes overseeing a major enterprise in distant locations more and more feasible. However, penturban businesses must invest significantly in this technology. In 1988, Wal-Mart Stores completed the installation of a $20-million Hughes satellite network that today links about 1700 stores to its Bentonville, Arkansas, headquarters and the company's 14 distribution centers. This futuristic system, which the Pentagon would envy, electronically logs every item sold at the checkout counter, automatically helps the warehouse identify merchandise to be ordered, and directs the flow of goods to the stores and even to the proper shelves. The company's state-of-the-art inventory-control system helps spot sales trends quickly. "It has speeded up our market reaction time substantially," says Wal-Mart President and CEO David D. Glass.

Another high-tech apostle is 61-year-old Marvin Schwan of Marshall,

Minnesota (pop. 11,020). He directs an estimated $1.5-billion empire and a personal net worth of about $400 million from his headquarters in a modest third-floor yellow and brick building in the northland. Schwan's Sales Enterprises' major division delivers frozen foods, mostly to rural households in 49 states. In 1988, the firm's 2300 drivers rang up an estimated $90 million in operating profits on sales of $750 million. Delivery people routinely log 12- to 15-hour days visiting almost a thousand customers every 2 weeks. To rein in his far-flung network, Schwan equips his drivers with portable inventory and pricing computers. These hand-held units allow those on the road to check out-of-stock products and recommend ready substitutes while they are taking orders at a customer's door. At the end of the day, drivers unload their computers in the firm's mainframe in Marshall, where staffers analyze everything from revenue forecasts to the popularity of new entrees. "In effect, Schwan has brought to the home delivery market the kind of powerful computerized inventory controls that Charles Lazarus created at Toys 'R' Us," writes *Forbes*'s Michael Fritz.

However, no frontier firm demonstrates a greater commitment to technology than does Mrs. Fields Cookies. Each of its 520 or so units, scattered from San Francisco to Sydney, is tied to Park City, Utah, through Tandy computers. One software package called *Retail Operations Intelligence* connects computers at each store to an IBM AS/400 minicomputer at the head office. The system dispatches baking schedules, logs workers' hours, records maintenance activities, and periodically tests employees' product knowledge. Another system answers telephones, takes messages, and plays them back to the parties for whom they were intended. A related package called *Form Mail* enables store managers to speak directly to the senior management. These programs have worked so well at Mrs. Fields Cookies that the company is now selling its software to retail chains such as Fox Photo.

Cofounder Randy Fields is the genius behind these elegant systems. "If we had an MIS guru, it would be Mr. Fields," said *INC.* magazine in selecting him as a board member on its 1989 "Dream Team." Few American executives better understand how technology can change the way a company is managed. Randy is using technology to remove the rote work of running a business, to strip away management layers that usually intervene between retail stores and headquarters, and to bring hundreds of store managers into almost direct contact with CEO Debbi.

"MIS in this company has always had to serve two masters," Randy explained to me, "better control and better decision making." By linking control and decision making, the talented husband-and-wife team is transforming their global retail enterprise into an information-based network organization. "Randy's theory," says Debbi Fields, "is that the eighties [were] a time of power dispersal, of moving from the center to the edges, with businesses dependent on computer terminals and communications satellites. This technology has allowed us to live a country life while enjoying the sort of convenience that used to be exclusively confined to large cities."

It is not unusual for Debbi and Randy to log up to 350,000 miles a year in commercial airplanes en route to their galaxy of stores. Even when winging around the world, the Fields are never out of touch with Park City. The centerpiece of their office on the go is an NEC Ultralite laptop plus a fax card and a cellular phone. The whole kit weighs only 7½ pounds—in the air, on the road, anywhere. The fax card allows them to receive documents through their computer without worrying about a logjam at a public or hotel fax facility; the modem permits them to receive electronic mail on their computer via phone link. Debbi and Randy also use the cellular phone to receive voice mail. Their portable office enables them to make important decisions, access data, or sign a contract electronically with the push of a button or the play of a fax card.

Modern technology, in effect, stretches the Fields' business horizons while giving them time to enjoy a frontier lifestyle. "Living in Utah has helped us focus on family, and on each other, without the distractions of life in more populous and busy places," says Debbi. "These quiet, peaceful times are a great relief from our other world, where there are always decisions to be made and problems to be solved." Stanley Davis, author of *Future Perfect*, believes that the next wave of American companies "will have to reconceptualize space, transforming it by technology from an impediment to an asset." That is exactly what Mrs. Fields Cookies and many other denizens of the new corporate frontier are doing. They are redefining distance.

Having It All

The chance for a better job, a better education, and a better home. This is what every generation tries to pass on to its children. This has been the American dream for over 200 years, and penturbia is fulfilling this dream.

With the help of advanced telecommunications, the burgs are becoming the bigs. Working Americans can now have it all: the qualitative benefits of provincial living without getting off the fast track. Frontier companies offer people the full range of career opportunities, not the limited menu of sales office or branch plant assignments long associated with small-town postings. Fast-trackers today can weave in and out of the firm's penturban headquarters over the course of their careers. Most probably, they will spend large blocks of their working lives in operating units scattered across the nation and around the world. But "home" will always be the corporate nerve center in the provinces.

Small towns are anything but small time when it comes to business. Increasingly, they are affording John and Jane Doe an ideal environment in which to satisfy their career dreams while sampling the good life. The next part examines how several leading corporations have achieved this balance.

PART 2
Stars in the Sticks

5
Boise: The Cowboy Capital

When Lewis and Clark discovered the rivers of Idaho flowing west, they sensed that they were on the threshold of something big. The famous explorers confronted firsthand the dynamic power of the Snake and Salmon rivers, the dizzying heights of the Sawtooth Mountains, and ice caves of spectacular beauty. The dramatic geology of Idaho (a Shoshonean phrase meaning "light on the mountains") was so overwhelming, so impenetrable, that it forced the Lewis and Clark expedition to turn back to Montana. The natural isolation of Idaho Territory made it the last territory to be explored and continues to make the Gem State something of an enigma.

Ernest Hemingway, one of Idaho's most famous part-time residents, said it well: "A lot of state, this Idaho I didn't know about." Most Americans today would be hard-pressed to form an opinion about the region. In many respects, its uniquely rugged geography—wedged between six states—makes it the last American frontier. "It's the great unknown, the unspoiled, the uncorrupted," writes David Lamb of the *Los Angeles Times*. Even the governor, Cecil D. Andrus,.has a tough time explaining the nation's ambivalence about Idaho: "Very few Americans seem to know what we are or even where we are."

No Small Potatoes

Recently, however, outsiders are forming more definite opinions about this part of the country, once known principally for its cowboys and white potatoes. The current perception: Idaho means business. Increasingly, Americans are identifying its capital, Boise, as a serious hub of regional business and commerce. For good reason. The only city in the nation more than 300 miles from another city, Boise ranks sixth in the nation, on a per capita basis, as a location for major corporate headquarters.

All told, nine leading companies—with combined sales approaching $25 billion—call Boise home. To name a few:

- Boise Cascade Corporation, the $4.2-billion forest products company, is a relative latecomer to the area. It was established in 1957 by the merger of two small northwestern logging companies—Boise Payette Lumber Company and Cascade Lumber Company of Yakima, Washington. After a period of headstrong expansion in the 1960s, Boise Cascade underwent a major metamorphosis, thanks to Chairman and CEO John B. Fery. Today, it is the country's second-largest producer of newsprint, the third-biggest supplier of uncoated free sheet (copier and computer paper, for example), and the fifth-largest supplier of coated magazine paper.

- Morrison Knudsen Corporation, a $1.7-billion global construction company, played a major role in building the Hoover and Grand Coulee dams, the San Francisco–Oakland Bay Bridge, the Kennedy Space Center, and the Cam Ranh Bay military base in Vietnam. The giant multinational began 1912, when Harry W. Morrison, a 27-year-old employee of the U.S. Reclamation Service, and Danish immigrant Morris Hans Knudsen, 50, plunked down $600 in cash and a bunch of used equipment. Nowadays, MK is concentrating on construction management and design work, marine construction and tunnel projects, railcar manufacture, and environmental management.

- Albertson's Inc., one of America's most admired supermarket chains, saw its sales nearly quadruple in the 1980s by stressing big, big stores kept surgically clean and very price-competitive. The $8-billion firm not only made the superstore the industry standard but also proved that high gross margins (24 percent) were possible in a notoriously low-profit business. Its founder, 84-year-old Joseph A. Albertson, opened his first store in Boise on July 21, 1939, at the corner of 16th and State Streets. Unit One continues to operate successfully today.

- J. R. Simplot Company, the diversified food processor, made its founder, Jack Simplot, one of this country's wealthiest individuals. A high school dropout who started with nothing at the age of 15, Simplot became the largest single supplier of potatoes to the military during World War II. After the war, he pioneered frozen french fries and became the major supplier to McDonald's restaurants. Today, the

Simplot Group is a $1.5-billion-a-year operation, with businesses rang-ing from fish farming to silver mines.

- Ore-Ida Foods, an $870-million potato processor and manufacturer, is Simplot's crosstown rival. Several years ago, it was acquired by the Pittsburgh-based H. J. Heinz Company, where it is now part of the Weight Watchers frozen foods division. Ore-Ida employs over 500 local residents.

- Micron Technology Inc., a $333-million semiconductor company, is a darling of America's techies. Although most computer chip makers are located in California's Silicon Valley, two brothers had a different dream. The Parkinson twins made their home in the wilds of Idaho, far from the Porsches and hot tubs of northern California. With the help of nearby potato farmers and sheep ranchers and, more recently, the U.S. government, Micron competes fiercely with the Japanese in dynamic random-access memory (DRAM) chips.

Clearly, Idaho's capital city is more than just spuds. Complementing its home-grown businesses are the operating divisions of several national companies, including Hewlett-Packard Company (the town's biggest employer, with 3500 people), IBM, Consolidated Freightways, and Sears Roebuck & Company.

The City of Trees

Boise has earned its reputation as a serious business center over many years. In the early 1800s, French-speaking fur trappers were so im-pressed by the abundance of trees along the river in southwestern Idaho that they called the area *la rivière boise*, the wooded river. When the town was established in 1863, it was named for the river. Its strategic location, near the point at which the Boise River comes out of the Rockies into the valley, was a natural for the new town. Even the earliest pioneers could see the river's tremendous potential as a power and irrigation source. Incredible wealth from the nearby gold and silver mines poured into the city, and the community emerged as a bustling hub of com-merce and culture for all those who traversed the Oregon Trail. Eventu-ally, Boise was selected as the capital of the Idaho Territory.

Growth continued through the late 1800s and early 1900s as Boiseans spread westward into the large tracts of agricultural land and the timber-land to the north and east. These bold initiatives enabled the commu-nity to lessen its dependence on mining, and because logging and agri-culture generally took place far outside the city, Boise became a community devoid of heavy industry. Gradually, its reputation grew as a headquarters and service center.

Although many outlying communities today are fighting hard times, Boise is growing—thanks to its diversified economy. L. J. Davis, a contributing editor of *Harper's* magazine, describes the city as "an island of prosperity in a state whose economy has only now begun to recover from the recession in agriculture, mining, and timber." Few would dispute the fact that Idaho's isolated capital boasts an improbable bumper crop of blue-chip corporations. "Boise is unique," says Leland F. Smith of Grubb & Ellis, the California-based real estate consulting company. "You don't expect to find head offices in an isolated city of that size—or, for that matter, the sort of business drive you associate with a place like Los Angeles."

The pioneers who followed Lewis and Clark brought with them the drive and enterprising frontier spirit that thrive today. "There's a strong work ethic here, and the Old West heritage of self-reliance is still very strong," says former Boise Cascade President Jon Miller. "We don't have a 9 to 5 mentality." Fellow Boisean Joseph Parkinson, 45, cofounder of Micron Technology, concurs: "We have a highly productive labor pool that we draw on from the local area—the farms and the surrounding community. These people want to work and they're willing to work any shift." Interestingly, because of Micron Technology's phenomenal growth, its local staff has been increased by newcomers from Vietnam. CEO Parkinson has skillfully blended these new Americans with third- and fourth-generation Idahoans. Micron is able to "run around the clock, seven days a week," he says. "We don't even stop for holidays!"

Overall, however, local firms report few difficulties in recruiting top-notch talent. Just ask the people at Hewlett-Packard, whose largest manufacturing complex outside of Silicon Valley is located on the outskirts of town. "Boise is very conducive to attracting people, especially engineers," claims Mary Schofield, the plant controller. First and foremost, she believes, are the many quality-of-life attributes that the area offers; but technology, too, is critical. "Telecommunications and video links are extremely important to our professional staff," Schofield says. "They must keep up to date in their fields and not feel cut off from the major learning centers." To ensure that its techies stay in touch, HP maintains elaborate video connections with the University of Idaho and with Stanford University and its Palo Alto Technical Center.

"As long as you have telecommunications and computer technology, you can run a company from anywhere," argues Gerald R. Rudd, senior vice president for human resources at Albertson's. Because of the vast distances between many of its operations, the 450-unit chain pioneered computerization in the supermarket industry. Out of sheer necessity,

Boise Cascade became another proponent of high tech. Imagine the challenge of managing the 6.7 million acres of timberland scattered across the country. Boise Cascade does it with its widely heralded geographic and management information systems. Foresters in the company's 10 timber regions have computer power at their beck and call to help them get answers to complex questions relating to yields, roadways, waterways, and almost any other timber or logging issue. Variants of this software help the firm link its overseas and domestic operating units to the Idaho headquarters.

The city's air service also makes its natural isolation less of a problem. From the Boise Air Terminal, located less than 10 minutes from downtown, regularly scheduled jet transport is available to and from most anywhere—except international destinations. Private jets lessen, if not eliminate, this shortcoming, and virtually every major company has its own mini air force. "The airport issue is irrelevant," claims a former Boise Cascade executive. "Boise Cascade has three jets of its own, which it would need wherever its headquarters were located." (Idahoans also point out that Cleveland houses 13 *Fortune* 500 companies despite its lack of direct access to international flights.)

Land, Lots of Land

Idaho spells freedom and space. It has more high-mountain wilderness than any other state except Alaska. The area exploded in the 1970s as Americans fled the cities in search of openness and rural simplicity. Idaho grew by a third to nearly a million people in that decade, with the largest number of immigrants—more than 43,000 between 1975 and 1980—coming from California.

The capital city is the capital attraction. *USA Today* labeled Boise a "boom town of the 90s," largely because of its strong economy, good transportation, excellent schools, and recreational opportunities. Pundits predict that its population (125,738) will grow by 20 percent by the year 2000. Asked to explain Boise's benefits, Randy Nelson, a local planning official, says: "It's the size of community people like to go back to. There aren't long lines on the ski lifts. You can go fishing or camping and not be shoulder to shoulder." The merits of more elbowroom are enticing many newcomers, especially those wandering Californians, to the state.

Tom Korpalski, 46, took a pay cut to move from Sacramento to Boise, where he is an environmental health and safety manager at the Hewlett-Packard plant. Korpalski swears that he would not dream of transferring back to HP's home base in Palo Alto, California, to continue his career.

"It's not worth leaving the quality of life I have in Idaho to go back to California to the congestion, the traffic, 2-hour commutes, things like that." More important to him are Idaho's wide open spaces. The state's density is only 12 people per square mile; California's is 14 times higher. "Everywhere you went in California, there were people, too many people," recalls Korpalski, a father of two small children.

Jazz musician Gene Harris is another confirmed convert of Boise. The 56-year-old Michigan native migrated westward in 1977. Here, Harris— regarded by his peers as one of the greatest blues pianists in the world— found the good life, and he is eager to share it. "If you haven't seen Idaho," he says, "you don't know what heaven is." Strange sounds for a black man living in the rural Rockies. Yet for a decade, Harris has found contentment playing in the lounge of the Idanha Hotel, a Romanesque Gothic landmark in downtown Boise. Periodically, he ventures afar, traveling the nation and the world to perform his improvisations. He also regularly invites other stars to Boise to play with him—among them Ray Brown, Ramsey Lewis, Lionel Hampton, and the late Buddy Rich and Woody Herman. "There are no black or white communities here," Gene explains. "It's just all of us together, and I love it." When he is not on a gig, Harris is playing golf, fishing, or piloting his cabin cruiser on the sparkling waters of Lucky Peak Lake.

In the final analysis, Boise's natural setting is one of its finest attributes. "Let me put it this way," says Governor Andrus. "Nature in Idaho is spelled with a capital 'N.'" Located along the Boise River and snug against the Rockies at the north of the city, the area offers a splendid mix of urban amenities and outdoor recreation. On the outskirts of town are the foothills and, to the west, a vast agricultural valley. From a vantage point in the hills, Boise looks more like a large forest than a thriving regional hub. Within the city limits is the Greenbelt, a heavily wooded, 10-plus-mile stretch along the river. It includes a number of well-maintained pathways for strolling, bicycling, jogging—or just getting away from it all.

Boise provides infinite forms of recreation for serious outdoorspeople. Residents can schuss down the well-groomed trails of the Bogus Basin ski area, ride a raft through the churning rapids of the Payette River, fly fish in a clear mountain stream, or hunt big game. All these activities are within an easy 30-minute drive from center city. Less adventurous indoor types need not despair. Boise is blessed with a wide array of first-class entertainment and cultural facilities. The Morrison Center for the Performing Arts—established in honor of Harry Morrison, the cofounder of Morrison Knudsen—offers ballet, opera, and theater as well as a symphony orchestra. The 12,000-seat Boise State Pavilion plays host to various community activities as well as big-name entertainers. Simply put, Boise offers year-round activities to suit every taste. It is one of the few places where you can battle a rainbow trout within a 9-iron's distance of a Shakespearean play.

. . . And There's More

Best of all, Boise offers business folks a hassle-free lifestyle that allows them the time to absorb the area's beauty and culture. The average commuting time is less than 15 minutes; hence, more time for the family. Speaking of the family, Boise is a great place to raise one. Violence generally is confined to the national section of local newspapers. Idaho's crime rate is the lowest of any Western state. In Boise, the incidence of murder is only one-eighth the national average; the robbery rate, only one twenty-fifth.

Idahoans also take their schooling seriously. The state allocates close to 70 percent of its budget to education. Consequently, Idaho has the third-highest literacy rate in the nation and ranks among the top 10 states in the percentage of high school graduates and median school years completed. Its college-bound seniors consistently outpace their counterparts on national college entrance exams. All told, close to 95 percent of its schoolchildren attend public schools—proof of the popular support for the state's educational institutions.

Idaho's system of higher education builds on this firm foundation. There are six vocational-technical schools, two community colleges, and four institutions providing undergraduate and graduate programs. The state also offers comprehensive work force training as well as screening and testing services to business. In addition, prospective employers can receive instruction tailored to their specific industry needs through the New Industries Training Program.

Paychecks, too, go further in Boise. Affordable housing is readily available, utility rates are low, and state and local taxes are among the lowest of any Western state. As mentioned earlier, Boise's cost of living is one of the lowest in the West. What local employer could afford to pull up stakes? Not Morrison Knudsen, the construction giant. "At one point, we did look at moving our headquarters to San Francisco or Atlanta," recalls Samuel H. Crossland, MK's retired general counsel. "But studies showed the cost would be too great. Where else can we get real estate at these low prices?" (Single-family houses in Boise average an affordable $80,000.) Morrison Knudsen's crosstown neighbor, Boise Cascade, agrees. "We looked at moving the headquarters to San Francisco, Chicago, New York, or Denver," concedes former Chairman Robert V. Hansberger, "but Boise was the best place because of its low costs and its people."

For all the pluses of the capital city, people may be its greatest asset.

Boise's roots as a frontier town are discernible today in the entrepreneurial spirit and the humility of its leading citizens. Octogenarians Joe Albertson and Jack Simplot remain a force in the community. Despite their tremendous wealth, these fiery individuals have never lost their small-town ways. Neighbors recall that Albertson would get up every Saturday morning at 6:30 to mow the lawn, and Simplot would often toss loose change to youngsters during his frequent strolls down Warm Springs Avenue. Unlike other cities in the trendy West, Boise has not been yuppified or gentrified—thanks largely to the spirited likes of Messrs. Albertson and Simplot.

Blurred Boundaries

No doubt, the great outdoors affects the attitudes of local folks. "Mother Nature gives us a different perspective on values," says Robert Hansberger. "People here have a different relationship with the land and with each other." The boundary between company and community is almost indistinguishable, and one thing is clear: Boise takes care of its own.

Jack Simplot to the Rescue

Micron Technology was started in 1978 by the Parkinson twins. Ward, the engineer, had designed computer chips at Mostek Corporation; Joe was a lawyer, accomplished in high finance and deal making. With a few other Mostek engineers, the brothers set up shop in Boise. When big-city venture capitalists turned thumbs down on them, Ward and Joe turned to local investors: a machine shop owner, a sheep rancher, and a potato farmer.

The biggest investor in Micron Technology was and still is J. R. Simplot. Convinced by his son Don to take a gander at this new venture, Jack was immediately impressed. "I bought 40 percent of their company for a million dollars [but] it was just a gamble," he explains. "But we got in it and made a success out of it, I mean, a biggie." What an understatement! The Simplot family, which now controls nearly 19 percent of the chip maker, has made close to $150 million on its investment. (Recent purchases increased Mr. Simplot's personal holdings in Micron to 1,845,000 shares. In addition, his Boise-based Simplot Financial Corporation owns about 5.3 million shares, according to Micron officials.)

The patriarch of potatoes is not bashful about promoting Micron's stock. Last year, crusty Jack openly encouraged workers at J. R. Simplot to buy Micron shares. In an internal memorandum, certain employees of his potato processing company were told that "Mr. Simplot will make whole any loss" on the semiconductor company's stock. Participants in the plan—all salaried employees—were given the go-ahead to buy on margin, that is, using credit. Mr. Simplot further indicated that the "no-loss guarantee" would apply to interest charges of as much as 12 percent on funds borrowed to buy the stock. (Simplot Company swears that the Micron guarantee plan, while novel, is legal.)

Aside from its local benefactors, Micron Technology has been less successful convincing outsiders of its potential. During the 1980s, every U.S. semiconductor manufacturer experienced great difficulty competing toe-to-toe with the Japanese. Five of the seven American DRAM producers left the market; only Micron and Texas Instruments, Inc. remain. However, only Micron manufactures and assembles DRAMS almost entirely in the United States.

DRAMs are the most common type of chip used to store information in a computer. In the world of semiconductors, DRAMs are low-cost, high-volume products. Micron, to its credit, quickly became the low-cost producer, thanks in part to its Idaho location. The other key to the company's success has been its ingenious chip design. Semiconductor chips are made from circular silicon wafers, with the design of the chip etched photographically onto the wafer's surface. The smaller the die size, the more chips a single wafer can produce. Micron's designers have developed the smallest die size in the industry; the Boise-based company typically uses just 11 photomasks rather than the 16 or more employed by its Japanese competitors.

Micron is accustomed to swings in its fortunes, notwithstanding its cost and design advantages. The company posted losses in 1982 and 1983, when it brought its first products to market. Micron generated solid profits in 1984 and 1985, so much so that the firm was given near-legend status by author George Gilder in his book *The Spirit of Enterprise*. Unfortunately, Micron's fortunes waned the next year, losing $33.9 million, because Japanese companies flooded the market with cut-rate chips.

With the help of the local community, the company retaliated by soliciting the Reagan administration and Congress for protection from Japan's dumping practices. Micron's friends in high places, predominantly the Idaho congressional delegation, were invaluable in securing minimum prices for Japanese DRAMs as part of the U.S.–Japan semiconductor pact of 1986. "If it weren't for the chip pact," Joe Parkinson concedes, "Micron would not be in business."

The floor prices on imported chips, coupled with a surge in demand, sent prices and the company's earnings upward in 1987 and 1988. Over the 2-year period, Micron was the world's most profitable manufacturer, with profits of $200 million on revenues of nearly $750 million. However, since then prices have tumbled, as a new supply of chips from Japanese and Korean factories hit the U.S. market. Micron's response: slash costs, expand production in a new low-cost facility, and branch into customized DRAMs. Also, the company concluded a lucrative licensing arrangement with IBM that will enable it to enter the market for next generation: 4-megabyte chips.

Volatility will always be part of the semiconductor game. As technology leaps ahead and new competitors enter the fray, chip makers will be challenged to survive, grow, and remain profitable. But most observers agree that, buoyed by the deep pockets of J. R. Simplot and the mighty arm of Uncle Sam, Micron Technology seems well positioned for the future.

Return of the Prodigal Son

William Agee, 52, is living proof that you can go home again. After a meteoric career that began in Idaho and spread to Michigan and Massachusetts, the third-generation Idahoan returned to Boise in August 1988 to direct Morrison Knudsen Corporation, which was in dire straits. Crippled by the recession of the early 1980s and hobbled by an ill-advised diversification program, MK reported losses of $186.6 million for the 2-year period 1987–1988. Hence, the call to a favorite son and former director (for 11 years) of the company seemed only natural.

Coming home also offered Bill Agee a second chance. After graduating from the University of Idaho and Harvard Business School, he hired on with Boise Cascade. Robert Hansberger, one of the great deal makers of the 1960s, spotted Agee's first-rate talents and immediately put him to work on the company's expansion plans. At 31, he was appointed chief financial officer with major responsibilities for mergers and acquisitions. In fact, Agee served as an outside director of my own company (Theo. H. Davies & Company, Ltd.) for almost 3 years in the mid-1960s when the conglomerate was considering a takeover.

Boise Cascade's house of cards began to collapse in the early 1970s. Bill Agee fled to greener pastures—in this case, Southfield, Michigan, where later, at age 39, he became the chief executive officer of Bendix Corporation. At age 44, he found himself out of work and out of sorts—dabbling in venture capital on Cape Cod Bay. Understandably, the challenge of jump-starting another giant multinational, especially one in his old hometown, offered ready redemption to this former whiz kid.

More than pride was at stake, though. Bill Agee vividly recalls how Morrison Knudsen turned his father's life around. "MK saved my dad," he says. Three decades ago, he explains, Harry Morrison chipped in 50 percent to help Harold Agee buy a small interest in a small Idaho steel company where he had worked for many years. Without Morrison's intervention, the business would have been sold within 48 hours. Eventually, Agee senior ended up as chief executive officer, with 20 percent ownership of the company. For these reasons, MK and Harry Morrison, in particular, carry special meaning to the Agee clan.

A supercharged Bill Agee is breathing new life into the 78-year-old company despite a sluggish heavy construction market. He has directed a major restructuring program from his fourth-floor office in Boise. So far, Agee has gotten rid of most of the loss makers, pared the central staff from 449 to 329, flogged the headquarters building for almost $40 million, and unloaded many of the company's real estate holdings. Besides tightening the screws, he is directing the firm's energies to high-margin segments of construction and to lucrative global markets. Two recent victories: MK was awarded a hefty contract to manufacture 256 rapid transit cars for the Chicago Transit Authority and was selected to join in a $48-million building project in downtown Tokyo, an unusual coup for U.S. contractors.

Whether Bill Agee can restore the sleeping giant to its former days of glory remains to be seen. To date, however, the turnaround is turning heads. The company recovered strongly in 1989, posting $32.1 million in net income. Those earnings rose 7 percent in 1990 as the firm reported a record backlog of $3.9 billion in contracts. Therefore, a number of Wall Street experts consider Morrison Knudsen to be one of the hot performers of the 1990s. But the question remains: Will Bill Agee find happiness in Boise?

The inveterate traveler claims that he is home for good. "I've lived in Idaho over half my life," says the Boise native. "I have deep roots here." To be sure, Agee is experiencing the usual contentment of the prodigal son playing before hometown fans. Mary Cunningham Agee, 39, also seems well-ensconced in Idaho. From her office on Main Street in Boise, she oversees the Nurturing Network, a nonprofit organization formed 5 years ago to provide support for pregnant college and working women. From all reports, the talented husband-and-wife team and their two young children have repotted themselves comfortably in the Rockies—and are very much on the mend.

Cooperation without Coercion

The relationship between Boise and big business should not be misconstrued. Although there are strong linkages between company and community and, as we have just reported, between local enterprises, these relationships are well balanced. "Boise is definitely not a company town, but a very eclectic community," says Phillip M. Barber, a prominent local attorney. "Executives of corporations here contribute to the community, but they do not dominate it." No doubt, the seat of state government, including Boise State University, tends to buffer any potential for bullying that the private sector might display. And the dogged individualism of the area's feisty entrepreneurs makes it even more unlikely that a clannish "Idaho, Inc." could ever emerge in this part of the country.

Looking ahead, the challenge for the community will be to replace the Jack Simplots and Joe Albertsons with men and women equally endowed with the high country spirit. No easy task in today's era of the "paper entrepreneur." However, if Joe Parkinson is a precursor of things to come, the frontier tradition of independence and self-determination should live on. "You can fail, you can plod along, or you can prevail," he says. "It's a matter of persuading people that they can have an effect on their own destinies. I believe in personal responsibility, not only for problems but for successes." Parkinson's fierce dedication to individualism suggests that the legacy of the Simplots, the Morrisons, and the other business buccaneers is alive and well in the Cowboy Capital.

6

Heartland Heroes

Far from the shimmering Rockies sits America's heartlands. Once the proud breadbasket of the nation and the world, the Midwest has seen its agricultural might wither over the years. Around the turn of the century, the region fortuitously hitched its wagon to a new star: the Industrial Revolution. Henry Ford, Cyrus McCormack, John Deere, and other Midwestern entrepreneurs revolutionized the face of America and the world.

What follows is a tale of two heartland heroes, Herbert Henry Dow and Will Keith Kellogg, who transformed salt water and grain into new and exciting products, and the giant multinationals that bear their names. But this is also a story of the symbiosis between two famous companies and the tiny Michigan townships they call home. The phenomenal success of The Dow Chemical Company and Kellogg Company could not have occurred without the active support of Midland and Battle Creek, respectively. Hence, their case histories offer valuable insights to any big business interested in frontier living.

Good Chemistry:
The Dow Chemical Story

In 1890, 24-year-old Herbert Henry Dow, or "Crazy Dow," as he was known, chose the minuscule Michigan town of Midland because of its large subterranean brine deposits. A few years later, the young chemist from Cleveland proved that he could produce commercial amounts of bromide by electrolysis, and, in 1897, he founded The Dow Chemical

Company. Capital, however, was a problem. When local financiers skeptically turned him aside, Dow stumbled upon a most unlikely source: Hetty Green, an eccentric millionaire who had been tabbed the "witch of Wall Street." Known far and wide for her astute investment savvy as well as for her miserliness, the sixtyish spinster was visiting Midland in search of solitude and anonymity. During her short stay, she decided that Crazy Dow was not so crazy after all. Ms. Green bought 100 shares of Dow stock that brought to her estate nearly three-quarters of a million dollars in net profit when it was sold in 1936. Other Wall Street scions, knowing Hetty Green's sense for a smart deal, joined the fold, and the tiny chemical company in the Michigan backwoods never looked back.

In retrospect, it seems preposterous "to think that a small concern isolated from the major population cities and money markets of the country had any worthwhile future," writes Don Whitehead, a two-time Pulitzer Prize-winning author and chronicler of Dow Chemical's history. "[Midland's] only transportation links with the outside world were rutted roads and a single rail line. Its managers were scarcely more than upstarts only just out of the college classroom. They were not widely traveled or experienced in the ways of big business. In sophisticated industrial circles, they could have been rated little more than country bumpkins in the fields of finance, management, manufacturing, engineering, and selling on any large scale."

Yet for all its deficiencies—and often because of them—The Dow Chemical Company survived and grew. Herbert Dow's genius in mass production and mechanization coupled with an uncanny ability to attract talented young engineers and chemists to Michigan's lower peninsula enabled the flyspeck firm to take on the industrial giants of Germany, Great Britain, and the United States. Today, Dow is the sixth-largest chemical company in the world and, next to Du Pont, the biggest in the United States. Mr. Dow's rugged individualism produced a $18.9-billion empire, which insiders hope will reach $30 billion in sales by 1995.

The 93-year-old conglomerate is on a roll. Recently cited by *Business Month* magazine as one of America's five best-managed corporations, Dow Chemical earned $2.7 billion in 1989. Its return on equity, which has averaged a respectable 18 percent over the past decade, erupted to an incredible 35 percent during the period from 1987 to 1990. Will this trend continue? Most people feel that the company's return on equity will more likely be in the 20 percent range in the next few years. Nevertheless, most seers, including *Forbes* magazine, predict that the Midland firm will be the chemical industry's strongest performer for the balance of the century.

Branching Out

Diversification is the key. Over half the company's sales are overseas, and of its 1800 products, no single one accounted for more than 8 percent of 1990 sales. In 1987, then president Paul F. Oreffice moved Dow further into the specialty chemicals business, backing away from commodity chemicals. He remembered painfully the downturns of 1958 and 1970, which were caused by massive industry buildups in the supply of basic chemicals. By shifting toward the high-margin, specialty end of the business, the company buffered itself against the vagaries of the business cycle. Dow Chemical now gets nearly 40 percent of its earnings from specialty products, and analysts expect them to account for 50 percent of earnings by 1992.

Aggressive acquisitions paved the way into the specialty business. The Richardson-Merrell drug business, purchased in 1980 through a $260-million stock swap, was Dow's first major deal. Next came Morton Thiokol, Inc.'s Texize Division, adding products such as Spray 'N' Wash stain remover and Fantastik kitchen cleaner to a fledgling stable of household products, including Ziploc bags. Dow leaped into hair-care products in 1987, when it outbid Alberto-Culver, Inc. for Lamaur, Inc. It then bought Essex Chemical Corporation for $366 million, boosting its automotive plastics business.

In another giant step toward more sophisticated products, Dow Chemical acquired a controlling (67 percent) interest in Marion Laboratories, Inc. in August 1989 for $2.2 billion. Marion Labs, combined with the Merrell Dow unit, makes the Midland firm among the nation's top five pharmaceutical companies, ranked by annual sales. Another promising move: In 1990, Dow formed a joint venture with Eli Lilly to create a $1.5-billion agricultural chemicals company, the world's fifth-largest. Earlier, Dow teamed up with United Technologies Corporation to develop advanced polymers for automotive and aerospace uses.

The company's track record in branching out through acquisitions is the envy of the industry. "Dow has been the most successful of the basic commodity chemical producers who have tried to diversify into downstream products," concedes J. Lawrence Wilson, chairman of Rohm & Haas Corporation, a Philadelphia-based chemical company that tried—and failed—to diversify into pharmaceuticals and fibers.

Making the $30-billion goal will take more than eager beaver acquisitions. Much of the growth will be generated internally. Dow's research and development budget has increased by more than 200 percent since 1978. The company currently spends the equivalent of $13,910 per employee on R&D, nearly twice the industry average. Much of the money is targeted at finding new products, says President and CEO Frank P. Popoff, who succeeded Oreffice in 1987.

Recently, Dow Chemical established an incubator system for new ideas. One major breakthrough: Drytech, a chemical which absorbs fluids and has application, naturally, in disposable diapers. The firm earmarks $15 million a year for its scientists to pursue their own ideas—even ones that may not sound like big money-makers. Also, its Innovation Development Department identifies potential commercial applications for all basic research. The payoff of this unit is reflected in its new patents: Dow received 473 in the United States in 1988, compared to 330 earlier.

Besides searching for new businesses and new products, Dow Chemical has streamlined its basic chemicals business. During the 1980s, it wrote off $800 million in assets, reduced employment by 19,000 jobs, and lightened its debt load. The firm also lined up alternative feedstocks so that it is less vulnerable to rising raw material prices—saving as much as $100 million a year. On the manufacturing front, every Dow plant in the United States, Europe, Asia, and Latin America has been operating at 91 percent of capacity or better during recent quarters. In some specialty products, the units are pushing 100 percent. To meet future demand, Dow's capital expenditures average about $2 billion a year. Its long-term commitment to invest in facilities, R&D, and education and training has made the company's productivity the highest, by far, in the industry. In 1990, Dow's profit per employee was $70,000, or nearly double that of the next-best chemical company.

Tomorrow, The World

Diversification also means globalization. Historically, international markets have had a special appeal to the Midland crowd. Frank Popoff is the third consecutive foreign-born CEO to grace the executive suite. The 55-year-old native Bulgarian distinguished himself at Dow by steering the company's European operations into specialty chemicals during the early 1980s. Popoff, who speaks Bulgarian and German as well as English, is thoroughly at home in the foreign markets that are crucial to the most-multinational U.S. chemical company. Today, the firm counts about 55 percent of its profits, 50 percent of its assets, and 50 percent of its people overseas.

One of a handful of U.S. businesses to crack the tough Japanese market, Dow Chemical has been ringing up annual revenues of more than $650 million in the Land of the Rising Sun. Mr. Popoff says that he expects sales in Japan to climb to $1 billion "reasonably soon"—an opinion supported by the fact that Dow is the fifth-fastest-growing *gaijin* company in Japan. The company's objective "to maximize growth, to reduce cyclicality, to reduce the costs of developing new materials over the broadest market mix, to develop applications, to tap the global market for good people" has led Frank Popoff to conclude that "more emphasis overseas, not less, is appropriate."

The Dow president personally tries to sustain the firm's global orientation by making people comfortable with the idea that the world beyond Midland is where the action is. He warns new hires, middle managers, and top executives alike to expand their cross-cultural horizons and to be wary of "old fellows in the chemical industry" who still perceive Midland as the Middle Kingdom. "I say to our people: 'Watch out for stuffy old guys like that,'" Popoff states. "'And kick me in the shins if I come across that way.'"

Frank Popoff understands the challenge of keeping a fire lit under a mammoth corporation, particularly one that might fall prey to small-town lethargy. "Success breeds inertia," he says, "and that means a love affair with the status quo and an aversion to change." Nevertheless, Popoff believes that the company's current mix of new and old commercial activities should make the $30-billion sales target readily achievable. "I think the businesses we have in place will be our locomotive," he says.

Fortunately, Dow's locomotive is engineered by a deep and experienced management team that shares the boss's vision and values. The top six executives average 30 years with the company, and only three will reach the firm's normal retirement age of 65 in this decade. One of President Popoff's great strengths is his ability to put people at ease and to secure their trust and commitment to change. "Dow today has a very open management style," says one outside consultant. "When Mr. Popoff comes in, he's called Frank, and that tells you something."

The demeanor of the company is definitely small-town: relaxed and informal. "There is no sense of rush apparent," writes historian, Don Whitehead. "The executive offices are neither expansive nor expensively plush nor isolated in a remote penthouse sanctuary. There are no batteries of receptionists and layers of secretaries standing guard in the outer offices of the decision makers. The executives often have their lunch in the headquarters cafeteria and wait their turn in line along with lower-echelon workers."

Don't be misled by the laid-back look of the head office. "Dow Chemical people work harder than big-city types," says Herbert D. "Ted" Doan, a former president and CEO and Herbert H. Dow's grandson. "Or so it is locally believed." The company also demands that its managers display an active, hands-on involvement in every aspect of their jobs. The founder set the standard almost a century ago. "My idea of a big man is one who, after he is in touch with a small job, then becomes acquainted with another small job, and another, until he knows the game," Herbert H. Dow declared. Fierce attention to detail, coupled with a roll-up-the-sleeves attitude, is essential to any aspiring careerist at Dow Chemical.

From Macho to Mellow

A proud, self-righteous attitude characterized the company for years. Not that long ago, Dow regarded such groups as the Environmental Protection Agency and the Sierra Club as implacable adversaries and disclaimed compromise as a matter of principle. Turn the clock back 20 years or so. Dow Chemical Company went through the public outcry over napalm during the Vietnam War. Next came the discovery of dioxin contamination in the Tittabawassee and Saginaw rivers below the Midland plant. Then, it was the defoliant Agent Orange that incited a string of humiliating battles with environmental authorities and regulators.

Throughout these fights, Dow's reaction remained unchanged: part annoyance, part indifference. During the early 1980s, morale had sunk so low that long-time chemists and researchers actually removed their company's pins before boarding business flights. Worn down, the beleaguered organization surveyed 213 employees, managers, directors, and outsiders about Dow's public posture. The 1984 report concluded: "The current reputation of The Dow Chemical Company with its many publics may well be at an all-time low. We are viewed as tough, arrogant, secretive, uncooperative, and insensitive."

Since then, the company has shifted to a softer image—thanks largely to the tall, relaxed Mr. Popoff. Dow has opened its plant sites around the country to hundreds of tours. Its scientific "road shows" and its advice to line managers to join more community groups are raising its profile. The company also incorporates its *Public Interest Reports,* which lists Dow's philanthropic activities, in the annual report. And recently, it gave $375,000 to the University of Missouri to create a Science Journalism Center.

In a marked shift from the past, Chief Executive Popoff publicly supports a strong Environmental Protection Agency as well as waste reduction and recycling. Dow is leading an industry effort to demonstrate the feasibility of recycling plastic collected from homes and fast-food restaurants. For the company's endorsement of hazardous-waste reduction, Anne Woiwode, a member of the Sierra Club's Michigan chapter, said: "This is the first time the Sierra Club was on the same side of an issue as Dow."

Obviously, the company is now paying attention to constituencies that the "old" Dow would have disclaimed. Its reason over confrontation approach is being recognized, and not just by the Sierra Club. In 1990, the World Environment Center, a New York-based nonprofit group that oversees environmental issues, awarded Dow Chemical its gold medal for achievement. Yet Mr. Popoff remains philosophical about these kudos and the company's mellow ways. "I think we still have a fair amount of work to do in terms of the way we are viewed," he admits. "We know we'll never change Ralph Nader's mind. But Dow is at peace with itself."

Making Over Midland

Peace of mind was in short supply when Herbert Dow first came to Midland. He encountered a derelict community, its landscape dotted by tree stumps, abandoned by the loggers who had stripped the land of its towering pine trees. The dirt roads leading from the town wandered into nowhere and, it seemed, so did the future of Midland and its people. Fortunately, Mr. Dow pledged to convert this dying lumber town of a few hundred residents into a model city.

To that end, Herbert Dow worked tirelessly, transforming Midland into a respectable, cheery community. "He held Dow picnics for citizens of the town, crowned Dow Queens, and marched down Main Street in Dow parades," says Charles C. Mann, a New York-based business writer. "He taught Sunday School, created a music society, served on the local parks committee, organized a contest to put gardens in backyards all over town, and rode around on his bicycle inveighing against the rowdies on Saloon Row."

Under Mr. Dow's tutelage, Midland evolved into one of the proudest, most civic-minded burgs in America. Today, the modern town of 38,000 people stands in stark contrast with the old Midland. Attractive, affordable homes, 1200 acres of parks, and 500 acres of city forest dot the landscape. First-rate schools, libraries, hospitals, golf courses, and churches (all 55 of them) complement the community's well-endowed infrastructure. Midland supports its own symphony orchestra, an art association, and a theater guild, and its mammoth community center provides entertainment ranging from ballet to bowling.

Dow Chemical's involvement in Midland's educational system goes back to the days when Herbert Dow served on the local school board. Mr. Dow knew that the company's professionally minded parents would insist on building their careers in a community with a strong commitment to public education. Nowadays, platoons of highly trained Dow Chemical professionals (Dow boasts that Midland has more Ph.D.s per capita than any other town in the country) reinforce the pressure on area schools to perform. Their vigilance gets results. Midland students receive a disproportionately large share of national honors each year.

"We have a marvelous public school system in Midland," boasts President Popoff. "I look at my friends in the big cities who say, 'What, send my children to a public school—you've got to be joking!' We don't have that kind of attitude here. My kids have gone to the public schools, and I wouldn't have it any other way."

Besides nurturing the local schools, Dow's generosity has left an indelible imprint on Midland. Over the years, the largest contributions have come from the Herbert H. and Grace A. Dow Foundation, established in 1936 with a large chunk of Dow stock. It has underwritten hospitals, libraries, churches, and, of course, schools. Add to this the local courthouse, property for a municipal golf course, and a state-of-the-art tennis complex, as well as various donations to Kalamazoo College, the University of Michigan, and other higher educational institutions. The Dow Foundation and 15 other philanthropic organizations set up by the company's founding families have a total endowment of three-quarters of a billion dollars—or roughly $20,000 for every man, woman, and child in town.

Understandably, it is impossible to distinguish Midland, Michigan, from The Dow Chemical Company. The Dow name is on everything: the Dow Memorial Library, Dow Gardens, Dow High School. Nearly one-third of the local residents are employed by the company; many others are indirectly affected by its dominant presence. As one Midlander puts it: "Dow influences everything that goes on in this town."

Nevertheless, Midland is not the stereotypical company town of yesteryear. The reason, says Ted Doan, is because the executives and professionals are active members of the community—toiling alongside farmers, blue-collar workers, and office staffers on various projects. "Dow doesn't patronize the community," he argues. Frank Popoff also plays down the company's enormous power in local political, economic, and social affairs. "We'd lose a lot if we tried to impose ourselves like Big Brother," he says. "We try to be a supportive presence, but not an omnipresence."

The chances are that any boorish provincialism that might exist is offset by the cosmopolitan backgrounds of many Dow personnel. The town has seven cultural societies to cater to their diverse tastes. It is not unusual on any one day at the Midland Country Club, the favorite gathering spot for entertaining visitors, to hear conversations in Japanese, French, Spanish, German, or Italian. Dignitaries from around the world bring diversity, and the community is far more worldly, more sophisticated, than many big cities.

These cosmopolitan Midlanders declare that their town is devoid of snobbery. But the allegation is widely disputed. "Class distinctions are firmly drawn," says *Business Month*'s Daniel Forbes. "Blue collar plus white collar equals an uneasy mix in this town." More vocal still is Kathleen M. Schultz, a former Dow brat. "You could avoid the smell [of the chemical factories] if you lived on the 'right' side of town," she recalls. "Some people don't think that kids should know exactly where they stand in the social order of things by age six. My sister and I often said that Midland was the last place we would choose to raise our kids." To this end, Mrs. Schultz chooses to reside in Portland, Oregon.

Despite these countercharges, the great majority of residents, past and present, describe the Michigan township as a great place to live. Even Mary Sinclair, the local activist who surfaced the company's scandalous contamination of the Tittabawassee River, says: "The community is pretty livable, and Dow has done really good things for Midland. On the whole, Midland is a real nice place to raise your kids."

Kellogg Country: The Land of Snap, Crackle, and Pop

Landing at the W. K. Kellogg Regional Airport on the outskirts of Battle Creek, Michigan, one begins an odyssey that passes through the 1600-acre Kellogg Forest, the world-acclaimed Kellogg Bird Sanctuary, Kellogg Community College, the W. K. Kellogg Auditorium, and the Ann J. Kellogg School for physically handicapped youngsters. Almost every vestige of Battle Creek, the self-proclaimed "Cereal Capital of the World," contains some element of the "K word."

Will Keith Kellogg was a driven, unsmiling, introverted man who became known as the "King of Cornflakes." His success did not come easily, however. Brought up in a rigid, humorless household ("I never learned to play," he once admitted), Will was hardly impressive in his first dabble in commerce—selling brooms made in his father's Battle Creek factory. Later, he played second fiddle to his high-flying older brother, Dr. John Kellogg, who had founded a sanatorium to care for the health-conscious disciples of the Seventh Day Adventist Church, headquartered in town.

Titled "business manager," but in fact a gofer for Dr. John, Will spent 20 difficult years in his brother's shadow. To make things worse, both his first and his second wife and two children died. At age 45, Will confessed his fears that "I will always be a poor man." During this difficult patch, Kellogg vented his frustrations by concocting various recipes to make cereals and grains more palatable to the locals. By accident, he and his brother stumbled upon a unique process of producing cold wheat flakes. Will Kellogg sensed the tremendous opportunity to create a new category of light, nutritious breakfast foods to fit the American lifestyle. On February 19, 1906—48 days before his 46th birthday—he founded the Battle Creek Toasted Corn Flake Company, now known as the Kellogg Company. Six weeks later, he began churning out his first cartons of corn flakes.

Will Kellogg was the consummate marketer—one of the nation's best and brightest. In July 1906, he took out a full-page advertisement in *The Ladies Home Journal* that brought in more orders than the company could handle. The marketing whiz gave away free samples, increased his advertising budget, and watched sales climb to 1 million cases in 1909. Three years later, the company erected the world's largest billboard in New York's Times Square. Will's gimmickry paid off, for customers around the world woke up to Kellogg's cereals. To fill their insatiable appetites, he next ventured overseas, setting up plants in Canada (1914), England (1922), and Australia (1924).

Ready for Breakfast

The Kellogg Company today stands as a proud legacy to Mr. Kellogg. The $4.9-billion in sales giant is the world's largest producer of ready-to-eat cereals. Its stable of famous products includes Kellogg's Corn Flakes, Rice Krispies, Frosted Flakes, and Special K; but Eggo Waffles, Mrs. Smith's Pies, Whitney's Yogurt, and other goodies are also part of the line. Breakfast foods, though, account for over 80 percent of the firm's revenues. "Ready-to-eat cereal basically is our thing," says Chairman and CEO William E. LaMothe, 64. "We're dedicated to doing it better than anyone else in the world."

Kellogg's focus on cereals has produced handsome dividends at home and abroad. Its share of the U.S. market is 38 percent; General Mills follows at 28 percent. The Battle Creek multinational also commands 50 percent of the world cereal market—important because overseas markets have almost twice the growth potential of the United States. Certainly, the company has become a powerhouse in the supermarkets of the world—expert at introducing new products, sustaining existing ones, and dominating store shelves with the industry's broadest cereal mix.

What about the bottom line? Here, Kellogg's results have been spectacular. The cereal maker enjoys the highest margins in the industry. During the last decade, it was the sixth-most-profitable American corporation, with an average return on equity of 38.9 percent. Also, the company frequently hits the charts as one of the country's best-managed businesses. Kellogg's secret? "We try to stay focused on what we know best—and execute, execute, execute!," says Chairman LaMothe.

Kellogg begins executing every Monday at 7:30 a.m. LaMothe and other senior executives congregate at corporate headquarters to evaluate the lifeline of any consumer-products company: new product development. During its extended breakfasts, the top management team taste-tests a wide menu of current and new items. Always on the alert to put more snap, crackle, and pop into the company's offerings, these selective slurpers give the thumbs up to only 12 to 15 percent of the cereals presented at the Monday breakfasts.

Overseas products receive as tough a going over as those developed in Battle Creek. Unlike other U.S. companies, Kellogg is especially sensitive to the need to modify American products for foreign palates—and vice versa. For example, Just Right, a mineral-laden, multigrain flake now sold in the United States, was first created for health-conscious Australians, who are among the world's biggest cereal consumers. Kellogg's cooked up Genmai Flakes, made of whole-grain rice, for the Japanese market, where many people still eat fish and rice for breakfast. That product was introduced into the U.S. market as a rice-bran cereal called "Kenmei," which in Japanese means "wisdom" and "prudence." Normally, the company launches nearly 40 new cereals worldwide each year.

The cereal maker knows how to produce, literally. Its famous Building 100 in Battle Creek is the world's most sophisticated cereal-production facility. Each of its four floors is larger than a football field; each is highly automated. Seven days a week, 24 hours a day, computer-assisted machines perform every step of the production function, from mixing grains to packing cereal boxes. As a result, Building 100 can crank out 500 million pounds of breakfast food a year. Moreover, Kellogg's investments in its plants at home and abroad are yielding significant manufacturing efficiencies. The company's gross margins (total sales less cost of foods) now stand at 49 percent as compared to 41 percent in 1983. The food industry average is 35 percent. In addition, Kellogg's plant workers routinely generate productivity increases of at least 5 percent a year. "We have a highly motivated work force that believes in updating its skills to keep pace with technology," beams Mr. LaMothe.

For all its success, Kellogg can hardly afford to rest on its laurels. Competitors, especially number two, General Mills, are nibbling away at its kingdom with cereals aimed at health-conscious consumers. Industry observers sense that the Battle Creek gang may have lost some of its sizzle. They criticize the company for several new product duds and its tardiness in capitalizing on the oat bran craze. What concerns top management most is that its 37-year string of annual profit increases was broken in 1989.

In response, Kellogg is preoccupied with "rightsizing" (in the words of Joseph M. Stewart, senior vice president for corporate affairs). It has trimmed the white-collar work force by 5 percent, slashed debt, deferred capital spending, and accelerated new product development. This series of midcourse corrections is designed to get the cereal maker back on track toward its long-term goal: a towering 50 percent of the U.S. market. Also, Kellogg's rightsizing program has forced the company to reassess its corporate culture and to make some hard choices about its next generation of leaders.

Kellogg-centric?

In the process of righting his tilting ship, Board Chairman William La-Mothe decided to remove his chief lieutenant and heir apparent, Horst W. Schroeder, from the presidency of the company. The action, taken in September 1989, was not an easy one. The 48-year-old Schroeder was a 19-year veteran of the company and the prime mover of its international success. Nonetheless, the German-born executive was blamed for many of the cereal maker's recent setbacks, particularly for its deterioration in market share. However, insiders suggest that stylistic differences between the abrasive Schroeder and the diplomatic LaMothe may have brought these tensions to a head.

Midwestern consensus and collegiality are long-standing values at Kellogg. Although Brooklyn-born and Fordham-educated, William La-Mothe assimilated nicely into the heartlands. Like most Kellogg managers, he is low-key and serious—"a soft-spoken, no-nonsense high achiever," says former Ford Motors Chairman Philip Caldwell, who sits on Kellogg's board. "He doesn't go around beating his chest." The 64-year-old LaMothe, now in his eleventh year as chairman, consistently has approached his company with a combination of humility and toughness.

Horst Schroeder, on the other hand, was often described as heavy-handed, even imperious. After all, his methods had made Kellogg the star of supermarket shelves in Europe. Why change? Unfortunately, his rather cold style won few friends in Battle Creek. Allegedly, Schroeder rarely delegated authority but readily handed out blame. His apparent inability to listen may have also turned off several key marketing people, who left the company. "He was very abrupt—European," recalls Robert L. Nichols, Kellogg's retired vice chairman. "His personality was quite different from what we consider normal executive behavior." To widen the fissure between himself and his Midwestern colleagues, Schroeder committed the unpardonable sin: he spurned a Battle Creek lifestyle, choosing instead to live 20 miles away in more cosmopolitan Kalamazoo. By contrast, LaMothe was a longtime resident of Cereal City, where he and his wife, Pat, happily raised six children.

The blowup was inevitable. In the fall of 1989, Horst Schroeder left the company "for personal reasons." In an interview with *The Wall Street Journal,* Chairman LaMothe cited a failure of "chemistry" as the prime reason. He conceded that he erred seriously in choosing an executive whose background and style strikingly departed from the corporate norm. In retrospect, Schroeder had to deal with two sets of unfamiliar values: one, American; the other, Kellogg's—rough indeed for any outsider. "Not only do you come into a national culture, but a corporate culture that's nearly 100 years old," admits Mr. LaMothe. "Oh, boy, what a tall order when you're foreign."

The Schroeder affair left Kellogg and Battle Creek reeling, and rightly so. Putting aside the obvious clash of personalities, it remains clear that the cereal maker must do better at managing a multinational pool of managers if it aspires to global leadership. While Kellogg gets high marks for developing a worldwide staple of products, it has been less effective at developing a worldwide inventory of people. Frontier firms generally have a real need to avoid their natural insularity. They must work especially hard at managing men and women on the basis of their abilities, not the color of their passports or the twang of their accents. Kellogg, it seems, has yet to make the transition to a truly global company.

Commitment to the Community

If Kellogg is blinded on occasion by its small-town ways, it is easy to understand why. Physical beauty abounds. The Battle Creek Metropolitan Linear Park links natural waterways and sculptured parks with 11 miles of well-maintained pathways for strolling, bicycling, or jogging. Homes and golf courses are hardly more than a 10-minute drive from the downtown headquarters. Thirty minutes away are vast woodlands, lakes, streams, and, for those who want it, total solitude.

Battle Creek has the appeal of offering Kellogg executives and employees sanctuary from the pressures of the big city, the long hours of commuting, and the tensions of living in a crowded place. Its schools, hospitals, and other public services are better than average; overall amenities, though not first-class, are on the uptick. Life in Cereal City goes on at a comparatively leisurely and relaxed pace, and children roam the outdoors relatively free from the fear of urban crime.

Nevertheless, the recession years of the late 1970s and early 1980s hit the area extremely hard. Michigan was in a depressed state, and Battle Creek was no exception. During this period, Kellogg had outgrown its corporate headquarters and was considering a new downtown location. Yet the cereal maker and many other townsfolk were fed up with the fragmented local municipalities that bickered over jurisdictional control of the area. On May 26, 1980, Kellogg delivered its ultimatum. Unless the city of Battle Creek and the townships merged their governments, the company was leaving for greener pastures. Fortunately, area residents voted overwhelmingly in favor of the proposed consolidation, and, on January 1, 1983, the merger took place. To many, Kellogg's ultimatum was an outstanding example of proactive business leadership; but to others, the company's tactics represented corporate intimidation at its worst.

On balance, most longtime residents of the area, including non-Kellogg employees, describe the cereal giant as a firm that cares deeply for its community. This commitment to the region began in 1930, when Will Kellogg established the Kellogg Foundation and stipulated that it had to remain in Battle Creek. Mr. Kellogg's words, printed on the foundation's front door, say that the organization exists "for the application of knowledge to the problems of people." Ever pragmatic, the foundation believes in giving money to three basic areas: agriculture, health, and education. In 1990, for example, grants went to such grateful recipients as the City of Battle Creek for recreational and cultural facilities and Michigan State University for the development of projects that encourage a healthy lifestyle.

Today, the Kellogg Foundation is the nation's third-largest. Only the Ford Foundation and the J. Paul Getty Trust surpass its approximately $4.2 billion in assets. Kellogg gives away about $120 million a year (a figure that is expected to jump to $200 million in 1995); it makes about 300 grants a year; and, at any one time, it has 600 to 700 active projects. Like many other penturban companies, Kellogg singles out its own community for special attention. In Battle Creek, the $60 million in grants since 1931 have been pivotal in helping keep the town alive. In addition to the facilities mentioned earlier, the foundation has donated a civic center, an ice rink, and various clinics and training programs. Thanks to Kellogg's support, local teenagers maintain the lush Metropolitan Linear Park that winds through town.

As further evidence of its largesse, the Kellogg Foundation is building a new $60-million headquarters downtown, thus demonstrating its commitment to the center city. The much-debated facility, scheduled for completion in 1991, covers 14 acres of land, or close to 25 percent of the downtown area. From all accounts, it will be the shining star in Battle Creek's redevelopment program. Also, Kellogg is pitching in to help move older businesses and to upgrade the center city with new shops. "The first thing we wanted to do was to take the [existing] businesses being relocated and move them to a new place," said Russell G. Mawby, foundation chairman. "It helped strengthen another part of downtown, and we wanted our project to be big enough to have an impact. That's consistent with our objective of working with the community."

Common Denominators

With only 132 miles of interstate highway separating them, Dow Chemical and Kellogg have much in common. Both Michigan mighties survived the treacherous transition from small, privately held, entrepreneurial businesses to large, publicly traded, professionally managed organizations. Both firms expanded far beyond their provincial homes to join the ranks of America's leading multinational corporations. Neither company allowed rural living to stifle its creative juices; both became industry pacesetters in innovation and marketing. Most important, both organizations withstood the test of time: Dow and Kellogg are household names on several continents.

These heartland heroes revalidate the thesis of frontier living. They converted the disadvantages of size and distance to their advantage. When both firms felt the sting of intense global competition during the seventies and eighties, they withdrew to the safe havens of their hometowns. There, away from the din of combat, their leaders drafted clear, uncluttered decisions about the proper battle plan. For Dow, diversification away from commodity chemicals was the answer; Kellogg, on the other hand, shunned diversification—focusing instead on its basic business, breakfast foods. In each instance, the cozy confines of their heartland homes gave these companies time—time to regroup, to lick their wounds, to plan a counteroffensive.

These critical periods of introspection also became rallying points for the community. Each village's survival was linked inextricably to the company's survival, and vice versa. The lifeline between them enabled Dow and Kellogg to receive an extraordinarily high level of support from their neighborhoods in times of crisis. It is this close bond between company and community that, above all, distinguishes the frontier organization. The interdependence of Dow Chemical and Midland with Kellogg and Battle Creek is typical of many other small-town settings. In our research, we found similar behavior in Columbus, Indiana; Bayport, Minnesota; Zeeland, Michigan; and Peoria, Illinois. In those places, the beneficiaries were named Cummins Engine, Anderson, Herman Miller, and Caterpillar.

Obviously, neither Midland nor Battle Creek is nirvana. Both townships have serious shortcomings, and we should not pooh-pooh them. Executives bemoan the lack of decent shopping that frequently forces them to motor great distances to Detroit and Chicago to stock their wardrobes. Top-notch hotels, too, are in short supply. In fact, Kellogg was forced into the hotel business when the Stouffer's Hotel across the street from its Battle Creek headquarters was going under. Out of sheer vanity, the cereal maker bought the property to provide decent accommodations for corporate visitors. But problem number one? "Travel," everyone agrees. Dow and Kellogg managers uniformly criticize the region's two-bit airports and the difficulties in making commercial connections when corporate aircraft are not available.

How do Dow and Kellogg deal with these blemishes? Not by covering them up. Both organizations are unashamed of their rural roots; they discuss openly the pros and cons of provincial living with every prospective recruit. "We attract people who have small-town values," says Dow's Popoff. "And we try not to be secretive about the trade-offs of living in Midland."

Kellogg follows the same approach. The cereal maker emphasizes three things in selling itself to new hires. First, its leadership in the marketplace. ("We're number one in our industry, and we let people know it," boasts Senior Vice President Joseph Stewart.) Second, the friendly, family-style culture of a company where everyone is on the team. Finally, the many quality-of-life benefits of Battle Creek.

So far, both organizations have been able to recruit the stream of new talent needed to survive and grow. Nevertheless, recruitment remains a constant challenge. "Would we move?," asks Frank Popoff. "Only if we couldn't attract the right kind of people in sufficient numbers. But so far that is not happening."

Executives at Dow Chemical and Kellogg adamantly insist that a small-town headquarters is much less of a liability today than it may have been 20 years ago. The great equalizer, they contend, is modern technology. "We have every gadget in the world here," claims Dow's Popoff. "With satellite communications, it doesn't make any difference where you are." Credit, too, goes to the state of Michigan for its advanced system of fiber-optic transmission cables that links local businesses like Dow and Kellogg to their customers, suppliers, dealers, and financiers.

Naturally, penturban locations work best for corporations that have decentralized management philosophies. Advanced telecommunications enable these heartland heroes to manage their activities in an arm's-length way, and both companies are moving in this direction. With the help of modern technology, Dow Chemical and Kellogg are reducing the size of their central staffs and pushing additional responsibility and authority out to their business units. The relative isolation of both organizations forces them to redistribute power to their operating companies. This trend toward a more hands-off management approach is a national one—one that further strengthens the case for a smallish headquarters in frontierland.

7

Mail-Order Marvels

Cities are first and foremost places of business. For many years, corporate America rejected the notion that a company might put its people and plant far from the center of commercial activity. Proximity, closeness, and concentration were overriding concerns. But proximity is now superfluous, says William Safire, the celebrated columnist. "You can be close without being near."

No industry disdains proximity more than the mail-order business. True, urban-based oligarchs—Spiegel, Montgomery Ward, and Sears, Roebuck—dominated the catalog market for more than a century. But then, along came modern telecommunications facilities, with the ability to link suppliers with unseen shoppers; along came the computer, with its centralized accounting brain that eliminates the need to put employees and inventories in the same place; and along came zip codes, new and rapid parcel delivery methods, and the new services provided by the U.S. Post Office. Suddenly, the economics began to work against downtown catalogers, with their limited, high-cost space and poor supply of educated workers.

Today, direct-mail firms are thriving in the new corporate frontier. Remoteness actually enhances their ability to compete with retailers across the nation. "It makes sense to put plants and executive offices where the living is easier and the cost of land much lower," Safire contends. "If 'out of town' is the aim, why not all the way out? That's why L. L. Bean and Lands' End do their mail-order business from places most Americans never heard of."

Being off the beaten path helps in another important way. Mail-order shoppers are, by definition, hundreds of miles away from the seller. They need to be educated, informed, and, most of all, stroked. Provincial folks have time for them. Unlike many of their peers in the big city, they are never too busy or too brusque to soothe the spirits of an irate or a confused customer. Their slow, syrupy voices kindle the warm glow needed to win trust at a distance. In their own way, direct-mail firms are redefining the close-to-the-customer maxim with superior results.

Courting Unseen Customers

"What's in: mail order. What's out: Bloomingdale's!" So says *Business Week* in its survey of social trends of the nineties. Direct-mail houses offer instant gratification to increasingly impatient Americans. These companies thrive by selling their wares to baby-boomers who have no time to go to the mall. Many of their customers are busy executives and working parents who have all but given up on department stores. "Let your fingers do the shopping" is their motto.

If the truth be known, there are few products in any mail-order catalog that are not found in Bloomingdale's or the local mall. But what armchair shopping offers is convenience and service. Mail-order distribution lets these unseen consumers shop 24 hours a day, 7 days a week, from any location.

Over 10,000 U.S. catalogers will spew out almost 15 billion fancy brochures in 1991, or triple the number in 1980. As a result of their labors, more than half the country's population, 98 million people, regularly shop by mail. The $35-billion industry is growing at a rate of 8 to 10 percent a year, double that of general merchandise stores. Clearly, catalog companies are encroaching on traditional retailers. According to the U.S. Department of Commerce, as a share of total merchandise sales, mail orders jumped from 22 percent in 1985 to roughly 28 percent in 1990.

All sizes and shapes of mail-order merchants find America's outback to their liking. They include the offbeat, mom-and-pop operators like Louisiana-based DuSay's, which sells sunglasses and hats for pampered poodles; the Peruvian Connection of Tonganoxie, Kansas—a merchandiser of Andean textiles; Austad's of Sioux Falls, South Dakota, which flogs colored golf balls and left-handed clubs to the nation's duffers; Colorado's Life Force, a supplier of the latest in eavesdropping equipment for the home; and Brigade Quartermasters of Kennesaw, Georgia, which flogs "action gear"—sun block, snake bite kits, and the like—to U.S. soldiers in the remote deserts of Saudi Arabia. Also among the pack are celebrities like Robert Redford. In 1990, the 53-year-old actor launched a line of products and condiments with a distinctly Southwestern flavor. The 36-page catalog for *Sundance* offers Native American and regional specialties, such as dried wildflower bouquets and handmade cowboy boots. The Sundance Kid's corporate corral is, appropriately enough, in Sundance, Utah. More adventurous shoppers can call on the Shop the World by Mail Club, Inc. of tiny Cary, North Carolina, to fill their needs. The club acts as a clearinghouse for catalogers in 25 foreign companies—putting acquisitive Americans in touch with authentic replicas from the British Museum to Thai handicrafts from Bangkok's Elephant House.

There is something for everyone. Provincial postage houses are experts at capitalizing on America's shop-til-you-drop mentality. Yet these fledgling firms will have to sell a lot to match the industry's premier players: L. L. Bean and Lands' End. Let us examine the rise of these backwoods giants.

Boots, Backpacks, and Big Bucks

In 1912, Leon Leonwood Bean founded his legendary company in the small town of Freeport on the southeastern coast of Maine. Sick of cold, wet feet, he invented the Maine Hunting Boot by putting rubber bottoms on leather shoes. To his chagrin, 90 of the first 100 pairs were returned because they were defective. Fortunately, the fiasco did not deter L.L., who restored his customers' money and built his boots better the next time. In the process, Bean resolved never to disappoint his clientele again. "Above all things," he said, "we wish to avoid having a dissatisfied customer." That philosophy serves the company well today.

The eventual success of his boots, coupled with Maine's issuance of hunting licenses, prompted Mr. Bean to start the first-ever direct-mail marketing campaign in 1919. Over the years, he expanded the product line to include outdoor gear of all kinds, which he marketed through a colorful mail-order catalog, distributed twice a year. Today, the Bean signature includes chamois shirts, duck-hunting vests, and, of course, the ubiquitous rubber-bottomed hunting shoes.

L. L. Bean's insistence on product quality and service ignited its rocket ride. Recently, *Fortune* magazine and the U.S. Council on Competitiveness rated the company at the top of its field in the area of quality. Its customer acceptance rate is over 99 percent, with an emphasis on dependability that goes back to the days when L.L. would charge around the store when some product failed. Everyone within the organization understands this insistence on quality and service. Bean has always had an unconditional satisfaction guarantee on its products and consistently encourages its staff to treat the customer as family.

Leon A. Gorman, L.L.'s grandson, perpetuates the company's mystique along with a talented senior management team that includes many former executives of Gillette, Spiegel, Sears, and other top marketers. The 55-year-old Gorman has directed the company's dramatic growth since the mid-sixties. L. L. Bean's sales passed the $1 million mark in 1937; they remained a piddling $3 million in 1964; but they exploded to $600 million in 1989.

Lands' End is a relative upstart compared to L. L. Bean. (The correct spelling should be *Land's End*, but someone made an error in the company's early stationery, and the name stuck.) In 1963, Gary C. Comer, then a 36-year-old advertising copywriter at Young & Rubicam and an Olympic-class ocean sailor, launched the company in Chicago. Yachtsman Comer naturally picked sailing equipment as the firm's first merchandise. But when his clientele requested duffel bags, luggage, and then clothing, the accommodating entrepreneur met their needs. Today, Lands' End sells 10,000 moderately priced, basic staples—from Oxford-cloth shirts to Shetland crewneck sweaters to many-pocketed canvas backpacks.

In 1978, Comer moved the company from the Windy City to the rolling cornfields of Dodgeville, Wisconsin (pop. 3882). He reckoned that this pleasant rural community, 45 miles southwest of Madison, offered plenty of room for a 475,000-square-foot warehouse. The wisdom of Comer's relocation decision was reconfirmed in 1990, when the company doubled its existing capacity with a second distribution center. The middle American locale also gave the cataloger an ample supply of willing workers to staff its 575 telephone lines.

By concentrating on well-made, reliable clothing and accessories, Lands' End proved that it is not just corn that grows in Wisconsin. Since 1984, the firm has averaged an almost 30 percent annual increase in sales and profits. Its return on equity has hovered around 48 percent since 1986. In fiscal 1990, Lands' End's after-tax earnings were $14.7 million on revenues of $603.9 million.

Like its Down East counterpart, the country cataloger can attribute its success to its dedication to quality and service. "Quality in the apparel business, we learned early in our life, is an ephemeral thing," says Gary Comer. To satisfy its customers, who range from Midwestern farmers to New England yuppies, the company's buyers shop the world over for top-of-the-line merchandise. Still, nearly 80 percent of its line comes from the United States, and Lands' End maintains a fleet of three airplanes and a staff of pilots to fly quality-control personnel to its domestic suppliers.

In both cases, L. L. Bean and Lands' End blend an authentically backwoods aura with a fetish for quality, speed, and service. These attributes distinguish them from their industry rivals. But, in truth, every major cataloger has benefitted from dramatic changes in the business.

Riding a Rocket

Competition in the mail-order industry depends on speed. Hence, the reasons for its recent boom are obvious: the emergence of zip codes, the lower cost of toll-free telephone lines, overnight delivery service, computerization, and, as mentioned earlier, a greater emphasis on convenience shopping.

Without question, the six-digit zip code revolutionized the catalog business. It took the direct-mail industry about 10 years—from 1964, when zip codes became commonly used across the country, to the mid-1970s—to take full advantage of the system. Zips made it possible to send mass mailings of catalogs, each personally addressed, to prospective customers. As a result, mail-order sales exploded.

Besides zip codes, less expensive toll-free telephone lines contributed to the industry's spectacular growth. Since L. L. Bean started taking phone orders on its Northern Telecom system 9 years ago, sales are up 300 percent. Consumers now view these free-of-charge phone calls as a right, not a privilege. AT&T reports that the number of 800 calls on its lines soared to 7 billion in 1988, from only 1.9 billion 5 years earlier. Originally conceived as a way to satisfy customer complaints, 800 numbers are an integral part of marketing and customer service. L. L. Bean, Lands' End, and other mail-order houses employ hoards of part-timers, largely because watching a CRT screen and answering a telephone are not particularly conducive to full-time work. Homemakers, retirees, and students from the surrounding community often staff these "telecatalog centers," which usually average close to a thousand workers.

Also, the recent addition of major delivery carriers has enabled mail-order houses to extend their busiest trading season by permitting them to mail earlier and later. Buyers, too, find it a godsend. For procrastinators and impatient customers, Federal Express Corporation and United Parcel Service, Inc. offer overnight service for an additional fee (usually $6 to $12 a purchase). This brings incremental business to catalog companies, especially during the gift-giving season, which accounts for anywhere from one-third to more than three-quarters of their annual sales and profits. At L. L. Bean, public affairs assistant Catherine Hartnett estimates that about 5 percent of its orders are delivered by Federal Express—a trend that is likely to increase.

The deft use of computers has further fueled the industry's explosion. Speed is the name of the game, and computer-aided technology accelerates the time from retailer to recipient. Once a call comes in, various software programs enable telephone operators to learn, typically in less than 2 seconds, whether an item is in stock and, if not, whether an alternative is on hand. Computers also drive the ordering, processing, and packing systems. They separate out single-order items and then re-sort them so that all orders for a particular item are in sequence. They direct the warehouse's elaborate picking and packing stations, rearrange stock to minimize congestion in peak order seasons, put the right postage or UPS charge on a package, and reorder replacement items.

Wherever possible, mail-order companies are displacing labor with state-of-the-art technology. Lands' End, for instance, recently installed a computer-aided inseaming system that shortens the time needed to hem trousers. In 1990, the company also invested $25 million on upgrading—mostly on futuristic sorting and packing equipment for its gigantic distribution center. Likewise, L. L. Bean is a big spender on technology. New Age equipment has helped it slash the average turnaround time for filling its 11.3 million orders, from 7 days to about 3.5 days in the past 5 years. The company's computers even engineer those ersatz personal letters (with the small, but deliberate, error) that go to riled customers.

The lifeline of any successful cataloger, though, is its mailing lists. Lands' End's rostrum of prospective purchasers includes 10 million names. "The list is our gold," says President and CEO Richard C. Anderson. Catalog companies compile their precious inventories of would-be buyers by renting them from competitors and independent list brokers for about a dime a name or by generating them internally through magazine ads and records of past customers. After entering the names in their computers, mail-order houses match each customer to his or her likely purchases in order to determine which of a dozen or so catalogs a prospect should receive. When the final results are in, lists are constantly checked and rechecked for the frequency and size of customer purchases. Normally, catalogers purge from the list people who have been inactive for 2 or 3 years.

Both firms flood the mails with their spiffy catalogs—reaching over 8 million homes, or one of every 10 households in the nation. L. L. Bean sends out close to 100 million of its 22 different brochures; Lands' End distributes 91 million of its 13 catalogs. In their own ways, both businesses pioneered the process. L. L. Bean introduced the first direct-mail catalogs in 1919, while Lands' End was among the earliest to develop the concept of a "magalog"—a catalog so thick with editorial copy that it resembles a magazine. In the latter case, Cary Comer recognized that customers from afar needed to be educated about the Lands' End line as well as how to find the best bargains. Its catalog, which typically runs to hundreds of pages colorfully displaying its outdoor clothing, has become a model for many other direct-mail merchants. Says former head of merchandising Russ Gaitskill: "The catalogs are our sales team." Lands' End's skillfully crafted brochures have helped the company sell to 45 percent of its listed customers since 1988—an extraordinarily high purchase rate for the industry.

Like a Good Neighbor:
Conveying Trust at a Distance

L. L. Bean and Lands' End conjure up images of folksiness and value through their catalogs and magazine advertisements. The venerable Maine merchant stuffs its brochures with photos of Waspy yuppies clad in lumberjack wear. Page after page displays Bean's backwoods look; 6000 items, including down-filled parkas, tartan-plaid boxer shorts, and a wide variety of camping equipment, are featured. Badger Staters prefer to use company employees, not high-fashion models, to hawk their 10,000-line collection of traditional garb and casual clothes. Lands' End catalogs are sprinkled with real people, complete with midriff bulge and wrinkles.

Conveying trust over the telephone is what sets Bean and Lands' End apart. They cultivate a shamelessly folksy image, urging readers of their catalogs to place an order. Telephone representatives in Freeport and Dodgeville have made a career out of being nice on the telephone. "What Bean demands, and gets, is unwavering loyalty to the company's goal of complete service and an imperturbable, friendly manner in the face of customer rudeness," says biographer M. R. Montgomery. "The rules are simple: never get mad, never hang up, and listen out the problem. If all else fails, encourage the customer to write, and shift into that cooler medium of communications."

This keep-it-cool attitude has made the Down-Easters one of the best direct-mail organizations, with standards to which most others aspire. "L. L. Bean has developed customer service into a standard of excellence," says Direct Marketing Association spokesperson Chet Dalzell. "They stress the human element [which is] most important in the catalog business." Phone reps attend product seminars to keep up to speed on all merchandise, and they have comprehensive product information at their work stations. The golden rule remains: Make every shopper's experience as pleasant as possible. "We never want to dissatisfy a customer," says company representative Kilton Andrew, as if paraphrasing founder Leon Leonwood Bean.

Lands' End employees, too, are much like its catalog: warm and unpretentious. Within one and a half rings, a friendly southern Wisconsin voice will answer with a genuine offer to help you. Polite phone operators, many of whom are homemakers or students from the surrounding farm country, are famous for their willingness to chat, even about the weather. "We're trying to build a relationship with a customer, not consummate a sale," claims President Anderson. No high-pressure stuff in Dodgeville. "Our operators don't feel comfortable selling," adds Russ Gaitskill. "And we don't want it to be part of their job."

Providing service, though, is very much part of the phone operator's job. Lands' End authorizes its telephone staff to stay on the line as long as necessary to help a customer. Famous for its quick response, the firm is able to fill 90 percent of all orders within 24 hours of receipt. Every one of its 10,000 items is so safeguarded that the company's motto is only two words long: *Guaranteed, period.* "We've left ourselves no escape hatches," says Chairman Comer.

Then there is the support staff, including people like Margaret Dunbar. After feeding the calves and tending the Arabian show horses, Mrs. Dunbar heads off for Lands' End headquarters to open the company's mail. Home is a 239-acre farm 7½ miles from Dodgeville, where she supervises the company's 125-person Customer Service Department. After a full day of work preserving the firm's reputation for service, she drives home to handle the evening chores. "This kind of dedication is not rare at Lands' End," its national ads proclaim. "Because so many of our people like Margaret are rooted in the good earth of Dodgeville and its rural environs, their spirit infuses the company for which they work just as it enriches the lives they lead before and after hours." Adds Cary Comer: "The kind of people we are fits the kind of products we offer."

Too homespun? Maybe, but when you undertake to run a direct-mail business that depends so heavily on trust and dependability, would-be customers need to know that warm, friendly, down-to-earth people like Margaret Dunbar are there day in and day out. First, build relationships; then sales. That's the Lands' End way.

The Midwestern company's staff of nearly 1300 permanent employees ram home their folksy philosophy with the help of their Quality Assurance Group. It consists of more than 80 people and is one of the largest departments in the company. Also pitching in is the Correspondence Corporation, a group of 230 employees (including Comer and Anderson) who voluntarily write four or five letters a week to shoppers. Even workers in the packing house pen personal thank-you cards that purchasers find in their package. Lands' End insists that its customers always have the name of someone to call for help.

L. L. Bean follows the same good-neighbor strategy. "We guarantee it!" is its anthem. This no-questions, no-hassles attitude dates back to the founder. "Mr. Bean would do anything he could to make the customer happy," says company spokesperson Catherine Hartnett. "We never question anybody. If somebody bought a hunting vest they feel should last 25 years, and it hasn't lasted that long, we'll be glad to make good on it for them."

Stories of Beaners' penchant for service abound. One time, L. L. Bean drove 500 miles from Maine to New York getting a canoe to a buyer who was going on a boating trip. A few years ago, the company recalled

25,000 of its oxford shirts because the yoke in a few of them had ripped. Although only a handful of shirts were returned following the recall, everyone received a new shirt—on the house. Furthermore, company employees have been known to meet vacation-bound customers at highway tollbooths to deliver hiking or camping equipment.

This attitude carries through to employee relations in both companies. In keeping with their small-town values, L. L. Bean and Lands' End consider their work force to be part of the extended family. Bean's Yankee reticence prevents it from intruding into the affairs of its employees. Nonetheless, the paragon of preppiness is as famous for its company clambakes as it is for its generous employee benefits, including healthy bonuses to all staffers.

Lands' End tends to be more paternalistic. Regular luncheons bring small groups of office and plant personnel together with corporate bigwigs to discuss the company's strategy as well as areas of possible improvement. "It's a way of getting across to them how [President] Dick [Anderson] and I feel about doing business," says Chairman Comer. To demonstrate that listening is a two-way art, he built a $7-million, state-of-the-art activity center for employees and their families. The 80,000-square-foot complex includes a basketball court, swimming pool, aerobics rooms, weight machines, and an indoor jogging track. What's more, the company cafeteria specializes in low-fat, low-cholesterol food to bolster the health of its work force. To make it equally accessible to all employees, the activity center is centrally located between the firm's distribution facility, telephone center, and new office building. Underground tunnels encourage its use during inclement weather.

True Grit

Despite their impressive accomplishments, L. L. Bean and Lands' End are feeling the recent squeeze of tougher competition. Americans today are drowning in a sea of look-alike catalogs; a staggering 15 billion will be distributed in 1991. Every cataloger is seeing its sales wither as more and more competitors enter the market. The glut has forced companies like Montgomery Ward, Esprit, and Pier 1 Imports to exit the business. Furthermore, every mail-order house is faced with huge catalog costs for paper, printing, and postage. Third-class postal rates, for example, jumped 25 percent in 1991, while UPS increased its average price for residential deliveries by 16 percent. Worse yet, revenue-hungry state governments are escalating efforts to collect sales taxes from out-of-state direct marketers.

Nobody is panicking at Lands' End. Nevertheless, tougher competition and higher costs caused profits to fall 13 percent in 1989, the first decline in earnings since the Dodgeville gang went public in 1986. More distressing were complaints that the firm's line of casual clothes was starting to look stale in comparison with that of more fashion-conscious catalogers and retailers.

Lands' End's competitive response is taking several different directions. For starters, the company is focusing on new products, along with new ways of selling and of using catalog space more effectively. It is developing a line of children's clothing, petite and extra-large adult sizes, and bathroom and bedroom products. One new offering, rubber boots, sold 40,000 pairs in 1990 instead of the 10,000 expected. Also on the agenda: a new eye-catching series of catalogs. The catalog for May 1990, for instance, featured "Mom Packs" of complete outfits in wrapped gift boxes for Mother's Day. One consisted of a T-shirt and shorts; another featured an all-cotton polo dress with cotton scarf. The Midwesterners are not resorting to price competition. "We do not, have not, and will not participate in the common retailing practice of inflating markups to set up a future phony 'sale,'" says Gary Comer. Besides maintaining prices, the firm "will never, ever take quality out of a product as a means of holding price."

Even if these measures take hold (and the results so far suggest that they will), top management acknowledges that Lands' End is unlikely to grow 20 to 25 percent annually the way it did in the old days. Comer believes that a slower rate of 10 to 18 percent is more realistic. Most publicly held companies would wilt pursuing such a slowdown strategy. However, the chairman believes that the course he has chosen is the correct one. "We are building our customer base for the future, rather than compromising it to show a short-term profit," Comer says.

L. L. Bean is also reporting depressed earnings after years of rapid expansion. "Maybe we were a little too aggressive in our planning," admits Ms. Hartnett. Indeed, President Leon Gorman is shelving the firm's goal of reaching a billion dollars in sales by 1992. He projects that future growth in sales will be in the 5 to 8 percent range, compared with increases of about 23 percent a year over the past decade. Gorman actually *wants* to expand more slowly; recently he postponed the building of an additional distribution center.

L. L. Bean got another comeuppance when customers were cool about its newly expanded product line. So the mail-order gurus are turning back to the basics. The company is downplaying its trendiest lines in favor of the old reliables, such as their Maine hunting boots. It also has added toll-free phone service (a no-no for many years), refined its order-handling operations, and expanded its mailing lists and catalogs.

More troubling yet, the company has been plagued by a significant jump in merchandise returns. In 1988, dissatisfied customers sent back $82 million worth of goods. That represented 14 percent of Bean's total sales—plus $2 million in return freight charges. Therefore, the Freeport firm is scaling back to ensure that greater care is taken in inspecting and shipping goods. "We don't mind fewer customers as long as we do it right," Gorman says. Since about 65 percent of the returns involved wrong sizes, Bean is updating the size information in its catalogs and in order-taker's computers. It is also retraining 3200 employees in techniques that boost customer service and quality.

None of this restructuring has been easy, especially putting the brakes on the firm's incredible growth. Fifteen descendants of the Bean clan control the firm, which is believed to be worth over $600 million. Being privately held definitely helps. "It's a good thing we're not a publicly owned company," Mr. Gorman concedes. "We don't have to worry about earnings." For the balance of the century, more businesses—private and public—would be wise to follow L. L. Bean's example of committing to long-term service and quality.

Too Many Bean Sprouts?

Freeport and Dodgeville are two friendly company towns. Because of its longer history and much larger factory outlet, L. L. Bean is the more dominant force in its community, even in its state. "There is no L. L. Bean without Maine," M. R. Montgomery professes, "and . . . there may be no Maine without L. L. Bean, the state's best advertisement." However, some critics contend that the legendary outfitter's fame may be killing this lovely coastal town.

For years, Freeport consisted of a few ancient white clapboard houses and traditional businesses clustered around Bean's store and warehouse. The local post office was inside the corporate office on Casco Street. Until a decade or so ago, life in Freeport remained peaceful. But as the mail-order industry grew, so did L. L. Bean's cult followers. The company's 90,000-square-foot discount store became a magnet for hunters, fishermen, preppies, and yuppies. Shoppers came in droves and, just behind them, other upmarket retailers: Ralph Lauren, Laura Ashley, Oleg Cassini, Anne Klein, Benetton, Timberland, Dansk, and Gant. All told, at least 100 outlets of nationally known brands sprang up and down the streets of Freeport. The locals call them "Bean sprouts."

With the sprouts came the nemesis of so many Down East towns: traffic. Today, the formerly quaint New England village is being loved to death by one of the newest and darkest trends on the American scene, the total shopping vacation. Over 2.5 million shoppers annually descend on the eight-block commercial district of this once-tranquil seaport. "Shoppers have taken over an entire Maine town and turned it into a retail gold mine without so much as a lobster sandwich or a view of a boat," writes columnist Rob Morse of the *San Francisco Examiner.* "People would rather look at marked-down sweatshirts than a good sunset."

Understandably, the locals are concerned that the traffic crunch, especially acute in July and August, is destroying the area's livability. "The whole town is a horror," says Mrs. Francis Chiarini, an 82-year-old resident. "The traffic is horrible, and I can't even open my windows because of the fumes from the cars."

Freeport is paying a high price for L. L. Bean's notoriety. Property values have soared as the population leaped from 5800 in 1982 to approximately 7000 today. Retail space that sold for as little as $2 a square foot in 1982 now goes for $40 a square foot, plus a portion of gross sales. Houses have tripled or quadrupled in value over the same period. And local employers complain about the great difficulty they have in attracting entry-level workers at $8 an hour.

The "Freeport disease" has spread to other parts of the Pine Tree State. One infected community is Kittery, 70 miles south of Freeport and only an hour's drive from Boston. The southern Maine seaport, close to the New Hampshire state line, wanted to divert tourists traveling north to visit Bean's massive retail outlet. So the town encouraged the construction of 350,000 square feet of shopping centers along the lines of the ones in its sister city to the north. Its efforts paid off. Kittery has 20 percent more retail stores than Freeport, but it also has the same social problems as its northern neighbor.

Worried that overexpansion may threaten the character of southern Maine, community leaders throughout the state have enacted the usual moratoriums on development. Freeport, Kittery, and other townships are now highly regulated, with building permits, visitor parking passes, and the like tough to obtain. What's more, the academics are getting in on the act. In 1989, the University of Southern Maine, in cooperation with the state's newly created Department of Economic and Community Development, established a professorship in growth management—one of the first in the nation. Candidates are expected "to assist the state in providing technical assistance dealing with growth-management issues." According to university officials, L. L. Bean's hometown will receive special attention.

Nevertheless, most Freeport folks are justifiably proud of the local company that made good. They are convinced that the community will survive this latest act of God. Bean employees are equally sanguine about the company's impact on Freeport, and vice versa. Many contend that all the talk about country living and the good life in coastal Maine may be exaggerated. "There is enormous pressure on us," one L. L.

Bean manager says. "We're caught between making the company grow and managing growth so we don't strangle on it."

Handful of Howdys

Despite these inevitable tensions, Freeport and Dodgeville—as well as Boise, Battle Creek, and Midland—support the case for frontier living. Their hometown businesses defeated the apparent limitations of size and distance. Lacking scope and proximity to major markets, firms in the hinterlands were forced to develop the skills and technologies needed to compete at home and abroad. In many respects, their achievements are analogous to Japan's, where the country's isolation and lack of natural resources stimulated its rise in the world economy.

The case histories of L. L. Bean and Lands' End "represent just one specific type of business [mail-order] that flourishes in remote places," says Cognetics's President David Birch. "Think about all the magazines published within a few miles of Peterborough, New Hampshire (currently there are more than two dozen), or the numerous free-lance consultants who offer their services around the world. Remoteness encourages [these] kinds of businesses [as well as] trucking, telecommunications, air travel, warehousing, and specialty manufacturing." With New Age technology, an increasing number of industries are finding that distance makes no difference.

These powerful examples are causing U.S. business to reassess its former image of frontier life. Gone are the days when a game of checkers at the country store was the highlight of the day; gone, too, is the potbellied stove warmth of some rural dwellers; and gone are the uncomplicated times when dominating the local scene was all that mattered to small-town employers. From Boise to Battle Creek, penturban enterprises represent much more than a handful of howdys and a mouthful of much-obligeds. Tough, dedicated professionals—not the homebodies of a bygone era or the dewy-eyed exiles from the inner city—are hellbent on success. Whether it is Bill Agee at Morrison Knudson or Bill LaMothe at Kellogg, the new breed of small-town executive is anything but nostalgic. With derring-do, they are repositioning their companies to meet the challenges of the twenty-first century.

As mentioned earlier, the minimalist movement is an essential force in the growing force of the new corporate frontier. The smaller the corporate command post, the greater the call of the wild. The next part examines the miniheadquarters phenomenon and its effect on U.S. business.

PART 3
More Means Less

8

The Rise of the Minimalist Corporation

Famous for his brevity, General Ulysses S. Grant was equally stingy when it came to his headquarters personnel. No more than a half-dozen officers staffed the Union Army's command post. When experts were needed, Grant plucked them from the ranks of his fellow generals. His headquarters philosophy was, in the words of his biographer William S. McFeely, "studiously simple."

For most of this century, U.S. business leaders spurned the lessons of General Grant. Doing more with less was the last thing on their minds. Corporations were primarily concerned with expansion rather than efficiency. To capitalize on the tremendous growth opportunities of the post-World War II period, increasingly complex, multidivisional (or M-form) organizations evolved.

Ever-burgeoning headquarters staffs performed three functions: creation of strategy, specialized staff support, and intracompany communications and control. Intricate management information systems linked the operating companies, which managed day-to-day affairs, to the corporate center. U.S. executives espoused these organizational commandments with evangelical fervor. Their devotion paid off, as U.S. business enjoyed unprecedented growth during the postwar era.

The last 2 decades, however, made it painfully clear that M-form organizations had run amok. Headquarters staffs grew in size and stature, and operating companies were ordered to rely exclusively on their head offices for service needs. In many instances, strategic directions received by the field units were inadequate. At the same time, headquarters became bloated bureaucracies, arrogantly insisting on ever-tighter control. Corporate communications, when they did take place, were invariably one-way: downward.

Small Is Beautiful

The antidote for the era of command and control was the "mini-headquarters." Enter the Age of Minimalism. Companies large and small began to deemphasize the traditional dominance of the center, while encouraging a radiation of power throughout the organization. The basic tenet of this philosophy was that big was bad.

Nowadays, small is beautiful. From Avon to Exxon, more than half the *Fortune* 500 have slashed their corporate staffs. More than 1 million managerial and staff professionals have been eliminated since 1979, says Robert M. Tomasko, a partner at the management consulting firm of Temple, Barker & Sloane and the author of *Downsizing*. However, other estimates put the body count closer to 3 million people. What's more, universities, hospitals, and other nonprofit organizations have also jumped on the staff-reduction bandwagon. Even the U.S. Army, traditionally a rigidly hierarchical organization, has shifted to "light fighter" divisions—small, self-contained combat units capable of quick response. This strategy reaped handsome dividends during the Persian Gulf crisis.

Nor is structural sleekness strictly an American phenomenon. Foreign companies, from Sweden's Electrolux to Japan's Toyota, are scaling back their head offices. Even the massive Russian Army is trimming down. Despite some grumbling, Soviet military leaders have had to lay off 100,000 officers, many of them in the central command, in an effort to become more efficient.

Minimalism, therefore, is universal. And it is here to stay—in good times and bad. In a survey of 250 top corporate officials, Louis Harris & Associates concluded that further cutbacks in the central staff seem all but certain. The pollsters found overwhelming agreement on the need to "give serious thought to fewer levels of management to shorten decision-making time." Hence, the taboos against "downsizing" (slashing away at the corporate staff) and "delayering" (eliminating unnecessary levels of management) have been put aside permanently. Minimalist strategies are now "an ongoing corporate activity without regard to a company's economic performance," says Eric Greenberg, editor of the American Management Associations' research reports. He claims that a downsized firm is six times more likely to downsize again, for the process becomes one of constant refinement.

Big business's recent conversion to smaller, sleeker command centers has given new life to Small Town, U.S.A. Since leaner and meaner headquarters can be domiciled anywhere, penturbia becomes a serious contender in the competition to lure head offices. Indeed, the rise of the miniheadquarters offers provincial cities and towns an opportunity to enter the economic big leagues in ways unimaginable a decade ago. Given its profound impact on the frontier movement, let us examine the forces behind the minimalist phenomenon.

Financial Pressures

The recent wave of mergers, acquisitions, takeovers, and leveraged buyouts (LBOs) stimulated the shift toward smaller central structures. "Defrock the chairman, dismantle the corporate staff, sell off the bits— and shareholder value will double," says management guru Tom Peters. That is the logic behind these transactions. Since stand-alone affiliates also enhance the value of the holding company, there is added incentive to transfer power and staff personnel away from the center and to the various business units.

Has the takeover movement led to a leaner and meaner corporate America? Absolutely. The threat of hostile action triggers a variety of minimalist strategies. As corporate raiders search for targets, companies must put their houses in order to protect their independence. Firms that have successfully defended themselves from takeover attempts frequently incur large debts in the process—debts that are often paid off in part by reducing the central staff.

"There is a clear linkage between mergers and layoffs," says an official at New Jersey's Department of Labor. "We've noticed that once a merger occurs, some departments in the acquired firms are very quickly done away with. Many of these people [whose jobs are lost] tend to be professionals or from middle-management posts." Anecdotal evidence is pouring in of managerial job losses stemming from mergers and acquisitions, LBOs, and hostile takeovers. Take, for instance, RJR Nabisco, which underwent a massive LBO in 1988. Its work force shrank from 14,700 in 1988 to 12,360 in 1989 and from 15 departments to 8—despite the fact that revenues increased $200 million during this period. Much the same for General Foods. Since being acquired by Philip Morris in 1988, it dismantled its corporate hierarchy and eliminated many of its 2000 jobs in its head office.

Generally speaking, restructured companies end up smaller, more productive, and more profitable. A seminal study of American LBOs by Professor Steven Kaplan of the University of Chicago found that, during the first 2 years after they were bought out, companies' operating profits climbed 6 percent above the industry average. He also discovered that employment in LBO-ed firms was below general industry levels. One of the country's pioneers of this technique, Henry R. Kravis of Kohlberg Kravis Roberts & Company, argues that LBOs represent "America's secret weapon." He sees them as "one tactic among others to free U.S. business from the paralyzing clutches of hidebound corporate bureaucracies and to increase a competitive position in the world economy. We need companies that are highly flexible and able to adapt rapidly to changes in the global marketplace. This means corporate bureaucracies must be tamed." Kravis believes that LBOs generally result in more efficient, flexible companies with downsized headquarters.

To be sure, the stock market's recent volatility has tempered the takeover frenzy. Does this mean that LBOs are dead? Probably not. As long as individuals and companies think that it is cheaper to buy assets on Wall Street than to build them themselves, the takeover race will continue. However, the trend will be to finance these transactions with relatively lower levels of debt. While one era of corporate takeovers is ending, another era—that of less-leveraged buyouts—is beginning. Look for borrowed money to continue to play an important role—forcing U.S. firms to keep their central staffs thin.

The Technological Revolution

New Wave technology is also changing the nature of work in a minimalist direction. What Harvard's Shoshona Zuboff calls "intellective skills" have supplanted manual skills in contemporary America. The number of blue-collar workers in manufacturing has declined from one-third of the work force in the 1920s to one-sixth today. State-of-the-art technology and methods of production will continue to depreciate the importance of labor as a factor of production.

Five years ago, Peter Drucker described this transformation as the emergence of the "knowledge-minded society," where new ideas and technology are the primary productive resources. Information is the lubricant of this new world, which is dominated by service and high-technology industries. "Large organizations will have little choice but to become information-based," Drucker points out. "Demographics, for one thing, demands the shift. The center of gravity in employment is moving fast from manual and clerical workers to knowledge workers who resist the command-and-control model that business took from the military one hundred years ago."

The passwords of the knowledge-oriented society are speed and flexibility. Old-fashioned, slow-moving hierarchies can no longer compete in the new, lightning-fast world. "Increased international competition and the rapid pace of technology are favoring organizations that are lean, fast, and flexible," says Berkeley professor Raymond E. Miles. "In fact, not only are more organizations downsizing, discoupling, and disaggregating, the search for flexibility is producing a whole new organizational form that looks more like a network than a pyramidical hierarchy."

Variously referred to as "network," "switchboard," or "electronic matrix" structures, these new, fleet-footed organizations are far less bureaucratic, hierarchical, and static than their M-form counterparts. The theory of the network configuration is that a company is at heart little more than a cluster of people with specialized skills. With less bureaucracy, network companies can pounce more quickly on new markets or technologies.

"In the knowledge organization, *size* becomes a strategic decision," says Professor Drucker. "Bigness by itself is a competitive handicap rather than an advantage." Information-based networks are toppling the corporate pyramid in what represents a dramatic reversal of the historical belief in the full-blown headquarters and thick cushions of midmanagers. With computers, not hoards of people as the new conduits of informational exchange, areas of control can expand dramatically. By how much? "I say the right number is closer to 10 or 15," argues General Electric Chairman Jack Welsh. "With 10 or 15 reports, a leader can focus on big important issues, not on minutiae." However, Tom Peters argues that it may be feasible for as many as 50 to 70 people to report to a single supervisor.

Minimalist companies not only trim the number of job categories at each level, they also broaden job responsibilities. The net effect is to decentralize decision making. For instance, at Chaparral Steel, with approximately 800 employees, production workers are responsible for identifying new technologies, meeting with customers, maintaining their equipment, and training. Quite simply, Chaparral Steel is the nation's best-managed steel company. Its famous minimills are setting world records for productivity, turning out a ton of steel in 1.6 worker-hours compared with the Japanese record of 2.8 and U.S. Steel's 5.0. To preserve this remarkable track record, expansion at Chaparral depends on horizontal, not vertical, growth. When Chaparral has added new mills, it has "expanded management sideways," says company President Gordon Forward. "If we take on any more endeavors, we're going to continue to add horizontally to retain our shallow management structure. We have only 4 levels of management, General Motors has 17. And some big steel companies would have trouble counting theirs."

Elsewhere, integrated computer networks are allowing U.S. business to expand management sideways—linking factory floors and outlying offices to corporate headquarters. Advanced computer technology is completely redefining methods of production by simplifying the nature of work, reducing the number of manual jobs, and widening the span of control. Computer-aided design (CAD) and computer-aided manufacturing (CAM) software and hardware systems help to speed production, improve quality, minimize waste, and accelerate customer response; and, eventually, these systems can redesign themselves.

"Integration is the key word," says John A. Young, president and CEO at Hewlett-Packard Company. "It is the interaction of all parts of the organization across major functional boundaries—and even with vendors and customers outside the institution itself." It boils down to teamwork, and information-based manufacturing can be an important tool in fostering esprit de corps. Computerized networks make it possible to put together teams of people to work on projects of limited duration. Through local area networks, desktop systems that once functioned in isolation are being integrated with one another in departmental and work group environments that give individuals even greater computing power and ability to share information with others.

"Cooperative computing," as it is popularly called, is replacing conventional production management systems in aerospace, automobile, electrical equipment, food processing, and many other industries. One of the most impressive attempts to introduce the electronic network is taking place at Caterpillar. In 1986, the earth-moving equipment maker launched its "Plant with a Future" program to replace antiquated production methods with more flexible, computer-driven systems. Cat's goal: a 20 percent cut in total manufacturing costs (about $1.5 billion a year) when its plant update is finished in late 1992 or early 1993. The company is reconfiguring work into islands of automation where teams of operators can handle several manufacturing functions, many of them project-oriented. Caterpillar is also developing a computerized software package that will integrate factories with suppliers and dealers. Ultimately, Cat hopes to link its 30 plants, suppliers, and dealerships with worldwide information on product and parts availability, pricing, and competitive analysis.

Then there is the office with a future, sometimes called "the paperless office." With computer-aided systems translating and combining sales, financial, and personnel information more efficiently, there is no need for the phalanx of paper pushers at the head office. Integrated work systems are also converting many once-fragmented tasks into fewer jobs requiring multiple skills. "A lot of the functions of the corporation are no longer necessary in today's information-rich society," says Steve Walleck, a consultant in McKinsey & Company's Cleveland office. "And as these functions are dissolved, a tremendous amount of overhead is freed up."

Ironically, minimalist companies' rejection of bulky central staffs is offset in part by their need for more high-powered specialists. "Converting data into useful information requires knowledge, which, by definition, is specialized," says Peter Drucker. "The information-based organization requires far more specialists overall than does the command-and-control structure." But with a different twist. The specialists in a minimalist enterprise are often domiciled in the operating companies, not in the head office.

Always the decentralists, minimalist organizations attempt to disperse work to its lowest operating level. "The power of the individual, or a small network of specialized terminals, increases far faster than the power of a large bureaucracy," says George Gilder, author of *Microcosm*. "Rather than pushing decisions up the hierarchy, the power of microelectronics pulls them remorselessly down to the individual." In one swing, the electronic matrix is giving more power, more freedom to the minimalist manager than anything before.

No new technology could have a liberating effect if people were not ready to use it. "Technology does not drive change," says Paul Saffo, research fellow at the Institute of the Future, a think tank in Menlo Park, California. "It enables change." American managers raised on computer games want to exploit these high-tech resources. Indeed, the experts project that by 1995 at least one-half of all U.S. executives will be computer-literate (versus 25 percent today).

The new breed of technically savvy managers is committed to smaller, flatter organizational structures. Besides rejecting traditional notions of corporate self-sufficiency, they are calling on other companies to perform critical business functions.

Stategic Partnerships

U.S. firms are finding that, to be competitive, they must be cooperative. When business alliances are forged, significant advantages can come about, including whopping efficiencies at the head office. This discovery is reflected in the acceleration of what Professor Howard Perlmutter of the Wharton School and I have called "global strategic partnerships," or GSPs. These alliances have become an important new strategic option that touches every sector of the world economy, from sunrise to sunset industries, from manufacturing to services.

To illustrate:

- After decades in IBM's shadow, Hewlett-Packard has shown an uncommon readiness to work with outsiders. Since 1978, HP has teamed up with Hitachi (precision architecture chip technology), Canon (advanced typewriters and printers), Yokogawa (logic systems), Northern Telecom (microprocessor development systems), Sony (digital audio tapes), Samsung Electronics (work stations), and Arthur Anderson (computed-integrated consulting services). These alliances range from marketing and licensing agreements to ambitious joint ventures to develop new technology.

- In 1988, Toshiba Corporation and Motorola Inc. joined forces to swap technology in semiconductors. Toshiba is competitive in mass-market memory chips, which are an American weakness. But the Japanese giant is not strong in the logic chip market, where U.S. companies dominate.

- On a more macro level, America's high-tech companies formed two coalitions, Microelectronics & Computer Technology Corporation and the Semiconductor Manufacturing Technology Institute, or Sematech, to buffer the competitive shocks of similar alliances in Japan and Western Europe.

- Madison Avenue, too, has seen a wave of GSPs, triggered in 1981 by Young & Rubicam's linkup with Tokyo's Dentsu, the world's largest advertising agency. Their pact created a direct-marketing company in Japan and a global advertising consortium called "HDM," in which the French market leader, Eurocom, is also involved. Recently, Y&R's public relations affiliate, Burson-Marsteller, teamed up with Dentsu's PR unit to accelerate their expansion plans in the Pacific Basin.

- GSPs are also a way of life in the auto industry. General Motors turned to Japanese companies, including Suzuki, Isuzu, and Toyota to manufacture its small cars, and to Volvo of Sweden to bail out its ailing heavy-truck business. Overall, the company has concluded 50 partnerships since 1980. GM's competitors are equally bullish on these joint agreements. Chrysler's former Vice Chairman Gerald Greenwald once predicted: "No car company can dominate who will be successful in the '90s that doesn't learn to develop strategic international alliances."

No company, not even the behemoth General Motors, can afford on its own to design, build, and market the products or services it needs to satisfy all its customers. GSPs are "based on the premise that some markets are so huge and multifaceted that no single company can hope to control all critical technological elements," says Kenichi Ohmae, who heads McKinsey & Company's Tokyo office. Therefore, the pace of alliance building is becoming increasingly hectic as companies search frantically for the best possible set of corporate colleagues.

Strategic partnering leads to leaner and meaner businesses. By sharing the costs of research and development, new product introduction, and other expensive staff functions, GSPs lessen the need for large, independent corporate staffs. When the two giant pharmaceutical makers Philadelphia-based SmithKline Beckman Corporation and London's Beechman Group PLC came together in July 1989, Robert P. Bauman, the new chief executive, vowed: "There's going to be a substantial amount of jobs lost—how much I don't know." So far, the group's cuts in duplicative staff functions have produced savings of approximately $600 million. With so much to gain, these burden-sharing ventures represent a profitable route to future opportunities.

Outsourcing

Another minimalist tactic is to export costly work elements. The 1980s saw the rise of the "global factory." We discovered that shoe workers in Maine could no longer compete with their Portuguese and Filipino peers; Pennsylvania steelworkers were outgunned by Koreans feverishly working 12-hour, 6-day shifts; textile spinners in the Carolinas were feeling the impact of low-cost labor in Mexico and Brazil; and even Silicon Valley's haughty "techies" saw their skills challenged by their rivals from Japan and the "second Japans." Hence, U.S. manufacturers rushed to set up assembly lines in foreign countries where hardworking employees gladly accepted wages that are lower than those of their American counterparts.

Service industries soon followed suit. Today, everything from keypunching to record keeping is being assigned to cheap-labor countries. American cartoon producers, for instance, are turning to animation houses in Japan, Korea, Taiwan, and Australia to keep their costs down. While most cartoon stories are still created and edited in the United States, firms are sending storyboards and sketches abroad for the tedious process of drawing and painting the 20,000 or so individual panels that must be strung together to produce a typical TV show. Usually, overseas firms work at two-thirds the cost of their U.S. counterparts.

The growth of the "global office" could soon outpace that of the "global factory." Rapidly advancing telecommunications and growing sophistication among low-cost foreign work forces are creating a similar mobility for some white-collar jobs. The result: smaller central staffs back home.

Up to 70 U.S. companies—for as little as $50 a month in mainland China and only $2.30 an hour in Barbados—process credit card payments and other back-office functions via satellite. Insurance giant CIGNA Corporation, for instance, is opening a $5-million medical claims processing center in the Irish town of Loughrea, creating about 200 jobs there. Industry rival New York Life Insurance Company uses the rural Irish village of Castleisland to handle its insurance claims. Reportedly, processing costs are about 25 percent lower than those in the United States. Texas Instruments, Inc. has put a software development facility in Bangalore, India, linked by satellite to its Dallas headquarters. The Chicago publishing house R. R. Donnelley & Sons sends manuscripts to Barbados to prepare them for printing in the United States. The legal research service Lexis, owned by Mead Data Control, Inc. of Dayton, Ohio, now handles about one-third of its data-entry operations in South Korea, the People's Republic of China, the Philippines, and Jamaica. And Denver-based National Demographics Lifestyles, which conducts market research for Zenith, General Electric, and Minolta, processes as many as 10 million questionnaires a year at its Barbados facility.

In 1984, American Airlines set up a subsidiary called "Caribbean Data Services" that today employs 400 people in Barbados and 650 in the Dominican Republic, processing data for the airline, and, on contract, for other U.S. firms. American estimates that this program is saving in excess of $3.5 million a year. Similarly, Transfer Data, Ltd., based in Jamaica, represents a half-dozen U.S. companies—employing 160 workers in three shifts, and growing. Its showpiece: a new $8.5-million satellite center in Montego Bay. Lawson Narse, who heads the New York office of the Barbados Industrial Development Corporation, says: "Due to modern satellite communications, there's no particular advantage to [data-entry] processing in New York and beaming it to your computer in Dallas. It's just as easy to do in Barbados."

So easy, in fact, that there are now 40 computerized processing centers on a half-dozen Caribbean islands. Insurance claims are typed into computers in Barbados, traffic tickets from Florida are processed in St. Lucia, and 2 million dog pedigrees have been recorded in Grenada. The global office phenomenon has just begun. "You'll see a lot more of it," says Professor D. Quinn Mills of the Harvard Business School. "And there are very few real limits to how far it can go." Some experts contend that one of four *Fortune* 1000 companies now uses an overseas back office—strengthening the case for the miniheadquarters.

Contracting

As U.S. companies experience the advantages of having other firms and suppliers perform key business functions, they are pruning their permanent staffs—replacing them with contract, contingent, or temporary employees. Of course, American business has relied on temporary help for years. Firms like Manpower and Kelly Services are household names.

In fact, approximately 9 of every 10 companies use temps. In 1988, U.S. business spent $9.9 billion on temporary help—up from $4 billion in 1983. The number of contingent workers now stands at more than 6.5 million, while the temporary services industry has grown at an explosive 18.9 percent a year since 1970.

With growth comes specialization. "Businesses are just starting to realize it is possible to fill in higher skill areas with [part-timers]," says Samuel R. Sacco, executive vice president of the National Association of Temporary Services. Sacramento-based Legal-Staff, Inc., is a franchise that finds lawyers and paralegal professionals. Staff Builders, Inc., headquartered in Lake Success, New York, serves the $7-billion market in home health care and hospital staffing—a market that is expected to grow 15 to 20 percent annually through the 1990s. Now you can even hire a seasoned engineer by the hour.

The fast-growing Philadelphia firm CDI Corp. is striving to be to the factory floor what Kelly Services is to the typing pool. The leader in the "rent a techie" business, the company provides U.S. firms with engineers they don't want to keep on their own payrolls. "The reason this business exists," says CFO Edgar Landis, "is that companies want to control their variable costs. Engineering is one of those variables." Altogether, CDI's 14,000 or so engineers represent 12 percent of the pool of available talent in what is estimated to be a $5-billion industry.

U.S. industry is also turning to the large and growing pool of general managers made redundant by the downsizing movement. If there is an important project to be done, companies do not want to start fattening layers again. Although temporary fees may be comparable to full-time salaries, employers do not have to bear the responsibility of paying bonuses, benefits, or payroll taxes. These costs, which are often assumed by the recruitment firms, account for a considerable savings. The "rent an exec" movement allows minimalist companies to keep their overheads down.

Other employers, especially small businesses, are transferring entire departments to third-party providers. To be technically correct, the permanent employees are fired; then, they are rehired by an employee leasing firm; and finally, they are leased back to the company. Leasing fees often consist of cost (taxes, insurance, and so on) plus a markup based on a percentage of gross wages. Other firms charge cost plus a fixed fee per employee—usually $25 per week. "Leased executives bring with them not only a high degree of specialized knowledge, they are trained to handle many of the fine points and intricacies of their respective departments," says Edward M. Katz, president of Choice Management Systems, Inc., a leading leasing firm. Some of the best candidates for this alternative: mailrooms, delivery and transportation departments, in-house messenger services, copy centers, child care units, warehouses, parts distribution centers, and computer services groups.

An offshoot of leasing is job sharing, which means, for instance, that two part-time employees hold the same job, each performing it for only 4 hours a day. By fragmenting clerical and administrative positions, the firm gains the advantages of a part-time work force, while allowing some of their employees much-needed freedom to conduct nonwork tasks. Some banking and insurance companies rely on job-sharing employees to perform as much as 65 percent of their total administrative functions.

These new flexible work alternatives are not being used just for entry-level, low-skilled workers. "Except at the upper-middle and top management ranks, job sharing is occurring nearly everywhere at the professional and managerial level," says Stephanie Pinson, managing director of Gilbert Tweed & Associates' West Orange, New Jersey, office. Companies often get more productivity out of two people sharing a job than from a single individual. The reason? "There is no burnout factor and there's less stress," asserts Pinson. "And if you get two dedicated, aggressive employees really banging away, there is a synergy—and sometimes 1 and 1 will equal 3."

Today, part-timers make up 17.4 percent of American employment. And their ranks are swelling. Multiple job holders, people with at least two part-time positions, hit a record 7.2 million persons in 1990, up 1.5 million since 1985. Persons with two or more jobs reached 6.2 percent of the work force in 1990, the highest level in over 30 years. Nevertheless, the United States still lags behind many other nations in the use of part-timers. The contingent work force represents more than one-fifth of the employment base of Denmark, Norway, Sweden, Britain, and the Netherlands. Richard S. Belous, senior economist with the National Planning Association, argues that the United States will be at a competitive disadvantage unless it relies more heavily on these cost-efficient part-timers. Look for their ranks to explode in the years ahead.

Off-Premises Work

The final factor contributing to the minimalist movement is the booming trend to shift staff work to off-premise locations. Working from home is a well-established tradition for the self-employed, but nowadays it is a viable option for salaried corporate employees as well. When they are included, 18 percent of American households have at least one member who works at home, according to a survey conducted by Link Resources Corporation, a New York-based market research firm. That statistic rose about 10 percent in 1989. Link calculates that 26.8 million Americans—about 20 percent of the labor force—work at home.

Half of all people currently working from home are in professional or managerial occupations, typically performing part of their work at home and spending the rest of their time in an office. An additional 33 percent are in sales, technical, or administrative fields, and 7 percent are in precision production or repair fields. The rest are in various occupations, including services and manual work.

Paul and Sarah Edwards of Santa Monica, California, are gurus of the burgeoning work-at-home movement. Fifteen years ago, they left their jobs in law and social work to face the challenges and benefits of working at home. For them, the pluses include more control over their lives, less stress, fewer distractions, no daily commutes, and more time with the family. Putting their talents in tandem, the Edwardses run a business called "Here's How," through which they share information with 6500 subscribers on how to work happily and productively at home. Authors of a best-selling paperback, *Working from Home*, and producers of a videotape entitled "How to Succeed at Working from Home," this energetic couple still finds time to host a weekly radio show and write a column on off-premises work.

The pressure to work at home is coming from several directions. First, baby-boomers have reached the age at which they have dual responsibilities: careers and children. Clocking in at home is a most attractive option for the two-career couple trying to juggle jobs and home life. Parents, especially, are welcoming employment options that can help them compete in the business world while still taking care of the kids. The number of baby-boomers working at home will increase as they reach their late thirties and early forties—the peak age period for wanting more independence and more time at home—and as traffic and pollution problems worsen.

Second, as the labor pool shrinks because of the declining birthrate of the past 20 years, retirees, the disabled, and single-parent families are needed to meet the growing demand for workers in a variety of industries. Working from home is particularly attractive to these groups.

Third, the surge in downtown and suburban real estate prices make it prohibitive for firms to erect skyscrapers or rent offices in order to house workers for only 7 or 8 hours or so. Farming out work makes good economic sense.

Fourth, attitudes about physical proximity to the workplace are changing dramatically. For years, American industry harbored the Calvinistic belief that serious work could be conducted only on premises. Progress up the corporate ladder was measured by hours spent at the desk, irrespective of one's productivity. Managers who completed the annual budget or penned the latest marketing plan in the cozy confines of their homes or the public library were looked upon as misfits. That thinking no longer holds.

"If you do your job and do it well, then it doesn't matter where you work," says Sunny Bates, who runs a head-hunting firm out of her Manhattan kitchen. Adds Dorothy Denton, executive director of the American Home Business Association in Darien, Connecticut.: "Fifteen years ago, if you said you worked at home, people thought it was because you couldn't get a job. There's no stigma any more because so many people are doing it."

Increasingly, U.S. industry is growing to appreciate the merits of off-premises work. In record numbers, firms are sending their workers home. Observers estimate that at least 500 companies have work-at-home programs, with perhaps 900,000 employees participating. What's more, several firms (Pacific Bell, AT&T, IBM, Travelers Insurance, J. C. Penney, and others) have found that they can both save office expense and increase work output by as much as 25 percent. Although productivity can be hard to measure accurately, especially for white-collar workers, experts believe that increases of 10 to 20 percent are common when work is done at home. "There are a lot of reasons for it," says Gil Gordon, an employment consultant who works from his home in Monmouth Junction, New Jersey. "People at home often work for long periods without interruption. Also they tend to work during the time of day when they are most productive."

Finally, high-tech tools are spurring the work-at-home revolution. The office is moving out of the office. Faxes, PCs, cellular phones—in short, low-cost and easily available electronic devices—allow employers to get rid of the fat in the head office while liberating their white-collar workers to the comforts of home. Consider, too, the upcoming fiber-optic revolution, which will vastly increase the amount of audio, video, and computer data that can flow in and out of the home. Fiber-optic cables are already widely used in long-distance lines and between local telephone exchanges. Extending them into the home could create vast new opportunities for residentially based business networks. Visionaries foresee fiber-optic "superhighways" that connect home-based workers with large business and government employers.

Speed, flexibility, and independence are the theme song of the work-at-home movement. They reflect values so important to today's working generation. For instance, Nick Sullivan, senior editor of *Home Office Computing* magazine, works out of his home in South Dartmouth, Massachusetts. His office is a third-floor loft equipped with a computer, printer, fax machine, and a two-line telephone. Every two weeks or so, he travels to New York for a few days to link up with his colleagues and the publishing crowd. The pluses? "There's a big advantage being able to be around my kids when they're growing up," Sullivan reports. "I see more of them than if I had to commute and go into the office every day."

Or take the Graysons—Robert and Suzanne. They traded in their hour-plus commute from New Jersey to Manhattan for the sun and sea of Santa Barbara, California. Operating under the name of Grayson Associates, the couple publishes *The Journal of Consumer Marketing, The Journal of Business and Industrial Marketing,* and *The Journal of Services Marketing*—and act as consultants to the packaging industry. "The commuting time (to their head office) is 3½ seconds," says Robert Grayson. Articles for their three journals come in from professors around the country by computer modem or by mail on computer disks. The Graysons then send the pieces by modem to a typesetting firm 10 miles away. The typesetters, in turn, fax the galleys back to Grayson Associates to proofread and check. "We can do that anywhere in the country," Robert says of the family's publishing and consulting business. "Where you are doesn't matter any more."

Telecommuting is spurring the work-at-home revolution even further. Certain jobs that once had to be done in a downtown head office because of the large space needs associated with traditional information processing technology (paper, files, and mainframe computers) and because of the necessity of proximity for communication can now be decentralized. Paper has been replaced by more compact forms of storage; the cost of computer work stations has dropped; and electronic mail now facilitates remote communications. So firms are setting up satellite offices in the suburbs near the homes of their employees. Instead of driving downtown, computer staffers report to nearby work areas equipped with computer terminals, telephones, and fax machines that are hooked up to the head office.

Although there are only 200,000 full-time telecommuters across the country, the movement is taking the nation by storm. Consultant Gil Gordon estimates that 5 million workers could be telecommuting by the middle of the decade. Pacific Bell is a leader in this movement. Fewer than 1000 of its 65,000 employees now work on computers at home, but the number is expected to rise to about 5000 by the mid-1990s. Many of the current crop of telecommuters trade in the long commuting trek to the company's downtown Los Angeles office to drive to a "satellite work center" in Woodlawn Hills.

Most Pac Bell employees in the San Francisco and Silicon Valley areas weathered the 1989 earthquake by telecommuting. They avoided the quake's rubble, mud slides, and damaged roadways by staying home and working on personal computers, telephones, or fax machines linked to their office by phone lines. The Santa Cruz software operation reported that as many as 100 of its 700 workers were telecommuting on and off. In fact, the company trucked up to 50 computers to other employees eager to keep working. At Apple Computer, Inc., about 5 percent of its 5600-member Silicon Valley work force—most of them software developers and market researchers—telecommuted during the crisis. The company's policy of giving each worker a personal computer for home use after a year seemed "like one of the best things we've done," said spokesperson Ylonda Davis.

In 1990, the state of Hawaii established its Telework Center in Mililani, a Honolulu suburb. Participants from business and government use computers, fax machines, and the latest communications links to the head office. The state hopes that the electronic highway will ease Oahu's road clog. "We're looking to high technology to solve some of our transportation problems," says Edward Uchida, director of Hawaii's Telework Center Demonstration Project. "We feel that with computers and telecommunications technology, we can move information rather than people." Although the Aloha State's rush-hour blues are far less severe than California's or New York's, environmentalists and traffic planners hope that a good deal of work will eventually be transferred far from downtown Honolulu. Telecommuting could also alleviate the shortage of expensive inner-city office space and entice former homebodies back to the work force.

Working across time zones and continents, users of these new electronic networks are prompting corporations to recast their traditional concepts of employment. After all, if employees can operate with equal efficiency from the office, home, or a ski lodge—and be happier doing it—why shouldn't they?

Centrifugal Forces

To sum up, financial pressures, new technological breakthroughs, strategic partnerships, outsourcing, contracting, and off-premises work—all are promoting heightened interest in the miniheadquarters and, therefore, in Small Town, U.S.A. These elements, in effect, serve as centrifugal forces—pulling power away from the traditional corporate center and to the periphery. How this redistribution of power is unfolding is the subject of the next chapter.

9

Redefining the Center

"Dress me slowly, I'm in a hurry!" Napoleon once remarked. This describes the double bind of the minimalist company: the challenge of capturing the benefits of efficiency and flexibility without destroying the advantages of size and scale. The center of corporate command "will be small, centralized, and local," says Professor Ralph H. Kilmann of the University of Pittsburgh. "At the same time, it will be connected to an extended network that is big, decentralized, and global." Achieving this new organizational amalgam means that U.S. business must change its spots.

A Matter of Definition

Corporations have been likened to families for decades: headquarters represent the "parents," and the operating companies their "children." With network organizations and minimalist thinking, this sociological model is no longer appropriate. The children have come of age. These once-docile operating units are today's corporate activists. No longer do they pledge their allegiance blindly to the latest corporate directive. No longer do their managers stand awestruck in airport lounges, awaiting yet another visitor from the head office. Many affiliated companies regard the term *subsidiary* as pejorative; some openly rebel against the hierarchical premises upon which companies have evolved.

To fend off threats from the field, minimalist executives must come to grips with the new economic realities. Prolonged conflict between headquarters and subsidiary results in a negative-sum game. There are no

135

winners, only losers: companies themselves. Losses on one side do not represent gains for the other. Simply stated, there is no divisible quantum of power in a minimalist firm.

The real solution lies in discarding the notions that gave rise to hollow definitions of the M-form organization in the first place. After all, what is a *head office* in a network structure? And who is *subsidiary* to whom? As the firm shrinks its command center and disperses key functions to the field and various third parties, aren't conventional terms, such as *centralization* and *decentralization*, however handy, somewhat misleading?

Three decades ago, the principles for running an M-form organization probably made sense: Centralize strategic planning at the headquarters level, decentralize operations, and communicate effectively. But with operating companies clamoring for power and with modern technology feeding their needs, this prescription is outdated.

Therefore, minimalist firms must recast the headquarters-subsidiary relationship in terms of a partnership. Concepts of *power sharing* must replace those of *power over* a business unit. "Instead of creating cowboy competition, winners and losers, conquerors and colonized, or rivals for the same tidbits of power, postentrepreneurial corporations will raise the performance standards by building commitment to shared goals and enhancing the ability to work together," says Harvard's Rosabeth Moss Kanter.

Organizational thinking today embodies two principles: horizontal trust and vertical distrust. The operating units are equal partners in the minimalist galaxy. Indeed, they contribute most to the economic value of the enterprise. Hence, they deserve an adult role commensurate with their achievements and capabilities. The challenge, then, is to energize the subsidiaries—empowering them to participate in a variety of corporatewide activities and freeing them from their centrally forged shackles.

Headquarters or Hindquarters?

America's minimalist mindset does not mean the demise of corporate headquarters, though. Bureaucracy, not the principle of command, is the enemy. If anything, central leadership in an information-based enterprise must be better than ever before. Network organizations have fewer staff, wider spans of control, more diffuse business units, and looser amalgams of partnership arrangements. Add to this the new demands for job sharing, flexible hours, off-premises assignments—and more. Clearly, managing a minimalist enterprise requires superior leaders at the center. What we are advocating, then, is a gradual redefinition of the head office's role, with greater authority being given to the operating units. The slimmed-down miniheadquarters must continue to provide strategic direction, staff support, and intracompany communications and control—but with some major differences. Here are the most important ones.

Strategic Planning

Under minimalist philosophy, operating company personnel are considered to be the equals of their head office peers as strategic planners. Hanson Industries, for instance, proclaims in its national advertisements that "it's only common sense that the right people to run a successful specialist company are, of course, the experts who run it already. And that knowledge and expertise learned at the operating level are invaluable and impossible to gain sitting only at 'corporate headquarters.'"

Operating-level participation in shaping the corporate game plan is a natural outgrowth of the smaller headquarters staff. "No matter how good they are, no matter how well supported analytically, the decision makers at the center are just too far removed from the intricacies of individual markets and the needs of local customers," argues McKinsey's Kenichi Ohmae. Scaled-down companies entice subsidiary managers to work on major segments of the firm's overall strategy. When operating managers are given a role in corporate planning, they must have the skills and talents to make groupwide contributions. This, of course, means providing sufficient training for subsidiary personnel.

Downsizing zealots preach the "incremental school" of strategic planning. They contend that a downsized company's overall strategy is simply to consolidate its business unit plans. As espoused by George E. Hall, former senior vice president for corporate planning at SCM Corporation.: "The corporate plan is, and should be, no more than the sum of the business plans." After all, who needs high-powered—and high-salaried—headquarters people to conduct fifth-grade arithmetic?

However, incrementalism alone is not enough. In today's increasingly complex business environment, corporate survival often depends on bold, new strategies. Witness, for instance, the dramatic redirection of such companies as AT&T, Singer, Bell & Howell, Northwest Industries, and General Foods. Abandoning core businesses and acquiring new ones, entering global markets, and other major policy initiatives require penetrating analyses that lie well beyond the scope of incremental planning. Therefore, strategic planning in the Age of Minimalism must be more than a compilation of individual business unit plans. It should integrate operating companies and capitalize on their synergies. Declares

Harvard Business School's Michael E. Porter: "Companies that are on top of forging integrated strategies are the companies that are going to succeed in the future."

The objective is to get everyone to think strategically. But the last thing a minimalist company needs is a strategic free-for-all. "Managing participation down through the organization entails clearly defining roles and carefully creating opportunities for managers and key contributors to become involved," say Benjamin R. Tregoe and Peter M. Kobis of Kepner-Tregoe, Inc., a Princeton, New Jersey-based organization specializing in strategic and operational decision making. "A growing number of companies employ cross-functional task forces to stimulate creativity and commitment and to resolve key strategic concerns."

General Foods is an active proponent of the task force approach. Teams of GF managers meet bimonthly to discuss policy directions and possible implementation plans. Managers then report back the results of their assignments to headquarters; these reports are in turn folded into the company's overall game plan. These task force sessions bind together a diverse group of decentralized business units and ensure that their talents are working in tandem.

Staff Services

A streamlined head office necessarily offers its operating units a more limited menu of technical services—a menu that will tend to shrink as U.S. business continues to evolve toward flatter, less hierarchical structures. The issue is not whether the menu is too expensive, but whether the head office's services add value to the corporation. "Each staff person has to ask, 'How do I add value? How do I help make people in the line more effective and more competitive?'" says GE's Jack Welsh. "In the past, many staff functions were driven by control rather than by adding value." No longer. Corporate services now must prove their worth to the operating units.

"In the traditional corporation, a business unit would often have to justify itself to the parent corporation, to explain why the corporation would want to keep owning it," echoes Harvard's Kanter. "Now, in an interesting reversal, the onus is often on the corporate entity itself—the entity that exists above and beyond the business unit—to, in effect, justify itself to the business unit, to explain why the business should bother to belong to it."

How does the justification process work? Minimalist firms force their central staffs to compete with outside suppliers. Operating unit managers decide what corporate services—from public relations to tax consulting—they are willing to pay for out of their own budgets. If the head office departments cannot bring their costs for these activities in line with the market, they can find themselves out of a job.

General Foods, SKF, and Weyerhaeuser are devotees of the "internal market" approach. Weyerhaeuser, for instance, launched its program 5 years ago. Each of the 14 corporate departments calculates its expenses, computes the cost of the services it offers, and issues a statement of charges to its internal clients—the other units of the company. If an operating manager thinks that the charge is too high, he or she is free to shop for the service outside the company. The change in corporate attitudes is amazing. No longer do the headquarters personnel view themselves as mere consumers of wealth generated by the operating units; instead, they are partners providing an essential service to customers. Says Dennis A. Loewe, Weyerhaeuser's controller of financial services: "Corporate staffers used to be a little embarrassed around these lumberjacks, the guys in flannel shirts and hobnail boots. Now we have a partnership." By having this partnership, the forest products firm has reduced its head office costs dramatically.

As with strategic planning, firms with diminutive headquarters must call upon their line officers or the staffs of their operating units to perform many corporate staff functions. In many instances, affiliate-level managers are viewed by others in the company as "doers" who are more credible than their ivory-towered counterparts in the head office. Nevertheless, firms must be realistic about shifting the responsibility for complicated staff functions to already busy line managers. Companies cannot afford to skimp on training of operating managers in technical areas. When properly instructed, field personnel can often match the talents of the "professionals" in head office. Many frontier firms successfully weave fast-trackers from their business units into meaningful specialty activities on a 2- to 3-year basis.

The challenge is to leverage operating company talent to the hilt. Several firms do this by creating technical teams of subsidiary personnel to perform groupwide duties. The firms encourage information sharing, which, in turn, promotes a partnership spirit. "You want to set up an egalitarian atmosphere," says Harry V. Quadracci, president and founder of Quad/Graphics, a $400-million printer of magazines and catalogs. "You want technical people sharing information and acting on it."

Communications and Control

Building operating-level involvement in corporate strategy and staff services is only half the loaf. The other half is to reduce or eliminate the oppressive communication and control systems between an imperial head office and the field. But how?

First, the quality of contacts with the head office should be improved. An effective partnership culture lives or dies on person-to-person contact between those in the center and their peers in the operating units. The Wharton School's Howard V. Perlmutter and I advocate the so-called godfather concept, an approach adopted by several minimalist firms whereby direct, but informal, advice is available to every operating company. This approach recognizes the fact that every affiliate needs its friend in court, an ally or "godfather" with first-hand knowledge of the local scene.

Second, corporations should cut the number of headquarters visits to the operating units by one-half, while doubling the number of operating unit visits to the center. Far too often, field trips by head office executives are ill-conceived and unnecessary. And far too often, business unit managers receive the company's telephone directory as a substitute for vital first-hand experience.

Third, CEOs should alter the motivational systems of the head office staff. Instead of being rewarded on the basis of "How many errors or indiscretions did I uncover in Business Unit X today?" those at the center should be encouraged to ask, "What did I do to build a stronger partnership culture within our company?" Firms must ensure that employees who are in contact with subsidiaries possess this capacity to assist, not to impede.

Fourth, companies should institute a communications audit. Here, a joint headquarter-subsidiary team performs a content analysis on the quantity and quality of communications (telexes, correspondence, and the like) between the head office and the field. Are they timely? Are they too frequent or too infrequent? Are they antagonistic or supportive? Do they focus on the right issues? These and other questions surface potential stress points between headquarters and the affiliates.

Frequently, a major stumbling block in the communication process is a difference in perception. For example, operating company managers often overstate the differences between their own markets and the others in which the company does business. Conversely, those in the head office often tend to discount the alleged differences. Successful minimalist companies are those that are able to sort out the myth and reality in head office-subsidiary relations.

Fifth, business units invariably are too loaded down with demands for reports and information and are kept on too tight a leash. Operating managers should be allowed to get on with their day-to-day tasks with a minimum of bureaucratic interference. Minimalist enterprises should confine financial reporting from the field to the essentials—a balance sheet, an income statement, and an analysis of cash flow—and simultaneously let operating companies stand on their own legs: give them greater flexibility in capital expenditures, borrowing powers, hiring and firing, and other key decisions. Companies should replace the figurehead status of field managers with something far more substantive. If subsidiary personnel are not equal to these challenges, they should be replaced.

Finally, minimalist firms should promote the business units as the fast track. They should sell their high-potential candidates on the many pluses of working in a subsidiary: profit center responsibility, generalist experience, and the chance to run their own show early in their business careers.

These six steps offer the best hope for unleashing the power and potential of the minimalist movement. Companies that rely on their business units for strategy and staff services are more likely to adapt to their individual quirks. "I've learned that operating companies are like kids," says Charles Leighton, chairman of the CML Group. "There are certain ones you don't have to check on and others that you have to make sure have done their homework." Leighton should know. His Acton, Massachusetts, headquarters of only 12 people (including the secretaries) controls a diverse group of specialty and leisure businesses from California to New England.

CML and other minimalist companies are devoid of the overmanagement malaise that characterizes many American businesses. They support, rather than direct, their operating units and strive for a balance between bold creativity and effective operating controls. "Instead of formalistic baloney and out-of-touch leaders," says management expert Tom Peters, "the new 'control' is the energy, excitement, spirit, hustle, and clarity of the competitive vision that emanates from the corporate center."

No doubt, redefining subsidiaries as partners, removing their shackles, and motivating them to accept greater challenge will be no easy task. But is there any alternative? CEOs can either promote an effective minimalist culture or suffer the consequences.

A Cautionary Note

The scaled-down headquarters is no panacea. CEOs should be mindful of the potential downside before rushing off to prune their command structures. Here are four common pitfalls.

Loss of Control

Overly aggressive companies (those that remove healthy muscle along with bureaucratic flab) create staffs that are too weak to monitor and control their own business units. Such staffs tend toward overdelegation, a shortcoming that plagued President Reagan, particularly during his second term.

Minimalist companies are especially vulnerable to ambitious operating units. Some of these hard-chargers become independent fiefdoms, with little regard for central authority. Eventually, a weakened corporate parent encounters great difficulty in pulling in the reins on its muscle-bound business units. Even the staunchest advocates of the mini-headquarters warn against yielding too much authority or ignoring early warning signs of recalcitrant subsidiaries.

Effective management controls take on added importance as strategic partnering, outsourcing, and other third-party alternatives become more prevalent. Minimalist firms must develop an ongoing surveillance system to sense potential disputes between their strategic partners, associates, or vendors. Progress reports which analyze growing or declining mutual trust and respect should supplement operational progress and performance reports. Invariably, many of the initial expectations of the participating companies prove to be unrealistic. Disillusionment sets in, and the alliance eventually dissolves. Building mutual trust and respect is the key to forging a long-term relationship; strategic partnership, outsourcing, and similar third-party agreements depend on all sides sharing their expertise for mutual gain. This requires an in-depth understanding of the strengths and weaknesses of each participant and a commitment to build on the pluses while reducing the minuses.

Communications Breakdowns

As companies prune their command structures, they may also weaken another vital headquarters function: intrafirm communications. CEOs decry the lack of information following the loss of key staffers who could cut through reams of information and propose viable solutions. Now that capability is gone.

Companies tend to discount the organizational continuity that a professional staff provides. While line managers often shift from one assignment in the company to another, head office people generally stay put. They represent, in the words of one executive, "the bone marrow of the company." Elizabeth Hass Edersheim, a consultant with New York Consulting Partners, Inc., contends that staff experts maintain crucial "underground networks." Invisible on organization charts, these contacts help a firm run smoothly. When staff personnel are cut loose, they take with them vital sources of secondary expertise: contacts with their counterparts in other companies, trade associations, and professional organizations. A minimalist enterprise can quickly find itself cut off from the technical mainstream.

Corporate Brain Drain

The diminution of communications, internal and external, may produce another problem. As power shifts to the operating entities, the head office often becomes an organizational gulag—a repository of demoralized staffers, each anxiously awaiting the next cutback. These businesses experience a noticeable decline in dedication and productivity. The stars at headquarters wander off in search of a brighter future just when they are needed most.

False Economies

As a crowning blow, some minimalist firms are shocked to discover that the alleged cost savings of a skinnier central staff never materialize. Postmortems reveal three common reasons for this. First, as they slim down, companies tend to overuse expensive consultants and third-party providers. Second, operating units in need of crucial technical advice often replace terminated head office staffers with an equal or a greater number of their own experts. Finally, additional training dollars are required to bring line managers up to speed on strategy and other key activities.

Actions for CEOs

Caveats aside, the swing toward smaller, less centralized corporate staffs will continue for some time. The benefits exceed the costs for most companies, and the organizational expert who advocates a return to the days of Pentagonlike bureaucracies will soon be out of clients. Still, chief executives should let their gut instinct temper hardheaded logic as they evaluate whether their firm is a candidate for going the minimalist route.

If your company is thinking about downsizing and, with it, a home in penturbia, here are five important considerations.

1. Assess Your Commitment to Scaling Back

Do you really have your heart in a miniheadquarters? To be effective, some executives need strength in numbers at their side. Others are simply incapable of adopting the arm's-length management philosophy that a smaller headquarters requires. Each CEO should examine his or her own management style, as well as the corporate culture, before erecting an organization that will discourage hands-on involvement in day-to-day operations.

The acid test of senior management's commitment to minimalist living will occur when an operating company is not doing well, when its profits are declining. How does the head office respond to tough times? Does it seek to reaffirm its authority by descending on the faltering business unit with a rescue operation? Or does it undertake genuine efforts to lend assistance and play a supporting role in the turnaround? The answer can reveal a firm's true commitment to minimalist living.

2. Pick Your Spots

Pruning the headquarters staff works best for diversified companies with units capable of supporting themselves and also capable of providing technical assistance to the rest of the company. Successful miniheadquarters companies, such as Hanson Industries, Burlington Northern, Transamerica, and the CML Group, meet these criteria.

Many unitary businesses (insurance, airlines, banking, and so forth) possess neither the structure nor the personnel to permit interdivisional sharing. For them, the best prospects for a smaller head office lie in pushing increased responsibility and authority to key geographic units. Again, special care must be taken to avoid duplicating overheads.

3. Monitor Costs Carefully

Proper control systems are essential if savings are to be gained from downsizing and delayering. CEOs should conduct a zero-base review of staff costs at every organizational level—and monitor those costs closely.

The Aluminum Company of America rigorously adheres to the so-called value-added approach. "Every dollar spent must add value to product deliverable to a customer," says CEO Paul H. O'Neill. "If a staff function adds value, it should be retained; if it doesn't, it should be eliminated." The challenge for CEOs is to examine every function the firm is performing and determine whether it is necessary or could be done more efficiently.

4. Invest in Computers—
and People

Information technology plays a vital role in minimalizing. As the U.S. economy tilts in a more knowledge-oriented direction, firms must invest heavily in complex computer systems and bring their work force up to the task. The dynamics of flatter, less hierarchical structures will not be achieved without pumping big bucks into these systems.

State-of-the-art technology is not enough, however. No amount of video conferencing, telecommunications, or computer networking can fully replace human interaction. Research conducted by Professor John Kotter of the Harvard Business School shows that managers accomplish objectives by talking to people. Car phones and fax machines have little effect on relationship building. This, Kotter says, "tends to get done face to face." Therefore, CEOs also must concentrate on the human side of minimalizing.

To begin with, this means not skimping on the care and feeding of outgoing staffers. Money spent on outplacement counseling, early retirement programs, and other "soft landing" systems offers comfort and earns respect from redundant employees; it also tells the rest of the organization that the company cares about its people.

Most survivors in a minimalist company wind up with greater responsibilities and new reporting relationships. To ensure success, restructured firms must draft new job specifications, standards of performance, methods of appraisal, and compensation packages. These changes, in turn, must be communicated to the entire organization. Finally, affected staff must be trained to meet their new responsibilities.

Du Pont has been one of the most successful companies in managing this process. After eliminating many of its supervisors, the company informed employees of the rationale for the changes. It created work teams and rotated the management of each team to train its members to take responsibility for performing critical tasks. Du Pont also introduced incentive-based compensation tied to team performance. The result: a more productive, better- informed work force.

5. Think Long Term—or Not At All

Any minimalist strategy is, at best, a 5-year process. Anything shorter is an invitation to failure.

Most U.S. companies that undertook downsizing were pushed into it by serious economic difficulties. Some were on the verge of bankruptcy; others had already filed for Chapter 11. Even for corporations in less trouble, attacking overheads was a matter of short-term survival. Understandably, firms in this first wave of cutbacks never benefitted fully from their efforts. They failed to match restructuring with the carefully planned programs and investments needed to make the concept work.

Today, we are beginning to see more thoughtful, less-expedient approaches to scaling back. A few companies—Ford, General Electric, and

Citicorp, to name three—are pursuing the minimalist approach with clear-cut, long-term strategies for the redeployment of their human and physical resources. Their goals are realistic, and they are prepared to buy time. However, too many companies still view cutting back as a quick fix to financial trouble.

If CEOs cannot satisfy these five conditions, they should reconsider the minimalist route. After all, a smaller command structure is not for every enterprise. Eliminating bureaucratic flab is one thing; quite another is robbing the center of its vital capacity to provide strategic planning, staff support, and intercompany communications and control. Our advice: Don't make a hindquarters out of headquarters.

A Final Note

The term *minimalist movement* is somewhat misleading, since it suggests a change in the quantity, not the quality, of organizations. Decomposing the center, by itself, is not enough. Firms intent on pursuing the miniheadquarters goal must also change the relationships between their managers in decidedly different ways. For those companies that make this transition successfully, the benefits will be impressive: lower overhead expenses, less bureaucracy, faster decision making, smoother communications, and greater entrepreneurship.

With so much to gain, the minimalist movement continues to captivate those in the executive suite. In many respects, the shift toward sleeker command structures is both a necessary and a sufficient condition for a frontier location. Existing small-town firms, emerging ones, and others contemplating a move to semirural settings must adopt some measure of the minimalist philosophy. Otherwise, penturbia loses its allure.

For the first time in modern history, big businesses are, in fact, seriously embracing the prospect of operating from miniheadquarters based in relatively remote townships. Ironically, this lust for downsizing and decentralizing has given rise to a new set of factors that further strengthen the case for frontier living. The next part examines these issues and their effect on corporate America.

PART 4

Trust in a Small Town

10
Building a Frontier Culture

The minimalist forays of the eighties enabled the United States to fend off, at least partially, the competitive onslaught of Japan, West Germany, and other industrialized nations. Not without substantial cost, however. Downsizing and delayering unnerved many working Americans. For a generation raised on Kellogg's Corn Flakes and *Ozzie and Harriet,* the concept of lifetime employment became a thing of the past. Fear and anxiety set in as employees sensed that traditional work values—dedication and company loyalty—no longer counted.

Shocking Repercussions

A *Time*-CNN poll of 520 workers conducted by Yankelovich Clancy Schuman reported a sharp decline in belief in corporate loyalty as well as an increased expectation of future job hopping. Among those surveyed, 57 percent said that companies are less loyal to employees today than they were a decade ago, and 63 percent said that workers are less loyal to their firms. Asked whether they trust their employers to keep their promises to workers, 48 percent said "only somewhat." While 60 percent of the employees said that they would prefer to stay on the job they have now, 50 percent said that they expected to change jobs within the next 5 years.

In a parallel study, Carnegie Mellon's Robert Kelly found trust and loyalty at an all-time low. His survey of 400 managers shows that fully one-third of them distrust their own direct bosses and 55 percent distrust top management. Obviously, companies cannot expect much from workers who don't believe what their superiors tell them. "The most important thing to remember is that these people are going through an unbelievable culture shock," says Daniel J. Valentino, president of United Research, a New Jersey consulting firm that works on human relations issues. Shock, in turn, has flamed widespread resentment across the country. "The cynical Americans," Donald C. Kanter and Philip H. Mirvis call us. Their research reveals that one of four members of the U.S. work force mistrusts management; less than a third described management as trustworthy; and nearly 30 percent are dissatisfied about their places of work.

"It's no fun any more—it's just a job," is a frequent complaint today. More and more of America's cynical and shell-shocked workers are withdrawing their commitment from the enterprise. Looking after number one takes precedence. "Call it the middle-management malaise or the leaner-and-meaner blues," says *Fortune*'s Anne B. Fisher. "Managers joined a union called 'Me First.'" Who could blame them? After all, the role models of the time were the business buccaneers Ivan Boesky, Michael Milken, Leona Helmsley, Donald Trump, and others.

"The 1980s, above all, was a decade when everybody was reaching out to grab everything they could," claims Michael Marsden, a popular culture professor at Bowling Green University. Allegiance to the company, an unspoken covenant a generation ago, was replaced by personal loyalty. Many people concluded that the only way to achieve the American dream was to tough it out.

Enter a new class of young urban professionals—the yuppies. Work was their slave-god. "Americans came to worship career status as a measure of individual worth, and many were willing to sacrifice any amount of leisure time to get ahead," said futurist Selwyn Enzer. All work and no play characterized the last decade. Stress seemed a small price to pay to the yuppie generation. Independence and career came first as these high-flying big spenders obliterated the notion of "team." They personified the much- publicized "me generation" that had its roots in the sixties and seventies. Organized self-gratification, hedonism, and narcissism symbolized the times.

America's integrative institutions also lost ground. The death of compulsory military service, shrinking church membership, declining summer camp enrollments, and the rising divorce rate were but a few examples. The United States seemed unable to sustain, let alone build, the cultural or organizational connections needed to synthesize an increasingly heterogeneous society. One wondered: Would "My Country, 'Tis of *Me*" be more appropriate lyrics to the well-known song?

A Nation in Transition

The glib solution to a business world viewed as increasingly cold, uncaring, and hypocritical is to withdraw from it. Although a segment of today's young and middle-age generation is dropping out, a more popular career choice is to own or manage one's own business. "Running your own business means controlling your own destiny," says Cognetics President David L. Birch. While starting a company rarely is a bed of roses, it can promise great satisfaction, flexible working conditions, and control over one's lifestyle. Nevertheless, U.S. industry need not suffer the hemorrhaging of talent and prospective entrepreneurs from the traditional work force.

If corporate America is to regain the hearts and minds of people, it must reestablish values of trust and sharing. However, time is running out. Big business's preoccupation with tough-minded minimalism comes at a time when our global competitors are demonstrating the power of pulling together. Building esprit de corps is something the Japanese do best, as Ezra Vogel, William Ouchi, and others have pointed out in their best-selling books. Despite the sting of their messages, U.S. industry has been slow to follow suit.

Besides the challenge of foreign competition, the forces of demography also demand quick action. For one thing, America's baby-boomers are hitting middle age. For the rest of the decade, most of the boomers—those born between 1946 and 1964—will move through their forties: perfect ages for introspection and reexamination. Already, "fortysomething" issues are beginning to affect these aging Americans. They want to pursue new, less frantic careers. Community, family, security, and meaning of life are becoming distinctly more important to them, and this trend will continue. "A growing number of executives are looking for lifestyles more than just that constant striving and going higher and making more money," says Gerald Celente, national director of the Socio-Economic Institute of America in Rhinebeck, New York. "There's a strong desire for people to live long, happy, and healthy lives, and they realize that this is no longer attainable under present conditions. We're going to see a redirection of priorities, more toward human needs as everyone ages."

The seeds of change are taking root. The nineties is a transitional decade, and we are already seeing the emergence of important trends that will influence our lives well into the twenty-first century. Lifestyle concerns are beginning to outweigh the drive for materialism. The eighties "decade of greed" is giving way to the nineties "decade of creed." Working to live is more important than living to work. In large part, credit for this new credo goes to activist women in business. Working women, who now account for 45 percent of the labor force, will make up 63 percent by the end of the century. Plus, working mothers are the fastest-growing segment of the work force. By the year 2000, the Department of Labor estimates that 84 percent of all females of child-bearing age will be working.

Men and women alike want business's support in balancing corporate and human needs. More than half the U.S. work force believes that employers have an obligation to provide child care to workers with children, and an equal number want such care provided in or near the workplace, according to a recent *Washington Post*-ABC News poll. Finding help for younger children appears to be a somewhat greater problem. Among those with preschool-aged children, 47 percent said that it is difficult to locate a child care center, including 23 percent who said it is very difficult.

Repeatedly, Americans are demanding that their employers provide a new generation of amenities. They include in-house child, elder, or intergenerational care centers or financial aid for external care centers; grants for new babies; reimbursement for adoption expenses; in-home tutoring for kids; and extended maternal and parental leaves, with guaranteed return privileges, as well as similar leaves to care for elderly or seriously ill family members. They are also clamoring for more work-at-home options, flexible hours, part-time employment, new career-path alternatives, and more vacation time.

The demands of America's baby-boomers at fortysomething are not likely to evaporate. "People have no choice but to bring these problems to the workplace," says Dana Friedman, copresident of the New York-based Families and Work Institute. Employers must respond or lose any hope of regaining the trust and loyalty of their workers. Like it or not, corporate America will have to find new ways to inspire higher levels of commitment and productivity in their employees—from cradle to grave.

Then there is the added challenge of the shrinking labor pool. Because of lower birthrates, an average of only 1.3 million people will enter the labor force every year of the decade, down from 3 million in the 1970s. The growth rate of the labor force during the 1990s is projected at only 1.2 percent—virtually half the 2.2 percent growth rate between 1972 and 1986. By the year 2000, the Bureau of Labor Statistics predicts that there will be a shortage of 23 million workers. Hence, firms today must deal with a labor market that is no longer a buyer's market. It is a seller's market.

These demographics are revolutionizing the work force. American men and women of every age and race are insisting on corporate policies that enable them to act more responsibly toward their families, friends, and the community-at-large and still satisfy their professional ambitions. "Balance," therefore, is the watchword of the times.

Paternalism Redux

The nineties is a time when people are beginning to care. Americans today are less inclined to see money as the carrot. More important are a sense of personal fulfillment and time for family, friends, community.

Enlightened companies are restyling themselves to accommodate these changes in values. They recognize that employees are attracted to their organizations because flexible employment opportunities along with personal and financial rewards are offered. Farsighted firms are drafting a new social contract that balances work and family responsibilities. "Watch for these employers to use all kinds of flexible work arrangements, such as flextime, job sharing, job banks, retiree work programs, and project staffing," says David W. Rhodes, a principal at TPF&C, a Towers Perrin Company affiliate in New York City. "Watch for family and elder care options to proliferate, such as elder and child care vouchers and direct payment from companies for the care of dependents. Watch also as prospective employees turn to these companies because the actions of these 'corporate parents' will be consistent with employees' own aspirations."

Although downsizing unnerved many Americans, the quest for minimalism is permanent and, therefore, should not be understated. U.S. enterprise must be fast and footloose if it is to compete in the global industrial system. This means greater use of a contingent work force, more outsourcing and strategic partnerships, and other minimalist measures. "Companies want fewer obligations to their employees, not more," says Michael J. Piore, an economist at MIT

Working people, for their part, are equally intent on keeping their options open. Having witnessed the severe cutbacks of the 1980s, the present generation treasures its freedom and independence. "Flexibility will continue to spread, partly because people want it and partly because employers need it," says *Business Week*. "We are moving irresistibly in the direction of a more and more flexible society."

Despite all the heavy breathing about flexibility, employers and employees both want more stability than ever before. U.S. industry needs a well-trained, semipermanent cadre of highly committed workers to blunt the steady advance of foreign competition. By the same token, the country's aging and shrinking work force is prepared to sacrifice some of its freedom for those employers that truly care for them, their families, and the community-at-large.

The challenge of this transitional period is to forge a new kind of corporate culture—one that combines elements of independence (or flexibility) with those of interdependence (or community). The kind of conceptual framework we are describing might best be likened to a two-story house. The first floor consists of collective values such as egalitarianism, teamwork, participation, and caring; the second floor accents the need for individual and organizational freedom. The new paradigm is the sleek, highly decentralized organization that fosters a greater sense of "family"; hence, the foundation of this two-story house is decidedly paternalistic.

Corporate involvement in the external affairs of employees will increase, but not in the intrusive manner of bygone days. The evolving neopaternalism attempts to revalidate the legitimacy of the contemporary corporation and to remove the shroud of cynicism surrounding it. Its major components include (1) a shared vision of the enterprise, (2) egalitarianism, (3) esprit de corps, and (4) communitarianism. Where better to reestablish these virtues than in Small Town, U.S.A.? Historically, penturban employers have excelled at developing these critical qualities. Consider their track record.

Shared Vision

The rallying point for any organization is a formalized statement of its view of the world. This statement describes the enterprise's dedication to lofty ends beyond the normal conduct of business. Properly crafted, a vision statement commits all those in the company to common goals and shared values.

Frontier businesses are highly proficient at communicating an unambiguous vision of their purpose—a rarity for many U.S. companies. In direct and simple prose, their mottoes tell the world of their fierce commitment to excellent quality and service. To illustrate:

- "Sell good merchandise at reasonable profit, treat your customers like human beings, and they'll always come back for more," was Leon Leonwood Bean's golden rule in 1919. This maxim serves the company handsomely more than 7 decades later. L. L. Bean's employees are constantly encouraged to treat the customers as family, and the firm's unconditional guarantee on all products reinforces its value on customer service.

- At Steelcase, the credo is similar: "Give the customer a dollar's worth of value. Don't shortchange him. Don't argue with him. If there's something wrong, fix it!" Small wonder the Grand Rapids, Michigan-based company is the acknowledged leader in the $8-billion office furniture industry.

- "Give them quality," was Milton Snavely Hershey's charge to his employees 97 years ago, when he founded a small chocolate company in Pennsylvania's Amish country. Today, America's largest confectioner is best known for its ubiquitous Hershey bar.

The simple messages of other small-town companies transmit equally powerful signals. "Dow lets you do great things" reminds America's second-largest chemical company of its dedication to a high standard. The credo at Mrs. Fields Cookies is also straightforward: "Good enough *never* is." Another down-home business pokes fun at itself with its self-deprecating slogan: "With a name like Smucker's, it has to be good."

Invariably, the best vision statements are highly personalized, highly intuitive. "The critical component isn't a grand sweeping plan of how to respond to what the world will look like in the future," say James C. Collins and Jerry I. Porras of Stanford Business School. "No, vision is the ability to see the potential in or necessity of opportunities right in front of you. It's knowing 'in your bones' what can or must be done."

Food Lion, the country's fastest-growing supermarket chain, based in Salisbury, North Carolina (pop. 24,880), knows that strict attention to detail separates it from the rest of the pack. "We may not do anything 1000 percent better, but we do 1000 things 1 percent better," is the $5.6-billion company's motto. This keep-it-simple slogan has produced incredible results. Over the past 20 years, the company's sales have grown at an average annual rate of 37 percent, and earnings 55 percent, rewarding shareholders annual returns on equity averaging 24 percent. In fact, Food Lion stock has made millionaires of at least 87 investors who live in Salisbury and surrounding Rowan County.

Above all, a shared vision embodies strong, deep-seated convictions about the mission of the enterprise and its attitudes toward people. For small-town employers, old-fashioned values like quality, loyalty, and steadfastness often dominate their view of the universe. For instance, Maytag's fetish about product quality goes back to its founder, Frederick Louis ("call me 'F.L.'") Maytag. His presence still seems to dominate a corner of the bucolic corn country of Iowa called Newton, where the $3-billion appliance maker is headquartered. Its street address says it all: One Dependability Square. If that were not enough, many Americans have grown up watching national advertisements that feature the lonely Maytag repairman (played for 23 years by the actor Jesse White), who moaned that his phone hardly ever rang. "When you compete with giants as we do, quality is our edge," says chairman Daniel J. Krumm. "If we ever lose it, we lose our meal ticket." Surely, old F.L. must be smiling.

Invariably, Corn Belt conservatism creeps into these vision statements. But a bit of stodginess is no vice. "Our basic beliefs are quality, ethics, profits, growth, and people," says Tim Smucker, the 45-year-old chairman of the jelly company that bears his name. "Maybe that sounds like motherhood and apple pie." Perhaps, but the United States could benefit from more down-home thinking. "People in upbeat companies (like J. M. Smucker's) talk unabashedly about corporate ideals," say Donald Kanter and Philip Mirvis, authors of *The Cynical Americans*. They urge other U.S. executives to preach the gospel of "realistic idealism" if the cynicism that pervades much of the country is to be dispelled. What the United States needs most is a new generation of value-driven leaders—individuals like Tim Smucker who can articulate the American dream in everyday language.

Another penturban proponent of strong values is Tom Chappell, founder and president of the fast-growing Tom's of Maine, an all-natural toothpaste and deodorant company. He says that "what drives and organizes people are values, not strategy, or quantitative rewards. If I can organize people around a purpose, that is the most powerful form of leadership." What Tom Chappell and other penturban entrepreneurs are doing is pulling rather than pushing people toward a higher purpose.

Headquartered in a renovated railway depot outside Kennebunk, Maine (not far from President Bush's retreat in Kennebunkport), Tom's of Maine has survived the marketing muscle of Procter & Gamble, Colgate-Palmolive, and Unilever. Its stated vision is to respect, value, and serve customers, employees, the community, owners, and all others who "are in relation to us." The Down East firm recognizes that its survival, growth, and profitability depend on how it is perceived by external as well as internal stakeholders. Tom's views its customers, the community, and other outside groups to be equal in importance to the insiders—the owners, managers, and employees.

Shaping organizational vision and values is only half the battle; the other half is communicating the vision and values until they are shared throughout the enterprise. Small-town execs are experts in articulating corporate objectives and values to the rank and file. As company needs shift, they are able to fine-tune the original message and retain organizational acceptance. The key to their effectiveness is openness and trust.

"There are no walls," says Jim Stack, CEO of Springfield (Missouri) Remanufacturing Center Corporation, large refitters of diesel and gasoline engines and engine components. "Here we live in a house without walls, without barriers." Openness and candor come easily to Stack—one of America's most successful businessmen, who has been featured on the Public Broadcasting System and in *INC.* magazine. Since acquiring Springfield from the once-troubled International Harvest Company, he has directed the $50-million company's phenomenal growth of almost 40 percent a year.

Stack, 41, wears his heart on his sleeve. "I'm a shot-and-beer guy," he says. There are no mixed signals at Springfield Remanufacturing. Everyone knows what the boss is thinking and where the company is headed. So, when one employee was asked why he went along with what Stack was doing, he said: "Well, I guess I just *trust* him." This may sound maudlin to outsiders, but this is the heartlands—where people mean what they say.

Egalitarianism

Small-town employers are also generally free from intellectual, social, and economic snobbery. Distinctions are kept to a minimum. "Elitism is an expensive salve that doesn't work," says Dow Chemical's Frank Popoff. "You thrive by having smart, dedicated people. Don't ever think you can divide the company into haves and have-nots, thinkers, and doers." Debbi Fields of cookie fame agrees: "There is a lesson that lies in the foundation of my business—there is no such thing as an insignificant human being. To treat people that way is a kind of sin, and there's no reason for it, none."

Predictably, the executive offices at Dow, Mrs. Fields Cookies, and most other frontier dwellers are neither expansive nor expensive. Absent, too, are cushy executive dining rooms, for senior managers mingle daily with lower-echelon workers in the company cafeteria or beside the lunch wagon.

No doubt, the folksy persona of small-town CEOs contributes greatly to this egalitarianism. Take, for instance, Don Tyson, the 60-year-old chief executive of Tyson Foods Inc. Since his father died in 1967, he has transformed a small feed hatchery outfit in Springdale, Arkansas, into the biggest U.S. chicken producer (sales $4.3 billion). In October 1990, Tyson acquired rival Holly Farms for $1.5 billion, thereby boosting his market share from 13.5 to 25 percent. Despite his success, Don Tyson hasn't changed. Though he rules the roost at Tyson Foods, there is no pecking order at the Springdale headquarters. He and most of his employees wear khaki uniforms with the Tyson logo stitched near their hearts. "If someone wearing khaki comes up to you with an idea, you pay attention," says Jim Blair, the firm's counsel. "It may be the janitor—but it may be the CEO."

You won't find many local residents complaining about the company uniform. Tyson Foods has saved the best parts of its success for the hometown faithful. Springdale citizens who held on to the 1000 shares they bought for $1 each when the company went public now own 120,000 shares worth roughly $2.4 million.

Clifton Hillegass, 72, is another unpretentious hometown hero. For the past 30 years, he has made Lincoln, Nebraska, a minipublishing center, with his famous *Cliff's Notes*. At last count, America's "Patron Saint of the Marginal Student" had sold more than 90 million copies of the controversial black-and-yellow student guides. 1990's sales revenues were $12 million, with pretax profits just over $2 million. These impressive numbers have attracted many prospective buyers, including some offers as high as $50 million for the business.

Cliff Hillegass is not your typical publishing baron. He is a big, friendly, outgoing man whose literary tastes tend toward mysteries and science fiction. His attire features string ties and ultrasuede sport coats. Plush corporate offices? Hardly. The company operates out of a windowless corrugated steel building that is wedged between a billiard equipment company and a Goodwill Industries warehouse. Publishing power lunches? No way. Cliff prefers the restaurant at the Harvester Motel, just down the road from the Cornhusker capital.

Khaki uniforms and string ties symbolize what's important and what isn't to these heartland heroes. And the undifferentiated look is not just a superficial matter. In the end, though, the simplest ingredient in bringing egalitarianism to the workplace may just be plain old hard work, with top management setting the pace. Frontier firms cling to a roll-up-the-sleeves approach that permeates every level of the organization. At J. M. Smucker Company fifth-generation family members spend their summers on the loading dock, and every management trainee is expected to toil for years to grasp an understanding of the basics.

Dedicated is also an adept description of Rubbermaid managers. The tone is set by its slight, dapper, energetic chairman and CEO, Stanley C. Gault, who arrives at the Wooster, Ohio, headquarters daily at 6:30 a.m. and works 70 to 80 hours a week. At Rubbermaid, an employee badly needed to talk to Gault. Trouble was, the man got off his shift at 5 a.m. No problem; Gault gave up an hour's sleep to be there. Rubbermaid's vigorous 64-year-old chairman actively seeks out any employee who wants "to know everything that's going on in our business."

Fast-growing Food Lion, on the other hand, looks for potential managers with the "Food Lion personality," which, loosely translated, means a willingness to work hard. "You've got to produce, you've got to sacrifice," says Ken Barbee, an 18-year veteran of the company who manages its Albemarle, North Carolina, store. "They're there every day," says Jay Myers, a Charlotte-based stockbroker who tracks the supermarket chain. "They go in in the dark and they come out in the dark—they're very pale." No suntans here. Everybody at Food Lion reflects the work ethic. The most senior executives perform regular stints stocking shelves and walking the aisles of their stores.

Joining hands with the rank-and-file enables penturban businesses to listen to the employees they consider as coequals. Tim Smucker describes his regular listening routine: "Typically, I arrive at a plant a little early and try to meet informally as many plant people as I can. Once I sat beside a woman and asked her how long she had been with us and what shift she worked on. It turned out she had been with us for seven years and worked on the night shift. Noting that it was only 2:30 in the afternoon, I asked why she came in for this meeting. She said she wanted to know what the company was doing and that she appreciated being included."

J. M. Smucker encourages employees at all levels to discuss their jobs, priorities, and problems with their peers and supervisors on a regular basis. Many of Smucker's best products have emerged from these ad hoc sessions. The jelly maker knows the value of giving serious weight to the inputs of its dedicated work force.

So, too, does Techsonic Industries, Inc. of tiny Eufaula, Alabama. The country's leading producer of sonar fishing equipment is all ears when it comes to its employees. "We don't think we have all the answers," says Tom Dyer, president and CEO. "So we are very willing to listen." The company is famous for its formal program of getting feedback from the rank and file. Techsonic workers are heard from through forums such as the Error Cause Removal Committee, which makes wide-ranging quality control recommendations, to the Clean Team, which monitors neatness. Once a month, all 400 staffers get together to give out awards and hear management's responses to their written suggestions. "It's an atmosphere of open discussion," says Chairman Jim Belkcom. "You've got to identify every individual. We do that by listening."

Rubbermaid's second-place ranking (after Merck) by *Fortune* magazine for innovativeness is due largely to its sharp ears. The Ohio-based multinational introduces about 200 new products annually, thanks to the many inputs of its employees. Says Chairman Gault: "We want to actively encourage the genuine Rubbermaid family atmosphere that we've promoted."

Another frontier firm that has built its reputation on treating employees as equals is Quad/Graphics, Inc. Under its founder and president, Harry V. Quadracci, this Pewaukee, Wisconsin-based company is one of America's largest and fastest-growing printers—handling such magazines as *Time, Architectural Digest, INC.,* and *Business Month.* With more than $400 million in sales and 5000 employees, Quad/Graphics has mushroomed at an average annual rate of 40 percent, remarkable for a firm in a notoriously hidebound industry.

Egalitarianism pervades the company. Traditional nomenclature such as "boss" and "worker" does not exist. Employees are known as "partners," bosses are referred to as "sponsors" and "mentors," and the rank and file are "students," who are in the process of learning to become partners and mentors themselves. Don't expect to find the typical corporate trappings: organizational charts, procedural manuals, and time clocks. There aren't any. Just two layers of management separate the chief executive and the new hire. Quad's relative disdain of hierarchy breeds an atmosphere devoid of political gamesmanship and backstabbing.

In explaining his open management style (sometimes referred to as "Theory Q"), frontiersman Quadracci says: "I'd rather have 50 people out there all thinking profitably—being in conflict with ideas without conflicting in personality—and working together profitably to develop an operating policy that I can validate, than for me to sit up here from the top down and say, 'This is the way we are going to do it.'"

Like many other penturban CEOs, the 54-year-old Quadracci is big on rituals. Perhaps none is bigger than Quad's annual Spring Fling. That's the day when management plays hooky, leaving the rank and file in charge of the company. Quadracci launched the tradition in 1974, and every year he gives the workers free rein to do whatever needs to be done. "After all, Theory Q maintains that responsibility belongs to everybody, that workers don't always need somebody telling them what to do," says *Business Month*'s Daniel Kehrer. Quadracci also lets employees use the company rail cars—a parlor car, dining car, and sleeper—for parties.

In an increasingly atomized society, Quadracci takes unusual risks to engender camaraderie. One of them is the rejection of the traditional convention regarding nepotism. Quad/Graphics employees are encouraged to have their relatives join up. Why? In today's tight labor market, Quadracci believes that the best source of dedicated recruits are those with strong blood ties to the current team. Before the company expanded its printing operations to other states in 1985, more than a third of its entire work force was related in some fashion—husbands and wives, brothers and sisters, cousins, fathers, mothers, and daughters and sons.

By promoting the family concept, Quad/Graphics, Rubbermaid, Smucker's, and other members of the new corporate frontier are creating a neopaternalistic environment.

Esprit de Corps

Along with shared vision and egalitarianism, team building reigns supreme in the heartlands. "All together, boys" were the first words of English learned by the Danish immigrant Hans Jacob Andersen—while clearing tree stumps in central Minnesota. Togetherness became the guiding principle of the window-making company that bears his name.

In 1914, Andersen Corporation of tiny Bayport, Minnesota, encouraged company unity with a progressive concept for the times: profit sharing. Like many other small-town employers, Andersen has led the way in pioneering incentives to foster esprit de corps. "Make a product that is different and better. Hire the best people and pay top wages. Provide steady employment insofar as humanly possible." That is the clear-cut vision that Hans Jacob Andersen shaped and shared with his sons and subsequent generations of company managers. Six percent of the profits was enough, he reckoned, for those who created and managed the business; the rest should go to the workers.

Using this philosophy, Hans Jacob and his son Fred built the company into the largest and most profitable window and patio door manufacturer in the country. In 1990, sales approximated $1 billion. The firm routinely distributes over $100 million among its employees, with the average tab running at $28,600. Thanks to Andersen's special brand of paternalism, company employees can earn up to 140 percent of base pay. Their end-of-year profit-sharing payment is based on overall pay for the previous year—in effect, incentive pay compounded by incentive pay.

Besides profit sharing, Andersen was well ahead of its time in introducing other important benefits. For example:

- In 1916, Fred Andersen launched a health and life insurance plan for employees.
- In 1923, he added 2 weeks' paid vacation, a concept fashionable for office workers but not for factory hands.
- The following year, management began paying $2 to anyone who made a suggestion about product design, employee relations, or manufacturing systems that was adopted by the company.
- The same year, every hourly wage employee in the plant became eligible for bonus pay based on productivity.
- Also in 1924, after putting the issue to a vote of the workers, management decided to cut the workday from 10 hours to 9 without a reduction in pay. (Today, a standard shift is 8 hours).
- In 1975, Fred added the Employee Stock Ownership Trust, a plan formulated to buy stock each year for the workers. They now own 30 percent of the company.

In turn, Andersen has been rewarded for its generosity with a stable, dedicated work force. Many loyal workers have put in 25, 45, even 50 years of service. Like Quad/Graphics, Andersen encourages nepotism. Most new openings go to the children, spouses, siblings, or close friends of current employees. Everyone wants to work here. "I love my job, I really do," says 39-year-old Darlene Schultz. "I haven't missed a day of work in 2 years." She earns $11.41 per hour in base pay on a night shift crew that applies vinyl waterproofing to window frames. Typically, though, her annual profit-sharing check runs as high a $15,000—unusual prosperity in a region known for its economic dislocations. Understandably, there have never been any unions at Andersen. Employees know that the restrictions organized labor might impose would kill the golden goose. After all, where else can production workers make over $60,000 a year?

Based in Janesville, Wisconsin (pop. 51,250), Rath Manufacturing Company has also kept unions at bay with its incentive programs. The $50-million manufacturer of high-quality stainless steel tubing is the industry leader in productivity. The company offers special weekly bonuses (averaging $55 a week) based on the amount of tubing shipped. Although operators work close to 50 hours per week, turnover is extremely low—only six employees have left the firm in the last 5 years. An added inducement: Rath pays college expenses —up to $10,000 a year— for any of its employees' children attending the University of Wisconsin or any other school.

S. C. Johnson Wax is another Wisconsin employer that believes in aggressive profit sharing. Johnson Wax, as it is widely known, is one of the largest family-owned firms in the United States, with revenues reputed to be $3 billion. Chairman Samuel C. Johnson, the great-grandson and namesake of the company's founder, explained the philosophy of the Racine-based firm: "Our profit-sharing program has created a family atmosphere within the company. It makes the managers, the owners, and all the people who work here all in the same camp. All of our interests are the same. We all sit on the same side of the table, so to speak, so we don't have the confrontational environment between various groups of people who work here."

Profit sharing is largely responsible for Johnson Wax's low turnover and the absence of unions. "I think people feel that it's a rather personal tragedy if they are asked to leave the company," Johnson adds. "Other than normal retirement and the people in the sales force—who tend to be a close group—our turnover is less than 5 percent a year."

Employees at Quad/Graphics also know that if the company succeeds, they will share the rewards. *Psychology Today* magazine singled out Quad's employee stock ownership plan as "the ultimate ESOP." Employees as a group own about 22 percent of the company, the original employee-founders own about 60 percent, and outside investors own about 18 percent. Nonsalary benefits at Quad total 40 percent of direct compensation per employee—putting the firm among the top 2 percent of U.S. employers in terms of these benefits.

The generous incentive plans at Andersen, Rath Manufacturing,

Johnson Wax, Quad/Graphics, and many other small-town companies help to reinforce the idea that all employees are tied together as an extended family, with similar goals. They know that even modest fringes can pay off. Bur Jon Steel Service Center, Inc. of Springboro, Ohio, has found that money alone is not enough when there are pressures to put in long amounts of overtime. On the theory that families and friends suffer when people spend lots of time at work, Rick Johnson, the founder and CEO, augments overtime pay with flowers and dinner coupons—plus a personal note. "When somebody works hard," he says, "it's hard on everyone. We think it's important to say thanks."

Little things go a long way toward building a high-commitment work environment. Frontier firms want everyone to know that their personal concerns are shared by others in the company. Dow Chemical, for instance, has put in place several plans to help better accommodate the work style and lifestyle of its employees. Its family leave policy allows staffers up to 12 weeks of employment-protected unpaid leave. Possible reasons for this leave include caring for a newborn child or a seriously ill family member. In addition, Dow has devised flexible part-time schedules and job-sharing opportunities; it also offers an employee assistance program, which provides employees with confidential counseling about personal and work-related problems. Plus, there is a child care assistance program, which helps employees find adequate day care for their children. Other company-sponsored activities include a job search and placement program for spouses of relocated Dow employees and a wellness program that encourages company employees to participate in organized fitness courses.

Like Dow Chemical, Corning Glass Works, the famous cooking ware company, was cited recently as one of the best U.S. firms for working mothers. According to Thomas Blumer, the firm's director of human relations, Corning found that every employee with children was losing, on average, a day a week during the course of a year because of a breakdown in child care. Professional women were leaving in droves, costing the upstate New York company as much as $3 million annually. Corning responded with a comprehensive, family-friendly environment that has reduced absenteeism, tardiness, and turnover—while boosting employee morale.

Another important component of neopaternalism is affordable housing. Assemblyman David C. Schwartz of New Jersey, who is also a professor of political science at Rutgers University and director of the university's American Affordable Housing Initiative, believes that employer-assisted housing will become one of the most important personnel perks during the decade. "It will probably be the best benefit for attracting employees," he says, "while it will achieve home ownership for people who otherwise wouldn't have it." Given the relative cheapness of land, companies in the provinces have a distinct advantage in making low-cost living available to their employees, and several firms are exploiting this advantage.

R. L. Stowe Mills of Charlotte, North Carolina, is offering rental homes to lure employees to its textile mills. The company often cannot find and retain the 1300 workers it needs to keep its weaving machines spinning. So Stowe Mills restored the old mill town of Belmont, just south of Charlotte, into an enclave for new hires. During the next 5 years, the company plans to spend upward of $7 million to transform 70-year-old frame houses into modern homes with central air conditioning, dishwashers, double-pane windows, and vinyl siding.

In Belmont, mill-owned housing was always a way of life. But with the plantation days long gone, the firm feels that, rather than helping employees to own their own homes, it will repair them and rent them out at low rates (about $50 per week). Too much Big Brotherism? Not so, argues Professor Schwartz. "I really think the fear of the company town is a yesteryear story," he says. "After all, the workers are not brought in by bayonet. People who come in and rent these houses presumably know what their housing needs are and presumably could get a job somewhere else."

Other frontier businesses favor ownership over rental. Some techniques they are using are:

- Making low-interest loans to employees for up to 15 percent of the purchase price of the house. If the employee stays, say, for 5 years—during which time no payments are required—the loan is forgiven.

- Giving sizable blocks of corporate business to a friendly local bank in exchange for low-interest second mortgages to help their employees qualify for down payments.

- Pooling with other companies in a revolving loan fund for down payments for employees who buy homes in a targeted neighborhood close to the job site.

Whatever the method, the objective is the same: to put affordable houses within reach of the work force.

Small-town employers also foster organizational esprit by diffusing power throughout the enterprise. One company that has taken the "power-sharing" message to heart is Johnsonville Foods, Inc., a relatively small (1990 sales: $130 million) but rapidly growing specialty foods and sausage maker in Sheboygan, Wisconsin. Ralph Stayer, 47, CEO of the family-owned business, is an ardent fan of the partnership approach.

"Flattening pyramids doesn't work if you don't transfer power too," he says. "Real power is getting people committed. Real power comes from giving it up to others who are in a better position to do things than you are. Control is an illusion. The only control you can possibly have comes when people are controlling themselves."

Stayer created the Personal Development Lifelong Learning Department to empower Johnsonville's work force. Workers meet with a counselor who helps them articulate their goals and aspirations. Each receives a small allowance of $100 a year to spend on a personal-growth project. Some apply to college or graduate school; others join a cooking class. For big expenses like education, employees also may get scholarships.

What's in this for Johnsonville? A lot, says Stayer: "When people see that they can change something in their personal lives, they bring that attitude to work." By personalizing the process, Johnsonville employees on the line have accepted greater responsibility for tasks formerly in the domain of corporate headquarters. For the past 5 years, volunteers from the shop, not financial experts from the head office, have written the manufacturing budget. In 1990, when the sales department aimed at increasing volume 40 percent, the manufacturing group set—and achieved—a goal of providing the additional output, while holding cost increases to 20 percent. All this is consistent with Stayer's directive to set goals as far down in the company as possible. By sharing power more widely, Johnsonville, in the last 6 years, has doubled its return on assets, while sales have risen more than 15 percent a year—twice as fast as payroll expenses.

Weaver Popcorn Company of tiny Van Buren, Indiana (pop. 935), has borrowed several of Johnsonville Foods' management systems. In 1989, the $70-million company incorporated Johnsonville's peer-evaluation system—whereby employees judge one another's performance—which is tied to the bonus pool. After some initial skepticism, the process has jacked up productivity and morale. "It reinforces our overall message that [our employees] are responsible," says 38-year-old President and CEO Mike Weaver. "They are better at judging the quality of their colleagues than anybody else."

Harry Quadracci of Quad/Graphics is another power-sharing proponent. Part of his success is in firing up people to the fact that they can "become something more than they ever hoped to be, that they're as good as anybody else, that nobody is any better than they are." Quadracci lets people manage themselves and, through assuming that responsibility, achieve things they never thought themselves capable of achieving. "He has refined the concept of employee participation into an art form from which even the Japanese could learn," says *Business*

Month's Daniel Kehrer. Quadracci doesn't tell his operating units what they should be doing. "That's your responsibility," he tells his subordinates. He manages more by walking away than by walking around. Quadracci's "figure-it-out-for-yourself" leadership style has made shared responsibility a cornerstone of the company.

Don't be misled by these Corn Belt capitalists. Frontier firms are no softies. They are tough taskmasters—tough on themselves and tough on their dealers, suppliers, and other outside groups. At Quad/Graphics, "nobody goofs off and survives around Harry Quadracci," says Kehrer.

Bill LaMothe has also imposed a combination of toughness and tact on the Kellogg Company. Within the company's walls, sources say, courtesy reigns. Turnover is low, and esprit de corps high. "There is a Marine-like atmosphere there," says John M. McMillan, an analyst with Prudential Bache. "Everyone is intense and serious. But there is a feeling of fairness and stability."

There is the same sense of equity mixed with firmness at Rubbermaid. The company's annual financial goal is 15 percent, meaning that sales, earnings, and earnings per share are expected to double every 5 years. "We set very demanding and ambitious objectives," says CEO Stanley Gault, who will retire on May 1, 1991. "But we meet them—best of all we frequently exceed them." Statistics bear him out. Since 1980, Rubbermaid's sales have nearly doubled; its net earnings have almost tripled.

Softheadedness has no place in the new corporate frontier. A "can-do" determination combined with a sense of caring and sharing sets them apart from many of their more famous big-city counterparts.

Communitarianism

Businesses operating from a small-town base develop a sense of community rarely found in metropolitan companies. "In an era when the changing of corporate names and the moving of corporate headquarters and facilities seem to be more the norm than the exception, it is important to remember their heritage and the people and communities that have helped them grow," affirms J. M. Smucker in its published credo. "It is important not to lose their sense of people and place. Our company has recognized and respected [this] force of unity since its beginnings in Orrville [Ohio] nearly 100 years ago."

The same proud anthem applies to Milton S. Hershey, who built the chocolate empire in the Pennsylvania town that bears his name. After his beloved wife, Catherine, died, Hershey, childless, gave his house to the community and moved to a small apartment. Upon his death in 1945, he left the bulk of his stock to the Milton S. Hershey School Trust, which remains the major stockholder in Hershey Foods.

Today, the Hershey School sits on a beautiful 10,000-acre campus with magnificent facilities, located 13 miles from Harrisburg, the state capital. More impressive than its bricks and mortar is the school's mission: to teach orphans and children from broken homes. Its 1150 students are clothed, fed, and given free medical and dental care from kindergarten through grade 12. Graduates of the Hershey School have made their marks in business, medicine, and the law. Several have become successful managers at the company, including William E. C. Dearden, who rose to the chairmanship and retired 4 years ago. "You can tell any organization by the product it turns out, and the product here is pretty good," says Dearden. He offers a simple explanation for the school's success. "We knew that people loved us." So renowned is the school, which is funded by Hershey dividends, that it—and the company—received *Business Week*'s "Best in 1989" award for public service.

Elsewhere, the Upjohn Company has made its mark on Kalamazoo County, Michigan. For more than a century, the pharmaceutical, chemical, and health-care giant has maintained its headquarters in Portage (pop. 40,430). Over the years, Upjohn has contributed greatly toward improving the health and educational climate of southwestern Michigan. Foundation grants and loaned personnel have enriched the public schools, Western Michigan University, and Kalamazoo College. Among its other contributions, Upjohn created the Math and Science Center, which offers a challenging educational opportunity to talented mathematics and science students from area high schools. Like Kellogg's activities in neighboring Battle Creek, Upjohn's have catalyzed the revitalization of downtown Kalamazoo by establishing its $122-million research and development hub in the center city.

In similar fashion, the publicity-shy Clark family has dominated the village of Cooperstown, New York, the birthplace of novelist James Fennimore Cooper. The fortune of the Clark Estates, Inc. was established in 1850 by the family's partnership with Isaac Merritt Singer, the inventor of the sewing machine. The venture later became the famous Singer Manufacturing Company.

Collectively, seven Clark-sponsored charities benefit Cooperstown to an extent probably unmatched in any other small town—an amazing $150,000 for each of the village's 2400 residents. The Clark Foundation, one of the nation's 70 largest private foundations, with more than $200 million in assets, spends nearly $1.8 million a year on college scholarships for about 900 area students, $100,000 for needy individuals, and $1 million to underwrite the lavish town athletic facility, named after a Clark. It even provides fresh flowers for Cooperstown's streetlight poles.

No doubt, the close proximity of company and community is a major factor in the philanthropy of these frontier companies. Andersen Corporation, for instance, casts a heavy shadow over Bayport, Minnesota, as well as the neighboring burgs of Hudson and Stillwater. Its 4000-person work force represents a large chunk of the area's population (22,000). So the window maker's image benefits directly from its generosity. Four company-controlled foundations, with a total endowment of $240 million, contribute significantly to the region. One, the Hugh J. Andersen Foundation, has outfitted the local fire department and helped build a hospital wing and a 231-seat art center in Hudson, a scout camp in Wisconsin, and a retirement home and library in Bayport.

Generally speaking, frontier businesses get high marks when it comes to forking out funds. "We have a long-standing rule that in the American parent company, our charitable giving should equal 5 percent of pretax profits," says Chairman Samuel Johnson of Johnson Wax. "Overseas, managers give 3 percent to the communities they work in. These are general figures; sometimes they may be bumped up a bit."

Tom's of Maine is even more generous. This year, the toothpaste and deodorant maker will donate 7.5 percent of its after-tax profits to charity. "This business is for the pursuit of goodness," says Tom Chappell. "But the business," he adds, "has to be a financial as well as a social success."

A positive community image is not the only benefit that comes from largesse. Tightly held foundations make their sponsoring organizations relatively bulletproof from predatory acquirers. The Milton Hershey School, for instance, owns 77 percent of Hershey Food's voting rights, and it is unlikely to sell without management approval. The arrangement does not quite make the company takeover-free, and occasionally rumors spread that a hungry giant is preparing an offer the trustees cannot refuse. But if a buyer appeared, a representative of the school trust would have to prove to the Pennsylvania attorney general that the orphans would be harmed by a refusal to accept the bid. So, in effect, the school trust keeps suitors at bay.

With the W. K. Kellogg Foundation controlling about 34 percent of the company, the world's largest maker of ready-to-eat cereals "is close to being takeover bulletproof," says Wall Street analyst Alan Greditor. Because a big block of stock is controlled by one group, a hostile takeover bid is almost impossible. At Smucker's, the family and company members hold about one-third of its 7.4 million shares; another one-fourth is held by institutions and pension funds; and the rest is in the hands of individual investors. Yet descendants of the founding family know that unfriendly corporate takeover attempts are always a possibility. To discourage such bids, stockholders receive only one vote per share until they have held on to their shares for 4 years. Then they get 10 votes per share.

At many small-town companies, large blocks of voting stock are held by friendly insiders who do not want to see the character of the firm or their tight little community disrupted by Gordon Gekko look-alikes. Such was the case when Phillips Petroleum and Bartlesville joined forces to fend off raids by T. Boone Pickens in 1985 and Carl C. Icahn in 1986. Fearing the loss of their economic mainstay, residents of the northeast Oklahoma town of 34,000 rushed to Phillips' defense. The Bartlesville Chamber of Commerce conceived a "cookie strategy"—sending thousands of heart-shaped cookies with the Phillips 66 shield on them to warm up the cold and distant institutions that held almost 50 percent of the oil company's stock. "Have a heart—vote for people" was the simple message that accompanied the gifts. No one knows how many financial hearts were turned by the chamber's tactics, but Pickens and Icahn eventually backed off. To shore up its defenses, Phillips later introduced an ESOP that gave employees 20 percent of the company.

Bartlesville's fight for its major employer is typical behavior for the new corporate frontier. In Phillips' case, the $12.5-billion conglomerate had the fervent backing of a community that is highly grateful for its support of local activities in culture, sports, health, and education. "Phillips is a perfect example of what a good corporate citizen is," said one chamber member. "Words such as 'outstanding' can't begin to describe the company."

Good citizenship takes many different forms. Frontier businesses are finding that volunteerism is an especially effective way to bond themselves closer to their hometowns. A growing number of firms encourage their employees to volunteer their services to charitable and community-service organizations. Some of the most-favored options are employee-release time (for service to schools and social welfare agencies during work hours), on-loan executives or staffers (for longer periods of time), community liaison officers (to hear complaints from outside groups), employee-volunteer recognition programs, communitywide telethons, and group projects (to improve the public schools).

Taken together, the shared vision, egalitarianism, esprit de corps, and communitarianism of penturban companies are restoring the legitimacy of U.S. business and recapturing the confidence of working Americans. The unique capacity of frontier firms to ally themselves closely to their employees, their families, and their hometowns gives them a special advantage over big-city businesses. The next chapter examines how five of America's best-managed companies are exploiting this advantage.

11
Five Frontier Favorites

Small-town companies are as different from one another as diesel engines and oven broilers. Nevertheless, they tend to have in common the vital traits of vision, equality, teamwork, and community. Let us consider five denizens of the new corporate frontier that excel at sustaining these important qualities.

Wal-Mart Stores Inc.

Nobody does it better than Samuel Moore Walton, 72, the cofounder and chairman of the $32.6-billion Wal-Mart Stores. Twenty-nine years ago, "Mr. Sam" (as he prefers being called) and his brother, J.L. or "Bud," opened the first Wal-Mart discount store in the Ozark hamlet of Rogers, Arkansas. Since then, 1573 units—plus 176 Sam's Club and Wholesale Club warehouse outlets and four giant HyperMart USA food and discount stores—have been added in 31 other states, mostly in the South and Midwest. Sales have mushroomed at a compound annual rate of better than 36 percent in each of the past 10 years, making Wal-Mart Stores the nation's biggest and fastest-growing retailer. Looking ahead, Sam Walton predicts that the firm could quadruple sales to about $125 billion by the year 2000.

Plaudits for the company and its feisty cofounder pour in. Tom Peters chose Wal-Mart as the best company of the eighties; *Fortune* ranks it number one in the retailing industry as well as one of America's 10 "most-admired" corporations; *Business Month* frequently puts the massive retailer on its "five best-managed companies" list; *Forbes* describes it as "one of the best companies for the 1990s"; and the United Shareholders Association of Washington, D.C., ranked it as the best U.S. company for serving the interests of shareholders. Likewise, kudos abound for Mr. Sam. They include recognition by *Financial World* as "CEO of the Decade," *U.S. News & World Report*'s 1990 Excellence Award in business, and placement on the best CEO rosters of *Industry Week* and *Business Month.*

The son of a depression-era farm-mortgage banker, Sam Walton grew up in the same four-state heartland where he operates today (Arkansas, Missouri, Oklahoma, and Kansas). After graduating from the University of Missouri in 1940, Walton did stints with J. C. Penney and, later, Ben Franklin Stores. Eventually, he began acquiring Ben Franklin five-and-dimes, and by the early 1960s, he owned 15 of them.

Sam's special vision was to bring a large discount store concept to Southern towns with a population of 25,000 or less. Established discounters, virtually all based in the North, generally avoided the market, believing that it would not provide adequate returns. However, the first Wal-Mart unit in Rogers proved Walton out. The rest is history.

The giant retailer's incredible success has made Sam Walton Croesus-rich. At one point, he held $8.7 billion in company stock, most of which was later distributed to family members. Amazingly, this lifelong resident of Bentonville did not change much as he got richer than his neighbors. Though fabulously wealthy, he abides by a feet-on-the-ground lifestyle. Mr. Sam drives a 1978 Ford pickup truck, with his two bird dogs in tow. He has lived with his wife, Helen, in the same ranch house for years, with furniture that has been described by visitors as "early Holiday Inn." When lightning destroyed an earlier home, Sam was content to live in a double-width trailer on the property until Helen protested. His home number, by the way, is in the phone book.

Fancy lunches? Not for Mr. Sam. He grabs a bite to eat at Fred's Hickory Inn and gets his hair cut at the local barbershop. Sam Walton has never forgotten his small-town customers' tastes, because they are his tastes, too. "The customers like our style of doing business," he says. "Lower the cost to the customers instead of taking it in the form of higher margins in profit. That's pretty much been our philosophy from the beginning."

Mr. Sam's keep-the-costs-down philosophy is reflected in everything the company does. Down past Keith's Body Shop, across the way from Colene's Beauty Chalet, sits the austere redbrick building that serves as corporate headquarters. The lobby is filled with 150 plastic-molded blue chairs, eight pay telephones, and a mounted giant fish caught by brother Bud. Topped off by yards and yards of pasty-colored linoleum tile, "Home Office" has all the charm of a Greyhound bus depot. Wal-

Mart's principal executives, including Mr. Sam, occupy small, unpretentious paneled offices on the building's ground floor.

The no-frills atmosphere permeates the company. Wal-Mart's selling, general, and administrative expenses, at just 16 percent of sales, are 10 percent or more below those of most of its competitors. This allows it to offer prices on everyday items far below what other discounters charge. Wal-Mart strives to keep its stores spiffier than those of any other retailer, doing major revamps on 70 units a year. That's why sales increases at Wal-Mart stores are nearly double the industry average.

Managing, Wal-Mart style, means active community involvement. When Governor Bill Clinton's public school reforms bogged down in the Arkansas General Assembly, he called on Mr. Sam to fix things. The Walton-chaired Arkansas Business Council Foundation responded, unleashing a bold set of recommendations to upgrade education in the state. "We have become absolutely convinced," Walton wrote, "that any significant improvement in the quality of life and economic welfare of the people of the State of Arkansas is inextricably tied to substantial improvement in our system of education. We see value in education for education's sake. In addition to preparing students *to make a living,* it is equally important that education prepare students *for living* itself." Arkansas's children will have a better chance to compete in today's global economy—thanks largely to frontiersman Sam Walton.

Wal-Mart is winning over the "greenies," too. In August 1989, the company became the first big chain to announce that it would push its suppliers to develop environmentally friendly products. Since then, Wal-Mart has attached green tags to its shelves to flag products using recyclable paperboard or fibers or products in which the manufacturer has eliminated chlorofluorocarbons or reduced solid waste. The company is presently considering making its store parking lots into collection points for recyclables, while hyping the environmental cause with a series of provocative TV ads.

The Bentonville retailer is one of the nation's staunchest flag-wavers. In 1985, Wal-Mart launched a "Buy American" campaign that includes chest-swelling television spots featuring factory workers and the patriotic pitch "We buy American whenever we can, so you can, too." In his open letter to U.S. manufacturers inviting them to take part in the "Buy American" program, Walton wrote: "Our American suppliers must commit to improving their facilities and machinery, remain financially conservative, and work to fill our requirements, and, most importantly, strive to improve employee productivity. Wal-Mart believes workers can make the difference, if management provides the leadership."

After 3 years, the company reckoned that it had spent more than $1.2 billion on U.S. purchases that otherwise would have gone to foreign vendors. Patriotic Wal-Mart saved many American jobs by aggressively jaw-boning its suppliers to produce domestically. "[But] the best part of the program, as important as any other," Walton claims, "is to try to get manufacturers to create a partnership with their workers the way we've tried to do with our people, and share the profits with them."

"Sam started out with the philosophy that everyone in the company could be a partner," says David Glass, the 55-year-old chief executive who assumed the title from Walton in 1989. "Some of our best ideas come from our people." Those people are called "associates," and if Wal-Mart did not originate the term, it has done a great deal to popularize it. What really makes Wal-Mart tick is its partnership philosophy. The basic theme is that customers deserve the best, and the way to deliver the best is through happy, satisfied employees. As Mr. Sam puts it: "If people believe in themselves, it's truly amazing what they can accomplish."

Top management is constantly in touch with its associates—and constantly on the lookout for new ideas. Walton, despite an ongoing battle with a form of cancer of the blood and bones, and other key executives spend 4 days a week in the field, visiting stores. (They are also required to work in a store several days a year.) The top brass compare notes on Fridays at the Bentonville headquarters. Next comes the famous Saturday morning meeting, a whoop-it-up 7:30 pep rally for 300 managers, complete with Wal-Mart cheers, awards, and occasional appearances by such groups as the singing truck drivers. It is a process rooted in small-town America, borrowing a bit from Andy Griffith and a tad from the Reverend Billy Graham. Nevertheless, every Saturday, Wal-Mart associates have the chance to tell the chairman, in person, what they think is important. These 3-hour, no-holds-barred meetings typify the level of trust and openness that flows through the company.

"Hey, if you've got a problem, talk to somebody. Don't talk about it in the lounge or the parking lot. Come to management," says Don Soderquist, vice chairman and COO. Opening up pays off. Wal-Mart department heads, who look after one or more of the 30-some departments ranging from sporting goods to housewares, see financial information that many firms refuse to show their general managers: costs, salaries, and profit margins. The company sets goals for each store, and if the store betters it, the hourly associates share handsomely in the incremental profits. (In 1990, the firm contributed 6.4 percent of an eligible employee's wages to its generous profit-sharing plan.)

To its credit, the Wal-Mart culture nurtured by Sam Walton lives on. The vision, values, and philosophy that Mr. Sam shaped are etched deeply in the current psyche. Moreover, leadership expert Abraham Zaleznik of the Harvard Business School cites Wal-Mart as the best example of an American company that has evolved into a major enterprise without the entrepreneurial vision of its founder having been destroyed. The present leadership, while perhaps less charismatic than Sam Walton, mimics him in many ways. "There are no superstars at Wal-Mart," says Chief Executive David Glass, a 13-year company veteran. "It is our people that make the difference *collectively*." Taking another page out of Mr. Sam's book, Glass drives a 4-year-old Mercury station wagon, works out in the corporate fitness center, and occupies a small, plain office equal in size to that of the other senior officers. Obviously, Sam Walton's legacy of vision, equality, teamwork, and community is alive and well in Bentonville.

Herman Miller Inc.

In 1923, Herman Miller and D. J. DePree founded a small furniture business in Zeeland, Michigan, on the eastern shore of Lake Michigan. Although the town has scarcely grown (pop. 5417), the business has exploded. Today, Herman Miller Inc. is the nation's second-largest office equipment maker, with 1990 sales revenues of $892 million. Over the past 10 years, sales have grown at an average annual rate of 17.3 percent, while the firm's average return on equity stands at an impressive 21.7 percent for the same period. By another measure, $100 invested in Miller stock in 1975 grew to over $5000 by year-end 1989.

"Good design sells" is the corporate password. Throughout its history, Herman Miller's outstanding designs have set it apart from its competitors. It is the top-ranked furniture maker on *Fortune*'s list of "most-admired" companies. Miller's list of design achievements is most impressive. More than 5 million copies of its 1956 Eames chair have been sold; the famous cup-shaped seat is exhibited in New York's Museum of Modern Art. Then came the outrageously successful Ergon chair, crafted by Bill Stumpf in the 1970s. More recently, the elegant Equa chair has been turning heads. However, the company's mainstay remains the Miller Action Office, the panel-backed system of shoulder-high cubicles in neutral beiges and grays offering the illusion of privacy to their occupants.

The firm's lofty reputation for elegant furniture and open office systems is well-deserved. Herman Miller outspends its industry competitors 2 to 1, on average, on design and research and development. The company has converted its remoteness in Zeeland—a frosty town with no bars, pool halls, or theaters—into a major advantage. Here's how.

Historically, Herman Miller has relied on a bevy of third-party designers for its new ideas. In many respects, it regards its outsiders as critical links to the world beyond clannish Zeeland. The company encourages them to live apart from its rural confines, while providing them private studios in the firm's so-called Design Yard. Retainers of $100,000-plus a year are not unusual, and many outsiders have grown wealthy on their royalties. In exchange, Herman Miller has benefitted from its association with some of the nation's most prolific designers: Charles Eames, Alexander Girard, George Nelson, Gilbert Rohde, and Robert Propst.

Creating sturdy bridges with people at all levels is what Herman Miller does best. For years, its chairman, Max DePree, D.J.'s son, has set the kind, gentle tone that characterizes the company. He defines the Miller mission as "attempting to share values, ideals, goals, and respect for each person in the process of our work together." He prefers "covenantal" to "contractual" relations. "To me a 'covenant' is a relationship that is based on such things as shared ideals, shared values, and shared agreement as to the processes we are going to use for working together. In many ways, they describe real love relationships." In contrast, he says, many U.S. companies mistakenly settle for contractual relationships, which "deal only with precedent and status."

Words such as *love, warmth,* and *respect* are embodied in the Herman Miller culture, and Max DePree is not embarrassed to use them. Workplace intimacy, he says, "directly affects our accountability and personal authenticity at the work process. And a key component of intimacy is passion." Passion and soul are critical values to DePree. He has little time for the hoards of antiseptic analysts that have invaded corporate America. "Managers who have no beliefs but only understand methodology and quantification are modern-day eunuchs," he contends. "They can never engender competence or confidence."

Herman Miller treats its 5400 workers not as adversaries but as partners in a shared enterprise. "Around here," says the 66-year-old DePree, "the employees act as if they own the place." And they do. Every full-time employee is a stockholder, and it is not unusual for close to 1000 staffers to attend the annual shareholder meeting. Herman Miller also provides "silver parachutes" to every member of the company. In the event of a hostile takeover, plant workers who lost their jobs would receive big checks right along with the top brass. Not surprisingly, there have never been any serious attempts to unionize the work force.

As further evidence of its egalitarian ways, Herman Miller limits the CEO's pay to no more than 20 times the average wage of a line worker in the factory. The COO's pay may not be more than 18 times that average, and this formula is prorated throughout the company. In supporting the policy, the company's President and CEO Richard H. Ruch, says: "One of the real keys of leadership is making sure you don't find yourself defending the wrong things, such as your own inflated salary." Despite the salary cap, Ruch earned about $470,000 in 1990, including bonus.

In the early 1950s, the furniture maker introduced a version of the Scanlon plan that was redesigned in 1979: When employees suggest ways to improve productivity, they are cut in on the financial gains that result from their contributions. Targeted are four general areas: customer service and effective use of money, materials, and labor. Teams of white- and blue-collar workers set mutually agreed-upon goals in each category, and 1 day a month is devoted to sharing information with everyone on productivity, profits, and the status of employees' ideas. Herman Miller receives nearly 2000 suggestions a year from this wide-open system and over the years has accepted an impressive 53 percent of them. Employees strive to gain admittance to the Idea Club. Membership is granted for 10 accepted suggestions a year, or for one suggestion resulting in a cost saving of more than $100,000 or a material savings of more than $25,000, or for suggestions resulting in cost avoidance topping $500,000. In 1990, President Ruch feted 24 club members at the annual awards banquet.

The bright ideas of Miller employees saved more than $12 million in 1988, cutting 3 percent from the cost of goods sold. "Thanks to Mary Boudreau's suggestion to renegotiate the pricing of Ethospace pedestals," said one company member, "we will save $780,000." Says another: "The Roswell tile team's idea to go from manually cutting Ethospace tile fabric to a new laser cutter will save $349,000."

Participative, not permissive, best characterizes the corporate culture. Max DePree confirms that the company is not a democracy: "Having a say does not mean having a vote. So managers have to be both firm in decision making and sympathetic in explaining why." Herman Miller views labor as neither chattel nor a mindless factor of production but as a partner in the corporate commonweal. "It's almost always worth the trouble to tell people why you're doing something," says President Ruch. "It's a wonderful way to get them committed to the company's goals."

Neopaternalism, Herman Miller style, means treating employees as extended family and recognizing their need for external support. "It isn't unusual for a worker to arrive on his shift and have some family problem that he doesn't know how to resolve," Max DePree points out. "We see people coming to work purely to get healed because they've got a handicapped child at home. They need the 8 hours at work just to get a little bit healthy again so they can handle that child overnight."

The spirit of sharing and caring has done wonders for Herman Miller. Therefore, DePree argues that the United States must adopt a similar spirit—and quickly. "If we don't find ways to get the capitalist system to be an *inclusive* system rather than the *exclusive* system it has been, we're all in deep trouble," he says. "If we don't find ways to begin to understand that capitalism's highest potential lies in the common good, not in the individual good, then we're risking the system itself." Always the philosopher, the 66-year-old DePree proves that big ideas, too, reside in the new corporate frontier. "If every company in America were managed like Herman Miller, we would not be concerned with the Japanese right now," argues the University of Southern California's James O'Toole, author of *Vanguard Management.*

Steelcase Inc.

An easy half-hour drive from Zeeland sits Herman Miller's arch rival, Steelcase. Located on the grassy outskirts of Grand Rapids, the nation's number one office furniture maker is twice as large as its next competitor, Miller. The company's roots go back to 1912, when Peter Wege and Walter Idema founded the Metal Office Furniture Company to make, of all things, indestructible safes. Later, it shifted to fire-resistant metal furniture and conceived the Metal Office of the 1930s. In fact, the Japanese surrender documents were signed aboard the *U.S.S. Missouri* on a Metal Office table.

After its name change to Steelcase in 1954, the company diversified into wood furniture and office systems. Among its highly regarded product line is the ultraergonomic Sensor chair, designed by Wolfgang Muller-Deisig and introduced in 1986. Considered the Mercedes-Benz of office chairs, the ultraergonomic Sensor has a high back that shifts back and forth as the sitter moves. Despite its steep price ($500 to $2000 a copy), more than a half million units have been sold.

While chairs are the company's bread and butter, Steelcase aspires to become the leader in modern office systems. Its Context system's curvaceous, organic lines and innovative modularity helped the company win top design honors from the Industrial Designers Society of America and *Business Week* magazine in 1989. Teamwork, flexibility, and interaction are the hallmarks of Context, which allows furniture to be arranged in a multitude of configurations. To help customers choose the right one, Steelcase offers them a design software package that runs on Apple Macintosh II computers.

The Context system may be prototypical of the office of the future. Steelcase is using architecture and interior design to accommodate the minimalist needs of its clients. All its efforts are intended to flatten the business hierarchy, speed up decision making, and accelerate new product development. "What sets Steelcase apart," says Franklin Becker, a professor of facilities planning and management at Cornell University, "is a commitment to the idea that new ways of working require a building that supports them. It's what the office of the future could be."

Interestingly, Steelcase is its own guinea pig. The company forked out $111 million to build an avant-garde Corporate Development Center, which serves as its laboratory for testing new office systems. The 575,000-square-foot pyramidal facility, which rises 128 feet above the prairies, fosters teamwork and innovation among the company's 800-member design unit. Constructed with the help of three environmental psychologists (including Cornell's Becker), the center is where all the creative juices come together. Multidisciplinary business management groups, or BMGs, work in unison to encourage the free flow of new ideas. As Steelcase redefines itself, it markets its experience to *Fortune* 500 customers.

The firm's integration of architecture and team-oriented management practices means having a corporate culture in sync with these changes. "We're trying to remake a large company into a whole bunch of small businesses, to downsize the company without getting rid of a lot of people," says 48-year-old James Soule, a corporate vice president. "We really want to push decision making down to the lowest level." Under Soule's leadership, Steelcase is developing many of the neopaternalistic traits of the frontier culture. Already, the furniture maker is recognized as one of the leaders in implementing "flex" policies—those options, discussed earlier, that give employees a greater say in the work environment. The firm allows many of its 21,500-member work force the opportunity to work unconventional hours, gives them a choice of benefits, and offers attractive bonuses for individual effort and overall corporate performance. For its leadership, Steelcase rated a listing in the bestseller *The 100 Best Companies to Work for in America.*

Flexible personnel policies deserve a good deal of credit for the firm's success. Steelcase's nontraditional work schedules allow employees to balance the demands of home and work. For instance, Denise Francis, a payroll adviser on flextime, works a 9 a.m. to 3 p.m. shift. She is able to take time off if she needs it and is otherwise free to set her own schedule, so long as she puts in 40 hours a week. "It makes my life easier," says a grateful Francis, who is divorced and cares for two daughters, 13 and 16 years old. "If one of my kids is sick and the doctor says, 'Bring her in,' I can just go."

Job sharing affects a much smaller segment of the work force. Forty white-collar employees share twenty jobs. But already, there has been a significant drop in absenteeism, especially among working mothers. Steelcase finds that almost every job splitter eventually returns to full-time work. In 1989, the company also introduced the concept to its factory workers, albeit modestly.

In 1985, Steelcase became one of the first U.S. employers to offer a choose-it-yourself benefits package. Workers receive benefit dollars and are allowed to choose from a cafeteria-style menu of options. There are eight medical plans, three dental choices (including no coverage at all), and various forms of long- and short-term disability and life insurance.

Employees who have money left over can put it in tax-free accounts to cover out-of-pocket health care or off-premises day care. Unused benefit dollars can also be put away for retirement or taken home in cash.

"People are becoming good at choosing what they need as opposed to us playing God," says James Soule. The flexible approach also saves Steelcase considerable money. It stipulates, for instance, that as health-care costs rise, the benefits will go up only 80 percent as fast, leaving employees to fund the 20 percent difference.

Shifting to direct compensation, the basic $9-an-hour wage rate at nonunion Steelcase is relatively low—about half the rate at the General Motors plant in the area. Its 6000 factory workers earn an average of about $18,500 a year. However, like workers at Herman Miller and many other penturban companies, these workers can bring in an additional 35 percent in piecework incentives plus 69 percent more in profit-sharing bonuses. The combination brings average compensation to about $40,000 per year, and many workers earn considerably more.

Other Steelcase programs give employees a warm and cozy feeling. An unusual and popular provision allows people with a grievance to bypass their immediate supervisor and talk directly to senior management. Workers can also seek out free advice from the company psychologist, social workers, or day-care experts. Available, too, are the corporate gym, a new minihospital, and the spacious company park in nearby White Cloud. Workers can even order nutritious take-home dinners from the company cafeteria—to be picked up after work. Neopaternalism personified!

"We have families of products, families of dealers, and many of us have family working alongside us in our offices and plants," explains former President Frank Merlotti. "Our kinship with one another has done much to set us apart from other companies." He credits employee loyalty for the company's success and the absence of unions in the heavily unionized Grand Rapids area. "We don't work at keeping the union out," says Merlotti, a corporate director and head of Steelcase's executive committee. "What we work at is being fair to employees and keeping the benefit levels as high as we can, and sharing—whether its profit sharing or information or just good feelings."

Softies? Forget it. "Don't get the idea that [we're] easy," argues Frank Merlotti. "You've got to work your ass off when you get here." Steelcase insists on strict accountability at all levels and constantly creates pressure to work harder. Its tough "demerit-point system" is enforced rigorously, and accumulation of demerits leads to suspension and then termination.

Benevolence blended with firmness helps make Steelcase number one. Profits of the privately held firm were estimated at $180 million on sales of $2.3 billion in 1989; its market share hovers around a command-

ing 21 percent; and employee turnover is a remarkably low 3 percent a
year. "Everyone wants to work here," boasts Merlotti. "You can't go anywhere in this town without having a ticket taker, a movie usher, or a parking lot attendant see your company car sticker and say: 'Can you get my
sister a job there?'" By cleverly redesigning the work environment,
Steelcase should maintain its appeal for some time.

Ben & Jerry's Homemade Inc.

Ben Cohen and Jerry Greenfield also found their just deserts in Small
Town, U.S.A. The two maverick entrepreneurs launched their gourmet
ice cream business on a shoestring in upstate Vermont. With knowledge
gained from a $5 correspondence course, they opened their first scoop
shop in a former gas station in Burlington on May 5, 1978. Today, there
are 90-plus units in 35 states dishing out oddball flavors such as Cherry
Garcia, Dastardly Mash, and Chunky Monkey. In 1990, Ben & Jerry's
sold $68.7 million worth of superrich ice cream plus two recent addi-
tions: "light" ice cream and frozen yogurt.

The founding fathers, who look and sometimes act like hippies, make
a habit of thumbing their noses at the business establishment. "Growing
up in the 1960s, [Jerry and I] felt business was something that tended to
exploit financial returns," says Ben Cohen. "We had no intention of
being businessmen; we wanted to be ice cream men." In effect, both
men backed into business—and it shows.

The operative uniform at the Waterbury, Vermont, head office is T-
shirts, jeans, and L. L. Bean boots. Chairman Cohen's office is the rear
end of a leased trailer that shudders in the wind. If you are looking for
director Greenfield, he can be found chairing the "Joy Committee,"
which spreads happiness in the workplace. This unique forum does everything from bringing in a masseur to work the kinks out of over-
stressed factory workers to Jerry's using a sledgehammer to break ce-
ment blocks on the stomach of his partner, "Habeeni Ben Coheni." The
circuslike atmosphere that envelops the company, as well as its store-
house of superpremium ice cream, has made its headquarters the sec-
ond-most-popular tourist attraction in the Green Mountain State (after
the Shelburne Museum, world-famous for its early American
collection).

Despite their funky management style, Ben and Jerry are taken seriously. President Reagan named them Small Businesspersons of the year
in 1988. A year later, *The Wall Street Journal* listed the company as one of
56 "corporate stars of the future" because of its "potential to bring vision
and innovation to the marketplace of tomorrow."

What distinguishes Ben & Jerry's is its corporate philosophy of stimulating social change. "Some people feel that the company's first goal is to make as much money as possible and then spend it in a socially responsible way," Cohen explains. "I see those values as influencing the way the company does business in all facets, and influencing how it makes all its decisions." Cofounder Greenfield expresses it slightly differently. "I see business as nothing more than a rich neighbor, and rich neighbors ought to help their neighborhoods," he says. "You can fuel your business with certain ideals and principles . . . [to] make the world a better place."

Evidence abounds of Ben & Jerry's commitment to make the world a better place. When the frontier firm went public in 1984, it offered the first shares only in Vermont, to Vermonters, thereby wedding itself to the community. It also deliberately set the minimum buying price of the stock low. "We wanted to make it available to all economic classes," Ben Cohen says. "We were seeking somewhat to redistribute wealth."

The ice cream maker is also a pacesetter in "public-purpose marketing," whereby a portion of its advertising revenues is devoted to social causes. It created, for instance, Rain Forest Crunch ice cream to support the advocacy group Cultural Survival, which is dedicated to preserving Brazil's trees. In 1990, Ben & Jerry's launched the Peace Pop to stimulate the reallocation of 1 percent of America's defense budget for other projects, such as international cultural exchanges. As a further statement of its commitment to the community-at-large, Ben & Jerry's gives 7.5 percent of its pretax profits to charity—among the highest of any public company and well above the national average of 2 percent. Instead of donating to traditional charities, it prefers gifts to children's rights programs and community self-help groups. Every year, the firm doles out tons of its all-natural ice cream in the hope that recipients will turn around and host a function, thereby generating a multiplier effect for its largesse. For its external efforts, Ben & Jerry's scooped up the 1990 Laurence A. Wien Prize in Corporate Social Responsibility from Columbia University.

"We're all in this together," says Ben Cohen. To bolster its communitarian bent, the company limits the salary of its top-paid executives to 5 times the salary of its lowest-level plant worker. In contrast, the average CEO's compensation at major U.S. corporations is nearly 100 times the average factory worker's. The salary cap, currently at $81,000 a year, fosters esprit de corps. "We believe the person who is working on the line, making our ice cream, filling the pints, is a very important person," CEO Cohen says. "[And] it's our general feeling that executives in this country tend to be overpaid . . . and self-serving." Obviously, there is a down side to this thinking. The company's search for a CFO lasted many months, largely because of its tight salary constraints.

Nevertheless, Ben & Jerry's takes excellent care of its people. It puts 5 percent of its profits into a profit-sharing plan—according to seniority, not rank. The firm treats every employee as an owner, with liberal employee stock ownership, stock grants, and stock purchase plans. As you would expect, participative management is the norm. Every month, Ben & Jerry's holds companywide employee meetings, when everything screeches to a halt so that divergent views can be aired. In addition, it orchestrates occasional Outward Bound-type camps to bring people closer together. If this isn't enough, there are therapy sessions, including confidential alcohol and drug counseling, for any employee who needs it—plus rock-'em, sock-'em all-day excursions to baseball and hockey games in Montreal.

Too much vanilla? Not so, says Fred Lager, the recently retired president. "Ben is looking to show other people that you can run a business differently from the way most businesses are run," he says, "that you can share prosperity with your employees, rewrite the book on executive salaries, rewrite the book in terms of how a company interacts with the community—and you can *still* play the game according to the rules of Wall Street." Those rules involve protecting the company's turf, and, if challenged, Ben & Jerry's is a tough street fighter. When competitor Häagen-Dazs tried to keep Ben & Jerry's products off the shelves, the Vermonters waged a grass-roots war against Pillsbury (the parent company of Haagen-Dazs), replete with bumper stickers asking, "What's the Doughboy afraid of?" Jerry Greenfield got so riled up that he picketed Pillsbury's headquarters in Minneapolis. Nor is Ben & Jerry's prepared to become takeover bait. In August 1987, the company instituted Class B supervoting shares to tighten insider control. Look for Ben & Jerry to rule the roost for some time.

Battle fatigues are not the uniform of the day. Whenever possible, top management prefers to nip potential problems in the bud, and "mellow" best describes the corporate culture. "That Ben, Jerry, the board, managers, and employees work hard at having fun and ensuring that the upbeat atmosphere in the company is kept alive makes them, in our view, a model of a culture that counters cynicism," say *The Cynical Americans'* Donald Kanter and Philip Mirvis. Will growth compromise Ben & Jerry's high-minded ideals? No one knows, but chances are the company will continue "to make the world a better place."

Cummins Engine Company

Driving through Columbus, Indiana, one discovers an American Florence, with its Medici, Cummins Engine. Under its former Chief Executive J. Irwin Miller, the company agreed to pay the design fees for schools and other public buildings and provided the community with the expertise of some of its top professionals. As a result of these contributions, close to 50 works of such prominent architects as Eero Saarinen, I. M. Pei, Cesar Pelli, and Harry Weese dominate the landscape of Columbus. This self-proclaimed "Athens of the Prairie" draws 50,000 tourists a year.

The close bonds between Cummins Engine and Columbus have been forged over 7 decades. At least one of every 10 Columbusites has worked at the company. And the giant engine maker has never lost sight of its responsibility to this Corn Belt community of 32,000 people. Besides its help with architectural fees (almost $10 million, at last count), Cummins sponsors arts and educational programs and supports the United Way, homeless shelters, and drug counseling programs—to the tune of $1 million a year. "A paradigm of the benevolent side of capitalism," is how Robert Johnson of *The Wall Street Journal* describes the world's largest independent manufacturer of diesel engines.

The benevolent employer is a leader in team building. Beginning in 1974, top management organized workers on the assembly line in teams of 10 to 30 people. Each team is responsible for scheduling shifts, ordering materials, and hiring more workers when necessary. It is not unusual for these switched-on groups to cut costs by as much as 50 percent. But teamwork extends off the job as well. One example: Every Fourth of July, some 40,000 Cummins employees and families converge on their own recreation complex, the 345-acre Ceraland, which offers everything from camping to concerts.

The company has long been famous for its tender conscience. It was one of the first *Fortune* 500 firms to have black senior managers, and it allocates 5 percent of its posttax profits to charity. A few years back, Cummins astounded Capitol Hill by lobbying for *stricter* antipollution standards so that the company could produce a cleaner engine without putting itself at a competitive disadvantage.

The top brass continually drum home these high-minded ideals. Chairman and CEO Henry B. Schacht, 56, describes the company vision as "being fair and honest and in doing what is right even when it is not to our immediate benefit. . . . Some say the firm's main goal should be to maximize shareholder value. . . . I say no." To Schacht, other values— quality products, happy workers, and strong community ties—carry greater weight. Moreover, the company has always looked upon shareholders as just one constituency, with the other constituencies consisting of employees, the community, suppliers, dealers, and customers.

For years, J. Irwin Miller, then Cummins' chairman, set the do-gooder tone. A Rust Belt legend, the 81-year-old patriarch and great-nephew of the company founder, vented his beliefs in superior products, concern for employees, and involvement in the community—all qualities that made Cummins Engine one of America's most envied corporations. In 1968, Miller was one of few executives to champion the civil rights movement. He was also the first layperson to head the National Council of Churches, chaired Nelson Rockefeller's 1968 presidential campaign, and ended up on Richard Nixon's infamous "enemies list." *Esquire* magazine celebrated his accomplishments by putting him on the cover and suggesting that he be made president. Certainly, Henry Schacht could not have had a better mentor.

Continuing the Miller legacy, Schacht is one of the most highly regarded CEOs in America. "Mr. Rust Belt," *Business Week* called him. Schacht's influence extends far beyond the confines of the Midwest—or Cummins Engine. He is a major force in such organizations as the Ford Foundation, the Brookings Institute, and Clean Sites Inc., an agency that helps mediate disputes over toxic cleanups.

The last few years, however, have not been easy for Mr. Rust Belt. Faced with intense competition, nice guy Schacht initiated a massive restructuring program, which, among other things, led to unprecedented layoffs of a local work force accustomed to lifetime security. The firm invested $1.8 billion to upgrade its production facilities and product line and, in the process, cut factory space by 25 percent. Cummins Engine lopped off 22 percent of its costs, while retaining its dominant 54 percent share of the North American engine market. The company also spent heavily on research and development (averaging over $100 million a year) and pursued long-term goals at the expense of short-term profits. That has been the rub for Cummins—namely, that these changes have yet to show up in improved profits, leaving the organization vulnerable to a hostile takeover.

The first serious run at the $3.5-billion firm came in early 1989. Hanson USA, the U.S. arm of the acquisitive raider Hanson PLC of London, bought an 8.8 percent stake in the engine manufacturer, with an eye on the entire doughnut. To the rescue came the Millers. These descendants of the Cummins Engine's founders blunted Hanson's takeover effort—acquiring its share for $72 million. By doing so, the family took a whopping $5-million loss in order to save the town's largest employer from paying "greenmail." This was the first known instance in which a major stockholder has made a greenmail payment when the company made no move to do so on its own behalf. (Corporate policy at Cummins prevents such payments.)

Understandably, the residents of this southern Indiana community were overjoyed by the Millers' altruism. "I am elated," said Mayor Robert N. Stewart "E-l-a-t-e-d." For good reason. The diesel engine maker employs 6200 people; their jobs and Columbus's economic future hung in the balance—if hostile takeovers consummated elsewhere are any indicator.

To the Millers, their rescue mission was straightforward. "This town puts a high value on being needed," said feisty octogenarian J. Irwin Miller. "Losing Cummins," he added, "would be a kind of death." To his sister, Clementine Tangeman, giving up $5 million also made sense. "Five generations of my family were here," she said in a press release. "I am interested in the long-term health of the company and in having the company headquartered in Columbus, thriving and independent." In exchange for their buy-out, the Millers received a so-called standstill agreement from Hanson, requiring for 10 years the family's permission for Hanson to buy Cummins' share. The family, in turn, must have Cummins' approval to lift its stake for 10 years.

Hardly had Hanson been dispatched when another foreign predator acquired a major position in Cummins Engine. In July 1989, the Hong Kong firm of Industrial Equity (Pacific) Ltd. raised its shareholdings in the diesel maker to 14.9 percent. The new entrant saw its stake as a "long-term investment." But its view of "long-term" was different from that of either Cummins' management or the descendants of the founders. When asked to define the term, Industrial Equity's president and chief executive Robert G. Sutherland replied: "At least 6 months."

The problem at Cummins, of course, is symptomatic of that which many U.S. companies face: How to invest in a business that requires years to pay off, in an era when shareholders are primarily large institutional investors seeking the best quarterly performance. (Business historians point out that the company did not make a dime of profit in its first 18 years of operation.) "It became increasingly apparent to us," says Mr. Miller, "that the company's natural long-term needs are out of sync with the short-term nature of today's shareholder base. This is not an indictment of investment professionals for responding to the competitive environment. It's just a mismatch between the real world of institutional investing and the refinements of a cyclical capital-goods company. It's a large social policy issue."

"We built this country on long-term money, not on quarterly returns," says Harry Schacht, agreeing with the Miller philosophy. "The demands of being globally competitive mean the payback is over years, not months." In July 1990, Schacht found the "patient capital" he had been desperately seeking. In a complex series of agreements, Cummins Engine sold a 27 percent stake to the Ford Motor Company, Tenneco Inc. (which owns JI Case, the tractor outfit), and Kubota Ltd. (the Japanese tractor and construction equipment maker). The strategic partnership not only strengthened the company's balance sheet with a much-needed infusion of $250 million but also made Cummins virtually takeover-proof. In announcing the alliance, Schacht said: "We believe that, taken together, these agreements . . . represent giant steps forward for Cummins as the world leader in our industry."

Ironically, several Wall Street free-marketers criticized Schacht for or-
chestrating the company's defensive tactics. The market mechanism,
they argued, best determines shareholder worth, not the misguided efforts of community do-gooders or industry partners. Let Darwinism—
featuring the likes of Hanson and Industrial Equity—resolve these policy issues. But the libertarian view is seriously flawed. Wall Street
consistently ignores the reasons for the success of Japanese enterprise—
success achieved through long-term planning for new product development and market penetration, in lieu of a consuming emphasis on
short-term results. "It is ironic that [the] business leaders who are now
most dedicated to those values are Shoichiro Toyoda, Shoichiro Ir-
imajiri, and several other Japanese corporate executives who follow in
the tradition of the late Konosuke Matsushita," wrote Vernon R. Alden,
the highly respected former chairman of the Boston Corporation. "It is
encouraging to read that the Cummins executive group still shares Mr.
Miller's commitments. . . . [This] gives hope for the future of the American corporate enterprise."

Indeed, Cummins Engine best exemplifies the principle of multiple
responsibility: to its owners by making a profit, to its customers by producing excellent products, to its employees by paying fair wages and attempting to ensure semipermanent employment, and to the community
by returning some of its profits in contributions for civic betterment.
Capitalism at its best, that's the Cummins way.

Nice Guys Finish First

By almost any standard, penturban businesses are equal to or better
than their big-city counterparts. Wal-Mart, Herman Miller, Steelcase,
Ben & Jerry's, Cummins Engine and many other companies demonstrate that *success* and *small town* are not contradictory terms. The shortcomings of size and distance have been turned to each firm's advantage.
They are all on the leading edge of their respective industries; they all
enjoy the admiration—sometimes grudgingly—of their competitors
and American business generally; and they are all well poised for the future. More significant, these frontier favorites offer important lessons
for every segment of U.S. industry.

Corporate America could benefit greatly from their soulful passion.
Sharing and caring transcend the fixation on the fast buck. Frontier
firms view their employees and the community as family. To be sure, the
proximity of their major stakeholders enables them to forge this special
relationship. Nevertheless, the expertise of small-town employers in
molding partnerships goes far beyond close-knit neighborhoods.

The leaders of many penturban businesses—from Sam Walton to Max DePree—have etched the uniquely American principles of indivisibility deeply into the culture of their organizations. They never lost touch with their constituencies. When their companies were attacked competitively, they turned inward: to their employees, customers, suppliers, and the community. By doing so, they acquired new strength and resolve. They then reentered the competitive fray—and never looked back.

Furthermore, the communitarian values of outlying America spawn a corporate culture in which cooperation is in everyone's best interest—a culture in sync with the country's new mindset. The prevailing winds are in the direction of greater togetherness, and many residents of the new corporate frontier—Wal-Mart, Herman Miller, Ben & Jerry's, and others—have captured this mood swing. They deserve widespread emulation.

Let us emphasize that the shift toward small-town living is an emerging phenomenon—one of evolution, not revolution. Although this change is irreversible, there are important counterweights. The next chapter examines these forces.

12
Limitations of Frontier Living

Whether the lessons of the new corporate frontier will be adopted by sweeping segments of U.S. business is difficult to tell. Obviously, hamlet living is not for every business. Nor are all townships equal. Park City (Utah) is one thing; Yazoo City (Mississippi) is quite another.

With all the oohing and aahing about Small Town, U.S.A., it is easy to become excessively sentimental. Sherwood Anderson wrote fondly about his childhood days before the turn of the century. He described "a kind of invisible roof" where "people who lived in [small] towns were to each other like members of a great family." Frontier living is laced with warm nostalgia for many other Americans. Vestiges of the "invisible roof" still exist in many of the nation's villages. Nevertheless, Anderson's sentiments may chronicle a bygone era. Chain stores, interstate highways, and the demise of the family farm have all changed the character of the small town. For one thing, they stripped important communal institutions from the tapestry of rural life: hoedowns and sewing circles, volunteer fire departments and town bands, country fairs, and general stores. For another, they laid penturbia bare to many of the social ills of the big cities and the suburbs.

Today, the kinds of places once depicted in Norman Rockwell paintings have their share of serious problems: alcoholism, abuse, drugs, at-risk children, even the homeless. The spillover effects of the societal malaise affecting the cities and suburbs extend to small-town America. Therefore, any attempt to portray the nation's provinces as Utopia would be inaccurate as well as naive.

188

The Village Virus

Seven decades ago, Sinclair Lewis identified the parochialism of America's rural landscape as "the village virus." Today, vestiges of Main Street can still be found. Like it or not, many frontier folk still can be accurately described, in Lewis's words, as "a savorless people, gulping tasteless food, and sitting afterward, coatless and thoughtless, in rocking chairs prickly with inane decorations listening to mechanical music, saying mechanical things . . . and viewing themselves as the great race of the world."

The occasional self-righteousness, meanspiritedness, and uniformity are the dark side of Small Town, U.S.A. In his famous study of Park Forest, Illinois, William H. Whyte found that racial and social homogeneity bred mindless conservatism and conformity. Companies today desperately need the stimulation that comes from diversity. In his recent book, Stanford's Richard Pascale, the author of *Managing on the Edge*, forcefully argues that U.S. business must create organizational structures that encourage more conflicting viewpoints to be thrashed out openly. One wonders: Can the new corporate frontier stimulate such an open exchange?

Small-town societies long accustomed to unchanging habits can make life difficult for original thinkers or newcomers. In describing the tight-knit insularity of village life, *The Wall Street Journal*'s Dennis Farney says: "The small rural community can be a closed system that resists outsiders and their ideas as stubbornly as the human body rejects foreign tissue." Penturban immigrants sometimes find that the cold shoulder is proffered as often as a warm handshake. Local hostility, usually unspoken, manifests itself in people's body language. Even Dow Chemical President Frank Popoff, one of the country's biggest boosters of the boonies, admits: "If I were a free spirit, I might swallow hard before moving to Midland [Michigan]."

Just as Sinclair Lewis characterized his heroine, Carol Kennicott, as "a woman with a working brain and no work," professional women express the same frustrations in pursuing penturban careers. Good jobs are hard to come by, and the support network for working women in small towns, while improving, cannot match that of the big city. Nor is the social life for unmarried managers bristling with variety. "This is not a single person's paradise," concedes Boise Cascade's former president Jon Miller, "and that's a handicap when recruiting talent."

Underlying these trends is yet another potent issue: the age-old question prominent in the works of Lewis, Anderson, and other American authors about whether the hinterlands can provide adequate intellectual nourishment for serious thinkers. Peter Drucker views this as a major limitation and questions whether small-town businesses have sufficient drawing power to lure high-powered professionals to their midst. He may be right, because there is considerable evidence that moving technical workers away from the big cities can be difficult. Some companies lose a third of their senior professionals in such moves, says the management consulting firm of Edward Perlin Associates. Just as troublesome is the "out-of-sight, out-of-mind" syndrome. "It's just too backwoodsy," is a common complaint of talented urbanites who are unwilling to expatriate themselves to "the sticks."

Despite the wonders of modern technology, isolation remains a serious problem for frontier firms, particularly small businesses. "When you have problems, you're an island unto yourself," moans Adrian Sween, founder of Apollo Corporation, a Somerset, Wisconsin, maker of bathing equipment for nursing homes. Penturban entrepreneurs do not have access to the products and services their urban counterparts take for granted. Oftentimes, venture capital is scarce; local banks are inexperienced in commercial lending; and municipal red tape is oppressive.

Then, too, operations in a smallish enclave can suffer from overexposure. "We're like Gulliver and the Lilliputians" is how Randy Fields describes his company's role as the leading employer in Park City. Too much visibility can be confining. Even Garrison Keillor of Lake Wobegon fame moved from Minnesota to Manhattan, in part to have some anonymity.

Benefactors or Bullies?

If truth be known, many frontier businesses revel in their "big fish in a small pond" role. One disquieting element of the heartlands is the demagoguery sometimes displayed by provincial companies. These alleged pillars of the community can abuse their awesome power in many ways. Circumventing the conventional canons of right and wrong is but one example.

Fort Mills, South Carolina, recently reconfirmed the overwhelming might of the town's historical benefactor, Springs Industries, Inc. When Will Close, Jr., a descendant of the family founders of the $1.7-billion textile giant, was arrested for the third time for possessing and intending to distribute cocaine, he received a slap on the wrist, with no jail time at all. The court sent Close to his mother's Taralike estate, complete with a small lake, tennis courts, stables, and peach orchards. He was required to be home by 11 p.m. every night for 6 months.

Obviously, the Springs name means a lot in this company town of 5960. There is the Springs Hospital, the Springs Recreation Center, the

Springs Mortgage Corporation, the Springs Credit Union, and, yes, the Springs Visa Card. Even the streets of Fort Mills carry the names of the Springs and Close families.

"People really owe their lives and livelihood to the Closes and they know it," says correspondent Ken Garfield, who has covered Southern towns for 18 years. "Their grandfathers worked in the mills, their aunts and uncles worked in the mills, and their kids are going to work in the mills. And that's a hard tie to break." Accordingly, some townsfolk contend that favoritism could exist.

In any case, the Fort Mills story reflects the possible vulnerability of some small towns to corporate power. Biting one's lip is the expected behavior of the general populace. And heaven help the whistle-blowers.

Reinventing the Company Town

Many frontier towns recoil from their dependence on a dominant employer. They know that the loss of a Gulliver—a linchpin industry or a major corporation—can rattle any community to its foundations. The ramifications of a pullout or closedown are swiftly measured in thinning wallets and depression. Frequently, townsfolk give up when adversity strikes, and the community ceases to exist. But this doomsday scenario need not occur if civic and business leaders band together. As the following cases suggest, many small cities and towns have faced the loss of a core industry or employer and survived.

For more than a century, copper dominated Butte, Montana. In its heyday, the town's copper kings dined with Mark Twain and Lillian Russell. But when primary metals prices hit an all-time low in 1986, Anaconda Minerals Company shut down its last mine and announced that it was getting out of the business. The news of the closedown was devastating. Many residents believed that Anaconda was the vertebrae that held this fragile community together. "From a psychological point of view, it was the toughest blow Butte had ever had dealt to it," says W. Paul Schmechel, chairman of Montana Power Company.

Nevertheless, Butte withstood the bombshell. The community took control of its future and was determined to succeed. Actually, the loss of Big Copper stimulated some surprising expressions of optimism in this rugged mining town. "Under the enveloping blanket of Anaconda, there was no entrepreneurism," says Laith Reynolds, an Australian businessman who now runs a precious metals company in Coppertown. By diversifying out of copper, many locals felt, innovation and creativity might well blossom.

Residents also began to realize that a millstone had been lifted from their necks. If something were to happen, it would happen as a result of copper and Anaconda *not* being there. "We made a deliberate decision we would never depend on mining alone," says Donald R. Peoples, who is President of Montana Technology Company and a former chief executive of the combined city and county governments. Coincidentally, the community had already begun some introspection. Before the Anaconda shutdown, area residents set up the Butte Local Development Corporation. They discovered that the town was both a transportation hub and the center of a commodities-rich region that produced a variety of minerals, lumber, and beef and other farm products. Recently, Mr. Peoples has been encouraging Butte's transformation as a transshipment and food-processing center. Among the town's first recruits: pasta maker Montana Macaroni, Inc., which is negotiating with local farmers to grow wheat. Civic leaders also won over Montana Resources, Inc., which has reopened Anaconda's mines. Strong community involvement is paving the road to Butte's come-from-behind victory.

The plight of Pueblo, Colorado, produced similar good news. A few years ago, this city of 100,000 was a one-horse, smelly steel town—but a prosperous one. "We were fat, dumb, and happy," says Gene Wilcoxson, who owns a Buick dealership and once served as vice chairman of the Pueblo Economic Development Corporation. (PEDCO). He ruefully recalls years of hefty union wage hikes followed by the "massacre" of 1984, when the giant CF&I Steel Corporation steel mill cut 4200 jobs in a few months. The dwindling employer cast a huge shadow over this sagebrush community. But locals were ready for the crisis. Swarms of PEDCO scouts hit the road, enticing new businesses to the new industrial park located near the airport. In just over 2 years, Pueblo attracted Unisys, McDonnell Douglas, B. F. Goodrich, Atlas Pacific, and several others. Enough new firms arrived and old ones expanded to bring unemployment down from 18 percent in 1984 to less than 8 percent today. In the process, University of Kentucky researchers ranked Pueblo as the number one place to live in the United States. Happy endings do happen to communities prepared to reinvent themselves.

Similarly, Mineral Wells, Texas, found that life goes on after the troops depart. In 1973, the U.S. Army closed its primary helicopter school at Fort Wolters, on the outskirts of town. For years, 7000 or so soldiers had propped up this rural economy of 15,340 people. Undaunted, community leaders took control of their future and pulled together to rebuild the town. Today, the old Army post is the site of the Wolters Industrial Park, which provides more than 2600 new jobs for local workers, about twice the number of area civilians who had been employed by the military.

Mineral Wells actually did not have to work all that hard to attract prospects. Within months, new businesses began to appear, including the area's leading employer, Mepco/Centralab Inc., an electronics manufacturer, and Century Flight Systems, a maker of autopilots. Units of large companies such as Halliburton, Optek Technology, and Perry Equipment also made their homes in the Industrial Park, as did many smaller firms.

Like some other troubled enclaves, Mineral Wells proved that a town can bounce back. Most residents believe that the community is much better off today than when its destiny was controlled by the Pentagon. "That [Army] post couldn't be reactivated now," says Mayor Willie Casper. "The people here couldn't stand for it."

Self-renewal is a continual process for any company town. Lowell, Massachusetts, rediscovers this every day. The town was founded in 1826 by the business associates of Francis Cabot Lowell, a Boston merchant who in 1810 had chosen a Merrimack River site for America's first power loom. For years, Lowell, located about 25 miles northwest of Boston, lived and died for the textile industry, drawing its labor pool from European and Canadian immigrants. In the 1950s and 1960s, the major manufacturers closed down or relocated to the Carolinas for their low-cost, nonunion labor. In short order, Lowell became an economic basket case. To its credit, in the 1970s the town of 93,000 people transformed itself into a high-tech haven. However, the recent economic downturn in the Northeast as well as the slump of its leading employer, Wang Laboratories Inc., badly battered the Bay Staters. Lowell's peak employment of 31,600 workers in 1985 has dropped to 22,500 today, and the number could go lower. Even the more optimistic city officials admit that it will take a lot of growth to make up for the lost Wang jobs alone.

Unless towns like Lowell "can find a viable economic base or just retain what they have, they simply have no justification to exist," says B. J. Reed, an associate professor at the University of Nebraska in Omaha, who advises community and business leaders in dying towns. Indeed, many burgs are banking on somewhat radical, offbeat ventures to rebuild their dying economies. Deadwood, South Dakota, and Gary, Indiana, are promoting gambling. Chicopee, Massachusetts, wants to turn its Connecticut River waterfront into an Amazon jungle, complete with monkeys and exotic birds. And Leavenworth, Washington, once a thriving timber and mining town, now feeds on the hordes of tourists to its "authentic Bavarian village." Whatever the prescription, penturban towns must replace their old Gullivers with new ones, or put on their death masks.

No major corporation in the countryside can discount its tight grip on the community. Nor can it expect much anonymity. Executives who attempt to build a wall between their business lives and their personal lives will find the new corporate frontier a vexing place. As we have seen, the life of the community is often synonymous with the life of the company. This interdependency can lead to considerable tension.

Fights Along the Frontier

Ordinarily, most towns would go to war for a Disneyland. Indeed, the most heated battle in Europe since World War II pitted two powerful combatants, France and Spain, each vying for the site of Euro-Disneyland. Both countries reckoned that much more than national pride was at stake: precious investment capital, jobs, and the New Age technology that drives the futuristic entertainment industry. No wonder the French beamed when they learned that the theme park would be built near Paris.

But back home, Disney bashing is the "in" sport. "A growing number of critics in Orlando, Florida, home of the world's largest Disney park, contend that the company behind the lovable mouse is a political power motivated by greed, bent on growth, and nearly impossible to control," writes Faye Fiore of the *Los Angeles Times*.

Walt Disney Company's polished image began to tarnish around Orlando during the late 1980s, when it agreed to pay the county $14 million to help improve roads stressed to their limits, in large part because of the hefty flow of visitors to its theme parks. In exchange, the county agreed not to challenge Disney's building rights for the next 7 years. Later, the company announced its plans to construct seven more hotels, 29 new attractions, and a fourth amusement park—all of which could further strain the local infrastructure. This incident was one of several that has turned the tide of public sentiment in central Florida against the creators of Donald Duck and Mickey Mouse.

Nowadays, area residents refer to Disney as "the mouse that ate Orlando" or "the grinch that stole affordable housing." Orange County (Florida) Commissioner Bill Donegan, contends: "Those people are powerful and dangerous around here. The roads are jammed, everything is clogged and now we have to raise taxes to pay for Disney's business. . . . It's just plain greed." To be sure, the entertainment conglomerate remains popular in the Sunshine State. A recent University of Central Florida survey concluded that locals endorse the visitor industry 3 to 1. In Florida, *tourism* is synonymous with Disney. Many locals contend that Orlando would be nowhere without the company, which pumped millions of dollars into the economy and made a humid farm town the world's number one tourist destination.

Nevertheless, the Disney-Orlando squabble typifies the love-hate relationship that often exists between the community and its primary employer. As we have seen in townships ranging from Battle Creek, Michigan, to Freeport, Maine, the oppressive unidimensionality of penturban economies can miff many area residents. When this happens, the Lilliputians can tie Gulliver up in knots.

Understandably, townsfolk dependent on a mammoth employer usually avoid a frontal attack. Often, they prefer to put organized labor on the frontline and to vent their frustrations on the picket line. Austin, Minnesota, is an example of an old-fashioned company town ripped apart by a union's defiant strike against a paternalistic meat packer. In 1985–1986, a bitter and sometimes violent 13-month strike erupted between United Food Workers' Local P-9 and Geo. A. Hormel & Company. Initially, many locals delighted at seeing the $2.7-billion Spam maker get its comeuppance. In short order, the drama of war in this Midwestern burg of 21,907 divided high school classmates, neighbors, even families. However, as the conflict grew uglier and uglier, community support slowly shifted to Hormel.

The strike's bitter legacy continues today. Neighbors still scorn neighbors, and some residents grumble over issues long since resolved. Eventually, things in Austin will return to normal. Nonetheless, any large corporation domiciled in the hinterlands should be prepared for the possibility of bitter family-against-family confrontations.

Back to the City

These infectious strains of the "village virus" can dispirit the most bullish proponents of a frontier headquarters. Just as Sinclair Lewis looked at fictional Gopher Prairie, Minnesota, and dismissed it as "tediousness made tangible," several American CEOs have reached similar conclusions and abandoned their small-town roots.

"Bucolic" was F. Ross Johnson's backhanded description of Winston-Salem, North Carolina, the historic seat of RJR Nabisco, Inc. Feeling the need for a faster-paced environment, the controversial former RJR president and chief executive relocated the company to bustling, cosmopolitan Atlanta. Then, late in 1989, his successor, Louis V. Gerstner, Jr., moved the firm to faster-still New York City.

At Firestone Tire & Rubber Company, then chairman John J. Nevin sensed a similar need to break with tradition and traded Akron, Ohio, for Chicago, after denying that he would do so. Shortly thereafter, Firestone was acquired by Bridgestone Tire Corporation, a Japanese firm, and returned to Akron.

Chairman Robert E. Boni moved Armco Inc. from Middletown, Ohio, its home since 1900, to the New York City suburb of Parsippany, New Jersey. The shift, he argued, gave the nation's fifth-largest steel maker greater strategic objectivity. "There was a great deal of confusion about what was the Middletown Steelworks strategy and what was the corporate strategy," he says. Mr. Boni also wanted Armco executives "cast into the midst of their major corporate peers." There was not a great deal of this in Middletown, he alleges.

Therefore, the bright lights of the big city have not entirely lost their glitter. Witness, too, the recent happenings in Tokyo.

Countercurrents from Japan

For the past decade, numerous pundits have recommended that the United States emulate Japan's postwar industrial strategy. In their best-selling books, Ezra Vogel, William Ouchi, and other scholars elaborated the virtues and lessons of the Japanese model for U.S. business. Nowadays, many American executives, enamored with the East, monitor their peers in Tokyo before making any major policy changes, including where to locate the head office.

What corporate Japan is *not* doing is withdrawing from the inner city. Despite the government's protestations, decentralization of trade and commerce has not taken hold. Greater Tokyo firmly remains the hub of economic activity in the Land of the Rising Sun. Its metropolitan area, with a population of some 31 million or nearly one-quarter of the nation's people, includes two of Japan's five most populous cities: the industrial town of Kawasaki and the port of Yokohama. About 30 percent of the nation's gross national product is turned out in the capital city, and more than half of its financial assets are managed there.

The Japanese believe that economic progress, or quantity of life, is more important than quality of life. For them, the primary function of a city is to provide jobs and create wealth. "Tokyo is everything," says Wakako Hiranaka, a member of Japan's Diet, the national parliament. "The power is here. The money. The culture."

Every day workers flood into the city. They are fleeing faltering steel foundries and coal mines in the countryside made uncompetitive by a strong yen and drawing on new opportunities in the booming services and financial industries concentrated in the nation's capital. In 1980, the Tokyo area provided a livelihood for 13.4 million people. Today, that number has risen to approximately 16 million.

The jobs are there because companies want to be there. "Three things matter most to sizable Japanese firms: money, information, and contact with government," reports the *Economist.* "Tokyo, the home of government and the center of the country's financial markets, is the hottest place to get all three." More and more Japanese businesses are moving their headquarters to the nation's capital—not away from it. Those recently setting up downtown offices include Fuji Photo Films, Toshiba, Snow Milk Products, and Nissan Motors. The city appeals greatly to university graduates, who, like their counterparts in the United States, are becoming a scarce commodity. Numerous studies indicate that new entrants to the managerial ranks overwhelmingly prefer Tokyo because of the excitement and the job prospects.

The city's magnetism, though, is wreaking havoc on an already noisy, polluted, overcrowded, and expensive community. For one thing, costs are skyrocketing. The office vacancy rate in Tokyo has dropped as low as 0.2 percent in recent years, and rents in the central business district ($186 a square foot in 1989) are four times higher than those in New York. The world's most expensive commercial property in the central Maronouchi and Ginza business district is valued at $23,700 a square foot. Commuters in Tokyo are shoe-horned into rush-hour trains, sometimes 6 days a week. To buy a house in any of the 23 wards of the city requires a worker to save 9 years of a typical salary—one reason for Japan's high savings rate. Nor are downtown properties the answer. Despite a recent softening of the real estate market, many small two-bedroom apartments in Tokyo remain at $1 million, with rentals averaging between $6000 and $10,000 a month.

As a result of these astronomical property prices, the local infrastructure suffers dreadfully. Roads in and around the downtown area are choked; public parks, gardens, and open spaces are few and far between; and the first signs of serious crime, juvenile delinquency, and drug abuse are starting to appear. Furthermore, the rigid discipline of Japanese society that has kept the capital city from collapsing is also eroding. "Tokyo has the highest incidence of heart attacks of anywhere in Japan," says the *Economist.* "Every year one office worker in three needs treatment for mental disorders, stress, or alcohol-related diseases."

The government insists that decentralization is the answer. A pet project of former Prime Minister Noburu Takeshita was to move the national bureaucracy out of Tokyo. So far, the government has ordered 79 public offices to leave town. Eventually, all ministries could pack their bags and open up the low-rise downtown area to high-rise development. Under the Takeshita plan, Tokyo would remain the country's international financial and information center, with the seat of government shifted to a so-called New Capital in some rural area an hour or so from Tokyo. Many national planners cite Tsukuba as a useful model for the new city.

Located 37 miles from the Tokyo International Airport at Narita,

Tsukuba, the nation's designated Science City, is 28 years old. In about 10 square miles, Tsukuba houses 47 national research and educational institutions, 6500 researchers, and 120 companies in its web of three industrial parks and one research park. From all reports, the successful Science City should offer the New Capital advocates some support.

The Tokyo metropolitan government backs an ambitious scheme to relieve the inner city. Its soon-to-be-completed crosstown move will open up some choice downtown real estate. Far more radical, though, is the proposed Tokyo Teleport now being built on 1107 acres of islands in Tokyo Bay, about 3½ miles from the heart of the central business district. The area will be studded with "smart" buildings containing state-of-the-art automation, communications, and information-retrieval systems—plus hotels, sports arenas, and shopping arcades. On one of the islands will sit Aeropolis 2001, a futuristic 500-story building designed by Ohbayashi Corporation, one of Japan's largest construction companies. People will be whisked up to the top floor of the 6660-foot-high building in linear motor-driven elevators in 15 minutes. The cost: $362.2 billion, with start-up planned for 2015. The more modest, phase 1 segment of the Teleport will provide homes for 60,000 people and offices for 110,000; it is scheduled for completion by the year 2000.

By and large, Japan's business leaders have greeted the government's efforts to decentralize Tokyo with jeers, not cheers. If anything, the corporate community is becoming increasingly Tokyo-centric. Mitsubishi Estate Company has launched a sweeping plan for redeveloping Marunouchi, the present hub of downtown commercial activity. It wants to revitalize an area of just over 1 square kilometer bordering the Imperial Palace and including the Tokyo Train Station. The project, targeted for completion in 30 years, would add 200,000 people to this already highly congested district. Nevertheless, Matsuda Katsutake, one of Japan's leading urbanologists and author of *Visions of the City for the Twenty-First Century*, says: "Mitsubishi Estate's blueprint for upgrading Marunouchi may well represent a more realistic and constructive approach than the fanciful decentralization schemes emanating from the bureaucracy."

Undeterred by this criticism, the government hopes that high technology may also make Tokyo more livable. It is constantly jawboning the business community to replace commuting with computing. But regrettably, the national culture seems antithetical to telecommuting. "Japanese don't trust electronic information," says Takao Ogiya, planning section chief of the government's Small & Medium Enterprise Agency. "Business is built on interaction, and Japanese businessmen want to read each other's expressions." People get the most valuable information, he claims, through human contact. "It's risky for business to move out," adds Mitsuhide Shiraki, a professor of labor relations at Seisen Junior College. "In the Information Age, people still want to meet face to face."

The Rising Sun's passion for quantity of life over quality of life also manifests itself in its investments in U.S. real estate. In 1989, the Japanese bought an estimated $14 billion of American property—making the total they own worth some $57.7 billion. Their companies have rushed to New York, Los Angeles, and other big cities to fill the office shells vacated by their U.S. counterparts. To the Japanese, urban living is synonymous with corporate dynamism. Locating away from America's major metropolises is, in their view, sheer lunacy.

My decade-long research of Japanese locational decisions reveals an overwhelming preference for New York as a base for a North American headquarters. Los Angeles is second, with Chicago, San Francisco, Washington, and Honolulu barely given any consideration. Most significant to the Japanese are the economic importance of the locale (where the U.S. headquarters would be based), its supporting services, government attitudes toward headquarters companies, educational and medical facilities, political stability, and an international and multinational orientation. Least important are quality of life and cost factors. These findings mirror the Tokyo-centric syndrome. When coming to America, Japan's business leaders desperately want to emulate Tokyo's hustle and bustle. Where better to do this than the Big Apple?

Following a recent visit to Japan, Tom Wolfe, the writer, said: "New York looks like Wyoming compared to Tokyo." In addition to being far less crowded than Tokyo, "New York," he added, "has become the city of admiration," where Japanese dream of going "to become recognized as world-class artists or businesses." As a result, more than 550 Japanese companies make up the largest contingent of foreign businesses in New York.

While their presence is formidable and far-reaching, it is only since about 1985 that Tokyo's visibility and influence in Manhattan have risen along with the buying power of the yen. As city officials court them, Japanese in New York can stay within a virtually self-sufficient world—and this pleases them immensely. "They can send their children to Japanese schools, shop at huge Japanese malls like the Yaohan Plaza in Edgewater, New Jersey, read the next day's edition of Japanese daily newspapers printed in the United States by satellite, and watch Japanese soap operas and news programs on cable television," writes Susan Chira of *The New York Times*. New York City offers all the comforts—and discomforts—of Tokyo.

This explains why Japan's big property grab has been primarily in New York and other major U.S. cities. However, after the furor over the acquisition of the Rockefeller Center, American indignation has caused

Tokyo's Ministry of Finance to advise other Japanese moneybags to lay off high-profile inner-city property. The message: Either avoid the metropolis or run the risk of controls on foreign investment. Hence, Japanese investors are scrambling to buy buildings in midtier settings, such as Cincinnati, Indianapolis, Memphis, Phoenix, and San Diego.

Japanophiles in the United States might be well advised to heed these powerful countercurrents before rushing off to the new frontier. Big businesses in the "second Japans"—Hong Kong, Singapore, South Korea, and Taiwan—display a similar, though somewhat less intense, inclination to be part of the metropolitan mainstream. On the other hand, trends in Western Europe, most notably in Great Britain, Sweden, and France, follow the decentralist pattern that is unfolding in this country. In any case, Americans contemplating a headquarters relocation should consider the experiences of other nations.

A Matter of Perspective

The arguments against a frontier address are powerful and should not be ignored. Those in the executive suite would be well advised to reject any hometown boosterism that claims that its citizens are extraordinarily intelligent, beautiful, and so forth. Small-town settings are not for every company. Put in perspective, "the rural culture was never as kindly nor always as pleasant as legend would have it," says *Time*'s Hugh Sidey. "But necessity forced a concern for family and community and an interdependence that as often as not subdued meanness and selfishness. A certain virtue and hope were required for survival."

Although Small Town, U.S.A., may have lost its innocence, it still provides the "invisible roof" that Sherwood Anderson wrote about. Shelter, serenity, and sincerity live under this roof, and more and more Americans want to carve their careers in these safe havens.

13

The Re-United States of America: An Action Agenda for Business and Government

Joseph Schumpeter once argued, "Creative destruction is the inevitable companion of capitalism." The late Harvard economist's prophecy accurately describes the decline of traditional urban economies and the rise of semirural, exurban ones. Big business, for better or worse, is now inextricably linked to the dynamics of the penturban revolution.

Obviously, small-town living is not for every company. Financial services, media-related businesses, and a few other industries probably need a metropolitan address. As firms continue to downsize and decentralize their organizations, however, the case for bucolic, out-of-the-way locations keeps improving. Furthermore, corporate America is rejecting the half-truths about small towns.

Out of the mainstream? No way. Space Age technology, while not a substitute for all face-to-face contact, is shrinking vast distances. From fiber optics to fax machines, state-of-the-art equipment links frontier headquarters with far-flung markets and operating units. Blinders on innovation? Far from it. Penturban firms like Caterpillar, Steelcase, and Rubbermaid consistently achieve bold new breakthroughs from their rustic settings. Access to financial services? Absolutely. In today's competitive world, bankers, venture capitalists, management consultants, and others trek anywhere for a new piece of business. Global clout? Most certainly. Many of the nation's leading multinationals—Whirlpool, Maytag, Cummins Engine and Dow Chemical—are nearer to a farm than to an international airport. Good people? Definitely. Provincial firms are able to attract their share of the best and brightest. With rising concerns about lifestyle, young professionals (especially two-career couples) yearn for the hassle-free heartlands.

Increasingly, U.S. business is separating myth from reality as it updates its notions about small cities and towns. "It's safe to say," David Birch of Cognetics argues, "that remoteness isn't nearly the disadvantage it was as recently as 10 or 15 years ago." The new corporate frontier is no chimera. More and more companies are seriously investigating the merits of the outback.

There are, after all, many reminders of the critical importance of small cities and towns to U.S. industry. Every time Americans munch a Hershey bar or a Mrs. Fields cookie, shop at Wal-Mart or Albertson's, or wear the latest from L. L. Bean or Lands' End, they are fattening provincial wallets. Some of the nation's most famous logos—from Caterpillar to Kellogg—originate in the heartlands. In the process, we are discovering that the U.S. economy, once thought to be the exclusive province of the metropolis, is very much up for grabs. What's more, grass-roots America is poised to take its share.

Actions for Small Towns

The changing configuration of postindustrial society is resulting in a shift toward frontier values. The cities and towns that best fulfill these values will be the ones to attract corporate tenants. But even then, communities that would succeed as headquarters hubs must stalk their quarry aggressively. Here are 10 strategies for attracting new business to the penturbs.

1. Take Care of Your Own

Charity begins at home. That's the golden rule of economic development. Janet Turner, chief economist for California's Department of Commerce, estimates that "at least 75 percent of job creation comes from existing companies." Homegrown businesses are the best candidates for future expansion.

In their lust for new business, ambitious planners often turn their backs on local firms. As a result, they not only alienate existing enterprises but lose the invaluable support of these firms in wooing newcomers. If corporate recruits sense that indigenous companies are hostile or ambivalent, they will take their business elsewhere. So to exploit the home-field advantage, city officials must cultivate home-grown industry.

In fact, public officials should go a step further and adopt a grow-your-own philosophy, developing their own roster of local companies. This means working closely with state and local banks to stimulate credit for fledgling businesses and with regional universities to establish incubator centers for burgeoning entrepreneurs. Experience suggests that home-grown firms are far less likely to evaporate in tough times. Again, the centerpiece of economic development should be captive companies, old and new.

2. Leverage Your Existing Resources

Penturban Lilliputs must call upon every weapon in their arsenal. Most small towns don't have a ready inventory of prestigious corporate names to bandy about, but they may have a state capital, college or university, research laboratory, or similar landmark with which to mount a serious recruitment campaign.

In the 1950s, an academic, Howard W. Odum, and an industrialist, Romeo H. Guest, envisaged a high-tech zone in North Carolina, linking Duke University in Durham, the University of North Carolina in Chapel Hill, and North Carolina State University in Raleigh, the state capital, as a site for industrial research laboratories. Four decades later, their dream is the highly acclaimed Research Triangle Park—the R&D home of 57-plus corporate, governments, and academic tenants employing more than 33,000 people with an annual payroll of $1.5 billion.

The Research Triangle evolved from a critical mass of academic talent. Hampton Roads, Virginia, drew on the region's massive military presence: three Army bases (Fort Eustis, Fort Story, and Fort Monroe), Langley Air Force Base, the Fifth Coast Guard District, and the unrivaled Navy presence in Norfolk. These mighty citadels convinced many companies, not all of them military contractors, that the Tidewater area was primed for business. Among the most recent immigrants are Atlantic Film Studios, the soon-to-be opened Continuous Electron Beam Accelerator Facility (one of the world's premier physics research labs), and the regional offices of IBM, Hospital Corporation of America, Beatrice Company, and Aetna Life and Casualty.

The lesson to be drawn from these successes is that the frontier folk should seek out their own unique rallying point. Frequently, the resources are at hand. Leverage them to the hilt.

3. Sell, Sell, Sell!

Conversely, don't be lulled into thinking that your town will sell itself. "We have so much going for us," some local planners ask, "why jump on the promotional bandwagon?" These dreamers forget the harsh realities of headquarters competition. In Wisconsin alone, 265 local governments have economic development programs. Our advice: Either organize the sales effort properly or get out of the courtship business.

Development agencies can be public, private, or combined activities. Public entities are able to exercise their official powers to use special financial tools provided through federal, state, and local governments. Private corporations, relatively free from government interference, often receive greater support from home-grown businesses. Finally, quasi-public enterprises usually act with relatively little government supervision, while enjoying privileges in important areas such as eminent domain, sale of tax-exempt revenue bonds, and special assessments or levies. Which vehicle to use depends on the relative strength of local business and government institutions as well as their willingness to work together.

Once properly organized, the penturbs should sell their number one strength: quality of life. And as noted, "livability" is increasingly in demand in the 1990s. To cite one example, Durham, North Carolina, recently enticed Organon Teknika Corporation, a wholly owned subsidiary of a leading Dutch multinational, to shift its medical diagnostics operation from the pressure cooker of northern New Jersey to the rural environs of the Research Triangle. In explaining the move, a company spokesperson said: "We were concerned with relocating to a place where key people would want to live." Other locales should follow Durham's example. Keep the heat on and constantly market your town's lifestyle attributes to the outside world.

4. Don't Compete on Price

As a corollary, cost factors are usually not decisive when it comes to moving a company's head office. For most firms, the savings may be too small to have a discernible effect on earnings. Indeed, many corporations that left New York and other big cities for the suburbs and penturbs fully anticipated higher incremental costs for lease rentals, office staff, and professional support services, plus the costs of a physical relocation.

So, too, with location incentives—tax breaks, cash grants, industrial revenue bonds, and other gimmicks. They have little influence over a head office move. Contrary to popular belief, the location of a firm's headquarters does not substantially affect the total amount of taxes that a company pays. Most taxes are levied in the domiciles of the various operating units. Hence, chief executives think that tax and related benefits (of the head office locale) are of low utility.

Nor are savvy local planners eager to compete on the basis of price. As Ken Smith, former director of community development for Coral Gables, Florida, puts it: "A city or town relying on tax and other giveaways can always be underpriced. The headquarters business is volatile enough without introducing cutthroat price competition."

Townships do not have to ransom their souls by offering financial inducements. Performance, not price, competition prevails. But if a community is to be competitive, its general business climate must be positive. Here, public officials can play a key role by cutting red tape, accelerating the approval process, and sensitizing the bureaucracy to the needs of big business. An attitude that makes new companies feel welcome will go a lot further than price incentives in attracting business.

5. Adopt Niche Strategies

Small towns should think small and think specific. Given their limited resources, frontier communities cannot afford the shotgun approach. They should carefully target companies and industries in which they can exploit a differential advantage.

Waxahachie, Texas, for instance, is one high-tech "wanna-be" that hopes to match Silicon Valley and North Carolina's Research Triangle. Located 30 miles south of Dallas, this cattle and cotton town (pop. 18,770) is the future home of the $8.3-billion supercollider atom smasher. Waxahachie has already caught the eye of a number of firms seeking to capitalize on the next wave of space age science and technology. Area population should jump to 90,000 by the end of the century, when the supercollider is operational.

Recreational tourism is the preferred niche for such other penturbs as Aspen, Santa Fe, and Park City. Over time, they have become major destinations for fun-seekers and, more recently, corporate resettlers. Now, a number of other towns are getting an economic boost from sports. A flood of skiers, hunters, hikers, and kayakers has turned Jackson Hole, Wyoming, into a penturban favorite. The peaceful little town of Hood River, Oregon, situated on the Columbia River 100 miles east of Portland, is the Aspen of wind sailing. Similarly, Bishop, California, in the Owens Valley on the east side of the Sierras, attracts people interested in hiking, hang gliding, fishing, and skiing. Moab, Utah, is the mecca of mountain biking, while Boulder, Colorado, pulls in hundreds of serious runners and technical climbers.

Whatever a community's special niche, hamlets must play the "people first, companies later" game of economic development. First, they must convince individuals and their families of their town's merits. Eventually, employers will follow—initially, with sales or branch offices and, later, with larger regional and corporate headquarters. So don't overreach, especially in the early years. Temper your enthusiasm with reality.

6. Think Globally

"The world has shrunk to the size of everybody's hometown," says H. Brandt Ayers, editor and publisher of *The Anniston* (Alabama) *Star.* Aided by state government, small towns like Anniston are planning major initiatives to befriend multinational corporations.

Oregon, too, has been seeking overseas investment. It has reduced workers' compensation rates, streamlined land-use regulations, and appointed an economic "action council" to expedite commercial negotiations. Today, this once-antibusiness state is the darling of the multinationals, especially high-technology firms. With the arrival of four leading Japanese companies—NEC, Fujitsu, Seiko, and Kyocera, Oregon is now known as "Silicon Forest." Says John C. Anderson, the state's former director of economic development, extolling the merits of global interdependence, "We're going to share Oregon with the rest of the world."

Aggressive outreach programs can produce handsome dividends at the local level. After a decade of globe-trotting, Battle Creek, Michigan's, persistence paid off. Japanese firms have invested nearly $700 million in the Cereal City, manufacturing everything from auto parts to machine tools to chewing gum. But James Hetlinger, president of Battle Creek Unlimited, Inc., the economic-development group courting global companies, warns: "If you're looking for a quick fix, don't even consider it. You can count on throwing your money away."

Obviously, not every burg can play the international business game. Nevertheless, any linkages a town can forge with world-class companies should be explored seriously. In an increasingly interdependent world, our greatest challenge, the late Buckminster Fuller once suggested, is not how we get on independently but how we get on together. For future generations, peaceful coexistence will be most successful in world-oriented communities.

7. Forge Partnerships

Small cities and towns can do only so much on their own. "Growing numbers of towns are forming regional alliances, convinced that collective enterprise, like old-style barn raising, has its advantages," writes Ross Atkin, a columnist with the *Christian Science Monitor.* There are seemingly endless possibilities for teaming up with other interested parties. For example:

- Community "clustering," which links expansionist villes with state organizations, university extension services, and rural advocacy groups.

- Tomorrow's Leaders Today, which is sponsored by the Kellogg Foundation and administered by Iowa State University and is a series of workshops in which young managers share experiences in economic development.

- Thriving Hometowns Network, an anecdotal database maintained by the National Association of Towns and Townships in Washington that includes more than 100 case studies on probusiness practices.

- Economic profiles of small cities and towns that can be matched electronically with prospective companies.

Add to the list the vast spectrum of partnerships: within state governments; between federal government and the state; between state and local governments; between the public and private sectors; between government, industries, and universities; and between different civic organizations. They can be tremendously helpful to any penturb on the prowl. Here are five state-level alliances that have benefitted penturban cities and towns:

1. Technology Development. Pennsylvania's Ben Franklin Partnership offers a wide range of programs aimed at accelerating the development and commercialization of technology. The coalition is managed by a 15-member board consisting of representatives from the private sector, education, labor, and the state legislature. Since 1983, the partnership's $155 million in state funds has attracted over $350 million in private support. More than 1400 businesses have joined the group; an estimated 5000 new jobs have been created; 585 new firms have been launched; and 304 existing businesses have been helped to expand—many of them in small towns.

2. Financial Assistance. The Michigan Strategic Fund (MSF), a state agency guided by a board with a majority of members from the private sector, offers seed capital to budding entrepreneurs. Four privately managed capital funds, with up to $6 million in private equity and $8 million in MSF funds, plan to invest in approximately 80 Michigan start-ups over the next 3 to 4 years. Launched by former Governor James Blanchard, MSF also oversees a $50-million fund to support outstanding research centers.

3. Labor-Management Cooperation. West Virginia's Labor Management Council was created in 1980 to promote harmony between industry, labor, education, and government. Reporting directly to the governor, the council assists businesses in improving their work environment by upgrading product quality, productivity, and job conditions. It helps local communities establish their own labor-management committees.

4. Small Business Development. Ohio's Small Business Enterprise Center (SBEC) coordinates support for emerging businesses from local companies, chambers of commerce, universities, and vocational institutes. Resources include managerial and technical know-how, legal help, incubator programs, procurements expertise, and export trade counseling. To date, 31 SBEC units exist.

5. Economic Diversification. Iowa's Community Economic Preparedness Program trains business and civic volunteers on strategies for attracting and retaining business. Towns willing to be certified for their commercial potential must undergo rigorous screening by the state's Department of Economic Development—culminating in an on-site final examination by two state employees posing as prospective entrepreneurs. Graduates report that the program significantly sharpened their economic-development skills.

America's villages need not go it alone. These are just a few of the successful partnerships helping them entice big business. They should collaborate whenever possible.

8. Fix the Infrastructure

Provincial cities and towns must be in good working order to win over corporate newcomers. This means having a first-class plant, including transportation, communications, energy, water supply, and waste management. A comprehensive physical infrastructure is a major plus; and the more integrated the service network of any frontier environment, the greater its likelihood for success.

For many locales, the starting point should be the local airport, a town's most important link to the rest of the country. Corporate executives simply will not tolerate mediocre air service or country bumpkin facilities. City officials must make every effort to attract an array of national and even international carriers. They should also try to secure "satellite" status for their airfield—meaning greater direct linkages to the major feeder airports.

Charm and friendliness make great selling points, but major corporations also want big-city amenities. Responsive townships must offer first-rate restaurants, entertainment, libraries, and other facilities. Outdoor activities, golf courses, and parkland are other key essentials. Heartland communities can't afford to skimp on their physical plant.

Bricks and mortar—and well-tended parks—are not enough, though. Without a well-trained, well-educated work force, no city or town can expect to attract corporate headquarters. "Human infrastructure is more important than highways," says George Autry, president of MCD Inc., a consulting company based in Chapel Hill, North Carolina. "There is a closer correlation every year between education and prosperity." Take for instance, Tupelo, Mississippi. For decades, it has pursued a strategy of educating its work force and diversifying its economy into service industries. In the 1930s, it was the poorest city in the country by several measures. Today, the town of 31,000 has more than 900 businesses, including branches of 17 *Fortune* 500 companies.

Nowadays, education is the prime long-range concern of big business. "It is difficult if not impossible for schools to be better than their communities, and yet it is equally difficult for communities to improve without better schools," says Henry Anatole Grunwald, former editor in chief of Time Inc. Consequently, newcomers must be convinced that public education is at the top of the community agenda.

Some companies located in the penturbs—for example, Dow Chemical and Phillips Petroleum—are taking matters into their own hands. Typically, their efforts are part of a more comprehensive educational reform program at the state level. The Minnesota Business Partnership, for instance, is helping improve the cost-effectiveness of kindergarten through twelfth-grade education in that state. Among the many business initiatives enacted into law was a modified choice (or voucher) system that, on a selective basis, allows students to choose the public school they will attend. Similarly, a South Carolina program, drafted in 1984 with the help of the private sector, led to a sales tax-financed 30 percent increase in the school budget. (Since the reforms were enacted, the average SAT score in the state has risen 128 points.) Whether through participation on local boards of education or support for higher funding levels, penturban leaders in business and government can and must continue to upgrade the caliber of their public schools.

9. Ensure Widespread
Community Involvement

The extent to which any city becomes a headquarters hub depends, in large part, on the rank and file. This process occurs only when its permanent residents are convinced that attracting diverse people and companies is essential to their town's survival and growth. Communities that attempt to become commercial citadels without co-opting their permanent citizenry court trouble.

Peoria Mayor James Maloof fully understood the importance of pulling people together. Before launching his "Forward Peoria" program, the backslapping, Lebanese-American launched a grass-roots campaign to tighten the community. Residents were drawn together in various ways—collecting food for those in need, planting flowers along the streets, and contributing their talents to nonprofit organizations. The town's two major hospitals, the St. Francis Medical Center and the Methodist Center, decided to stop competing and to collaborate. This done, Mayor Maloof could then confidently market Peoria to the outside world.

The commitment to become a corporate center requires endorsement from the entire community—the private and public sectors, labor unions, even religious and educational institutions. Without such broad-based support, potential new firms may run afoul of surly local officials, exploitive realtors, and a chauvinistic citizenry—with consequences that are all too obvious.

Experts at PHH Fantus believe that the most effective way to achieve such commitment is for the community to develop a long-term strategic plan for orderly economic growth. "It gives the town a sense of direction and better control over its own development," says President Bob Ady. "It's a most effective method for achieving community consensus toward the kinds of economic activity that are most desired by local citizen groups." To that end, PHH Fantus has assisted more than 100 penturban communities with their development plans. Its client list includes Colorado Springs, Colorado, Des Moines, Iowa, Lowell, Massachusetts, and Scranton/Wilkes-Barre, Pennsylvania.

10. Be Patient!

Finally, recognize that the competition for head office business is fiercely intense. With much the same zeal that state governments have pursued direct investment from foreign firms, cities and towns are vying for economic dominance. Nobody is more aware of the volatility of corporate relocation decisions than local planners. Their vocabulary is filled with terms such as *net additions* (the number of new headquarters gained minus the inevitable departures); their planning horizon is abbreviated (2 to 4 years is the usual gestation period for firms to reach a decision about the head office); and their effective sales rate may represent only 5 percent of the number of serious corporate inquiries.

Competing for the "gold chips" is no place for the fainthearted. As one director of business development puts it: "There's a lot more work than results in this business." City planners should be prepared for these stops and starts. Our advice: Think long-term, or not at all.

Taken together, these 10 steps should enhance a small town's economic prowess. Properly applied, they can promote the welfare of resident companies, stimulate the development of fledgling firms, and attract new businesses. To be sure, not every penturb is destined to be a corporate command post. Nonetheless, to survive the decades ahead, communities must develop a capability, defined in their own terms, to better serve a corporate constituency.

New Clothes for Business

As cities and towns remake themselves, corporate America must follow suit. The time for revisionist thinking is now. Working Americans are putting on a different face: They are less greedy, materialistic, and self-serving than the 1980s generation. People today are moving from a period of cynicism and apathy to one of optimism and commitment. Especially noticeable is a renewed interest in collaboration.

Business, for its part, has also been on a new heading. Competitive pressures at home and abroad have reversed a 70-year trend toward centralization and bigness. For the past decade, firms have been shifting to smaller, less hierarchical structures. With the withering of the pyramidal organization have come new attitudes about corporate power. *Power over* is being replaced by *power sharing*. The password is partnership as firms seek to balance freedom and flexibility with collaborative values: shared vision, egalitarianism, esprit de corps, and a communitarian spirit.

U.S. industry's new mindset carries a strong paternalism, but it is far different from the feudal relationship between employers and employees of yesteryear. The new paternalism attempts to instill a unity of purpose within the company and community while respecting the diversity of contemporary America. Farsighted firms are building this neo-paternalistic culture. While some of them are urban dwellers—

Honeywell, Control Data, Hewlett-Packard, Motorola, and Levi Strauss, for example—most now reside in the penturbs. Small cities and towns seem much better equipped to accommodate these emerging values.

In an increasingly atomized society, penturban firms are unsurpassed in fostering the people-oriented idealism needed to counter a decade of cynicism and distrust. From Wal-Mart to Herman Miller, firms forming the new corporate frontier are extraordinarily committed to their employees and to the community at large. "It may very well be," author Robert Levering reminds us, "that the most important contribution of good workplaces is social: providing harmonious community in a society in which few such opportunities exist." The unique ability of provincial firms to restore communitarian virtues separates them from their big-city counterparts. For this reason, Small Town, U.S.A., offers the nation its greatest hope for future success.

A Checklist for CEOs

Despite the benefits, penturban living is not for every company. What's your firm's small-town index? Here are 10 questions CEOs should consider if they are contemplating a move to the new corporate frontier.

1. Will relocating to a small town enhance your firm's survival, growth, and profitability? What is the likely impact to the bottom line?

2. Can you distance yourself from the rest of your industry and not be penalized? Will your key customers react favorably to your new address?

3. Can telecommunications adequately replace face-to-face contact in your business? If so, are you prepared to make a major investment in state-of-the-art technology?

4. Are you willing to spend possibly large amounts of time traveling to and from your small-town headquarters? Are your customers, suppliers, bankers, and other resource people willing to entertain a similar increase in travel? Are you willing to purchase corporate aircraft?

5. How much pruning can be done at corporate, regional, and divisional headquarters? Do you really have your heart in a mini-headquarters, or do you need strength in numbers at your side?

6. Are you prepared to adopt a decentralized philosophy that a small-ish head office in penturbia requires? Do the corporate culture and your own management style encourage delegation and discourage

hands-on involvement in day-to-day operations? How talented are your operating company personnel? Are they up to the task of managing with limited guidance?

7. Are you willing to trade off the anonymity of urban living for the fishbowl environment of a small town? Does your management team share this view?

8. Can future generations of top-notch talent in your industry be attracted to a frontier locale?

9. Would your small-town destination accommodate the two-career couples among your management? Are you prepared to assist with spousal employment? How will women, blacks, Hispanics, and other groups be received?

10. Most important, do you and your top executives really want to live and work in the penturbs? Are these values shared by all their family members?

If you answered "yes" to these questions, penturban living may be for you. If not, stay put!

Constant Ebb and Flow

There is, after all, nothing permanent about a firm's home. The head office can be the most mobile unit in the company. Recall that J. C. Penney recently shifted its headquarters for the third time in its history. James Cash Penney founded the company in Kemmerer, Wyoming, in 1902; 12 years later, he moved the head office to New York City. In January 1988, the mammoth retailer reestablished its Western roots in Plano, Texas.

J. C. Penney's movements are part of the natural life cycle of the modern corporation. "How can we justify in today's changing world having stayed in one location for 70 years?" asks Chairman William R. Howell. Where and when will the company move next? No one knows. But one thing is clear: As firms like J. C. Penney change their strategies, they outgrow "home."

Cities, too, are living organisms, subject to the ebb and flow of constant change. And while there is a definite shift in momentum toward penturbia, we need not begin wrapping our larger cities in black crepe. There will always be compelling attractions—theaters, museums, shopping—to living and working in major population centers. For those seeking a low profile, New York, Los Angeles, and other big cities provide a liberating anonymity. At the same time, high-strutters like Donald Trump, Leona Helmsley, and George Steinbrenner who seem to thrive on parade grounds exposure, for what William Whyte calls "the impulse of the center," gravitate to the metropolis. Bright lights, big city will continue to magnetize many Americans.

The dominant trend of the new decade, however, is to step back from the daily push and shove of metropolitan living. More and more working Americans want room to expand, to grow, to raise their families. Above all, they want to escape the emptiness of urban life.

America's new corporate frontier best satisfies the nationwide tendency toward greater togetherness. On July 19, 1989, for instance, we witnessed the incredible outpouring of support by the citizens of Sioux City, Iowa, for the surviving passengers and crew of United Airlines Flight 232. Even before the stricken DC-10 had skidded to a stop, hundreds in the Siouxland—where Iowa, Nebraska, and South Dakota meet—launched a massive rescue effort that saved 184 lives. Doctors and nurses rushed to the scene, some from 100 miles away. Counselors showed up unsummoned. Four hundred people immediately lined up to give blood. Local businesses donated food, clothing, and flowers without ever being asked. Nearby Briar Cliff College opened its doors to 54 survivors.

In the understated style of the Midwest, Sioux City's samaritans took their volunteerism in stride. "We expect this reaction," beamed Red Cross volunteer and Briar Cliff student Teresa Wolff. "When something like this happens, we *want* to be there." Nor did the heroics of this meat packing city of 80,000 surprise social worker Mike Esch. "Sometimes we underestimate people's goodness," he said.

Flight 232 underscores the down-home goodness of Small Town, U.S.A. There was no "who cares?" no "me first" thinking in Iowa that devastating summer day. Everyone cared, and everyone cared for one another. Sioux City's capacity to cope with disaster with such uncommon speed and grace serves as a hopeful reminder that the dynamics of pulling together can prevail over the forces of selfish individualism. In the provinces, neighbors in time of trouble can look to their neighbors for help. Indeed, one of the ironies of our times, demographer Michael J. Weiss points out, is that the farther we live from our neighbors, the more we seem to care for them. The ethos of a more caring and communitarian nation—a Re-United States of America—is alive and well in the heartlands.

"Be not simply good," wrote Henry David Thoreau. "Be good for something." In short, take a stand and get involved. Personally, professionally, as public citizens. That, in many respects, is the message of the nineties, the decade of community. That is the message of Sioux City, Boise, and Battle Creek: Be good for something.

"The history of a nation is only the history of its villages written large," Woodrow Wilson once remarked. Today, these villages seem best equipped to unlock the spirit of America's economic potential.

Notes*

Chapter 1: Overview

Page 1. For a comprehensive and still influential description of the small-town ethos and the perceptions of American writers, see Arthur J. Vidich and Joseph Bensman, *Small Town in Mass Society*, Princeton University Press, Princeton, 1968.

Page 1. There were no significant relationships between the after-tax profits of 1000 U.S. companies and cities (categorized as large, medium, and small) over the 5-year period 1982–1988. However, larger companies (as measured by annual sales) tended to reside in larger cities.

Page 3. L. Clinton Hoch is quoted in "Benefits of Moving to Suburbs Narrowing," *The Wall Street Journal*, February 11, 1988, p. 25.

Page 4. For more on this trend, see the excellent works of Robert Fishman, *Bourgeois Utopias: The Rise and Fall of Suburbia*, Basic Books, New York, 1987 (From *Bourgeois Utopias: The Rise and Fall of Suburbia*, by Robert Fishman. Copyright © 1987 by Basic Books, Inc. Reprinted by permission of Basic Books, Inc., Publishers, New York.); John Herbers, *The New Heartland: America's Flight Beyond the Suburbs*, Times Books, New York, 1986; and Kenneth T. Jackson, *Crabgrass Frontier: The Suburbanization of the United States*, Oxford University Press, New York, 1985.

Page 4. Professor Lessinger is cited in John Naisbitt and Patricia Aburdene, *Megatrends 2000*, William Morrow, New York, 1990, pp. 305–306. (Reprinted by permission of William Morrow and Company, Inc.) For additional information, see Lessinger's comments in *Snow Country*, February 1989, p. 68, and *Mother Earth News*, March–April 1988, p. 68. See also his *Regions of Opportunity*, Times Books, New York, 1986.

Page 4. Lessinger's definition of penturbia is discussed in Richard D. Lyons, "Scholars Predict a New Era for Small Town, U.S.A.," *The New York Times*, September 27, 1987, sec. 8, p. 2. See also "A Faster Heartbeat in the Heartland," *The Economist*, June 4, 1988, pp. 26–27; "A Burst of Rural Enterprise," *The New York Times*, January 3, 1988, p. F1; and Fred F. Worthy, "American Boomtowns," *Portfolio*, Fall 1987, pp. 35–63.

Page 4. For more on these alternative definitions of penturbia, see Robert Fishman, "America's New City," *The Wilson Quarterly*, Winter 1990, pp. 24–45.

Page 5. The Herbers quote is from *The New Heartland*, p. 10.

Page 5. For more on the rural decline in the most recent U.S. census, see Felicity Barringer, "Census Data Shows Sharp Rural Losses," *The New York Times*, August 30, 1990, p. A1.

Page 5. Professor Heslop is quoted in Scott Armstrong, "U.S. Population Report Draws Fire," *Christian Science Monitor*, August 31, 1990, p. 8.

Page 7. The triumph of ideology over pragmatism is discussed in my "The Case for Convergent Capitalism," *Journal of Business Strategy*, November–December 1988, p. 54. (Re-

---

*Unless indicated, quotations were from interviews with the author or his associates. The following references, in chapter sequence, complement those interviews.

printed with permission from *Journal of Business Strategy*, Summer 1984. Copyright © Warren, Gorham & Lamont, Inc., 210 South Street, Boston, MA 02111.)

Page 7. For more on the dispersal of political power, see Martin Tolchin, "States Take Up New Burdens to Pay for 'New Federalism,'" *The New York Times*, May 21, 1990, p. A1. Also: David S. Broder, "The Waning Days of Washington," *Washington Post National Weekly Edition*, February 26–March 4, 1990, p. 9, and his "States: Where the Action Is," *Honolulu Advertiser*, April 18, 1990, p. A14; "Washington Passes Paralysis on to the States," *Economist*, February 9, 1991, p. 27; Elaine Ciulla Kamarck, "U.S. Capital Is Becoming a Political Backwater," *Honolulu Sunday Star-Bulletin & Advertiser*, June 17, 1990, p. B3; Thomas W. Hoog, "The Power of Individual States Grows as Federal Bureaucracy Downsizes," *Executive Challenge*, vol. 2, no. 2, 1990, p. 17; and William H. Miller, "Watch Out for the States," *Industry Week*, August 20, 1990, p. 45; Philip Slater and Warren G. Bennis, "Democracy Is Inevitable," *Harvard Business Review*, September–October 1990, p. 167; and Alvin Toffler, *Powershift: Knowledge, Wealth, and Violence at the Edge of the 21st Century*, Bantam, New York, 1990.

Page 8. Congressman Matsui is quoted in my "Congress Rethinks America's Competitiveness," *Business Horizons*, May–June 1989, p. 14. (Reprinted from *Business Horizons*, May–June 1989. Copyright 1989 by the Foundation for the School of Business at Indiana University. Used with permission.)

Page 9. John Naisbitt and Patricia Aburdene discuss the "new electronic heartlands" as well as their move to Telluride in their *Megatrends 2000*, pp. 307–308. See also "The World's an Executive Suite," *Economist*, December 8, 1990, p. 72. Note that the couple commute between their houses in Telluride and Cambridge, Massachusetts, while the official business address of Megatrends Limited is in Washington, D.C.

Page 10. For more on Telluride's high-tech renaissance, see Frank Clifford, "City Office, Home on the Range," *Los Angeles Times*, October 29, 1989, p. 1, and M. S. Mason, "Selectivity Is the Word at Telluride," *Christian Science Monitor*, September 7, 1990, p. 13; and Ann Trebe, "A Pristine Paradise in Colorado," *USA Today*, February 4, 1991, p. D2.

Page 10. See David L. Birch, "The Hidden Economy," *Chief Executive*, May–June 1988, pp. 30–35. (Reprinted with permission from *Chief Executive* [May/June 1988]. Copyright, Chief Executive Publishing, 233 Park Avenue South, New York, NY 10003. All rights reserved.)

Page 11. For more on the minimalist corporation, see my "The Downside of Downsizing," *Journal of Business Strategy*, November–December 1989, pp. 18–24.

Page 11. Peter F. Drucker is quoted in "Peter Drucker's 1990," *The Economist*, October 21, 1989, p. 20. See also his *The New Realities*, Harper, New York, 1989.

Page 12. The relocation habits of U.S. business are examined in Alan Farnham, "Migratory Habits of the 500," *Fortune*, April 24, 1989, p. 400. See also George D. Hack, "Relocating Corporate Headquarters," *Area Development*, February 1990, pp. 36–139; Jolie Solomon, "Corporate Elite Leaving Home Towns for Headquarters in Faraway Places," *The Wall Street Journal*, February 21, 1990, p. B1; and Robert B. Reich, "Secession of the Successful," *The New York Times Magazine*, January 20, 1991, p. 16.

Page 12. William Safire's quote is from his "America's Next Direction: Out of Town, All the Way," *International Herald Tribune*, September 26, 1989. Also, see my "Is Big Business Heading for Small Town, U.S.A.?" *Journal of Business Strategy*, July–August 1989, pp. 4–10.

Page 13. See Donald L. Kanter and Philip H. Mirvis, *The Cynical Americans*, Jossey-Bass, San Francisco, 1989.

Chapter 2: Bright Lights, Dim Prospects

Page 17. Jane Jacobs, *The Death and Life of Great American Cities*, Random House, New York, 1961, p. 179.

Page 17. For a discussion of big city costs, see Spencer Rich, "The Biggest Problems City Officials See," *The Washington Post National Weekly Edition,* September 4–10, 1989, p. 37.

Page 18. The Survey of the National League of Cities is reported in "U.S. Cities Say They're Losing the War on Drugs," *Honolulu Star-Bulletin,* January 8, 1990, p. 1.

Page 18. James K. Stewart is quoted in Lawrence W. Sherman, "Small Merchants' Big Burdens," *The Wall Street Journal,* October 23, 1987, p. A17.

Page 18. The Urban Institute's Adele Harrell is cited in Anita Manning, "City Dwellers Fight Fear of Violence," *USA Today,* September 17, 1990, p. D1.

Page 19. See Ron Winslow, "Study Cites Burden of AIDS Caseload in the Inner City," *The Wall Street Journal,* August 11, 1989, p. B2.

Page 19. For more on the homeless, see Joe Davidson, "Survey Says Cities Meet Needs of Many Homeless," *The Wall Street Journal,* December 21, 1989, p. A16, and Alan Finder, "Homelessness in New York: Years of Plans, No Solutions," *The New York Times,* December 30, 1990, p. 1.

Page 19. The Carnegie Foundation survey is discussed in Gary Putka, "Education Group Encourages Reforms for Urban Schools," *The Wall Street Journal,* March 16, 1988, p. A16. Also, Rushworth M. Kidder, "Urban Schools Get a Near-Failing Grade from Carnegie Study," *Christian Science Monitor,* March 28, 1988, p. 18.

Page 20. For more on the U.S. Transportation Department's survey, see Denise Kalette and Lori Sharn, "Gridlock Is Creating 'Wall-to-Wall' Cars," *USA Today,* September 18, 1989, p. A1. The smog report of the U.S. Office of Technology Assistance is also discussed by Kalette and Sharn. See, too, "Big Cities Still Lagging on Clean Air, U.S. Says," *The New York Times,* August 17, 1990, p. A10.

Page 20. The National League of Cities survey is cited in LaBarbara Bowman, "Many Cities Running in the Red," *USA Today,* July 18, 1989, p. 3A. Also, "Big-City Costs Deterring Work Relocations," *Honolulu Advertiser,* July 10, 1989, p. D2; Jill Goldsmith, "Washington, Like Other Big Cities, Is Almost Broke," *Honolulu Star-Bulletin,* July 9, 1990, p. A8; and Michael deCourcey Hinds with Erik Eckholm, "80's Leave States and Cities in Need," *The New York Times,* December 30, 1991, p. 1.

Page 20. See Jacobs, *The Death and Life of Great American Cities,* p. 179.

Page 21. See Joelle Attinger, "The Decline of New York," *Time,* September 17, 1990, p. 36.

Page 21. See Bruce Frankel, "Bashing the Big Apple in Vogue Again," *USA Today,* March 23–25, 1990, p. 1A. Also: "Money Managers Are Short-Selling Big Apple," *USA Today,* March 10, 1990, p. 9B; Ron Scheer, "New York Mayor Faces Sea of Red Ink," *Christian Science Monitor,* January 9, 1990, p. 1; Kenneth Lipper, "What Needs to Be Done?", *The New York Times Magazine,* December 31, 1989, p. 28; "The Walls Keep Closing in on New York Developers," *Business Week,* July 2, 1990, p. 72; Richard Levine, "Job Growth in New York Shifts to Losses as Economy Slows," *The New York Times,* July 31, 1990, p. C19; Susan Chira, "School Days Test Parents' Ties to New York," *The New York Times,* September 14, 1990, p. A1; Alan Finder, "New York Real-Estate Slump Hits Biggest Builders," *The New York Times,* August 20, 1990, p. A1; William Glaberson, "Chilled by Violence, New Yorkers Are Questioning Life in Their City," *The New York Times,* September 16, 1990, p. A1; Neil Barsky, "Hard Times for Big Apple Real Estate," *The Wall Street Journal,* February 19, 1991, p. B5A; "The Naked City," *The Wall Street Journal,* September 11, 1990, p. A22; Ruthe Stein, "New York, New York, It's a Scary Town," *San Francisco Chronicle,* October 22, 1990, p. B3; and "Last One Out of Gotham, Close the Door," *Economist,* October 20, 1990, p. 21.

Page 21. For more on the Time-CNN poll, see Attinger, "The Decline of New York," *Time,* September 17, 1990, pp. 36–52.

Page 21. Felix Rohatyn is quoted in Sam Roberts, "This Is Not the City He Rescued," *The New York Times,* April 20, 1990, p. A17.

Page 21. William H. Whyte is quoted in Sam Allis, "Contrary to Previous Reports, Cities Are Not Dead," *Time,* August 7, 1989, p. 10.

Page 21. Thomas Repetto is quoted in Carlos Sadovi, "New York, Nation Face Rise in Crime," *Christian Science Monitor,* April 9, 1990, p. 7, and in Attinger, p. 39.

Page 22. See Barbara Howar, "You Take Manhattan, I'm Gone," *The New York Times,* March 19, 1990, p. A17.

Page 22. Camilo Jose Vergara, "Hell in a Very Tall Place," *Atlantic Monthly,* September 1989, pp. 72–78.

Page 22. The joint survey by Louis Harris & Associates and Cushman & Wakefield is cited by Mark McCain, "Bright Lights, Big City: More Firms Staying Put," *The New York Times,* March 27, 1988, p. 2RY.

Page 22. The Runzheimer International study is reported in "Why They Hate New York," *Forbes,* September 21, 1987, p. 189.

Page 22. For a discussion of transfer turndowns, see Howard Kurtz, "New York Costs Repel Firms, New Employers," *Washington Post,* September 6, 1987, p. A3. Also, Martha T. Moore and Mindy Fetterman, "Bottom Line: Big Apple's Too Expensive," *USA Today,* October 27, 1989, p. 1A; "Apple Crunch," *The Economist,* March 3, 1990, p. 26; and "Why They Hate New York," *Forbes,* September 21, 1987, p. 189.

Page 22. The Household Goods Carriers' Bureau data are discussed in Attinger, "The Decline of New York," *Time,* September 7, 1990, p. 44.

Page 22. Kenneth Rosen is quoted in "Which Cities Will Be Hot—And Not," *Fortune,* March 26, 1990, p. 150.

Page 23. See Charles Lockwood and Christopher B. Leinberger, "Los Angeles Comes of Age," *Atlantic Monthly,* January 1988, pp. 31–32. Also, Kevin Starr, *Material Dreams: Southern California Through the 1920s,* Oxford University Press, New York, 1990.

Page 23. See Fishman, *Bourgeois Utopias,* p. 155.

Page 23. See David L. Kirp and Douglas S. Rice, "Fast Forward—Styles of California Management," *Harvard Business Review,* January–February 1988, p. 75.

Page 23. The entrepreneurial breed is described in "The Case against Bigsville," *The Economist,* December 18, 1988.

Page 24. Information on L.A. traffic and smog-related problems is quoted in Robert Reinhold, "Parking: Even an Angel Would Cry," *The New York Times,* August 30, 1988, p. B7. See also Alan Weisman, "L.A. Fights for Breath," *The New York Times Magazine,* July 30, 1989, p. A15, and Judy Keen and Sally Ann Stewart, "L.A. Jams Are 'Sheer Terror on the Roads,'" *USA Today,* May 30, 1989, p. A1. For further traffic projections, see "Coming Soon: Regional Power," *Los Angeles Times,* February 11, 1990, p. M6; "At the Crossroads: A Special Report on Southern California's Environment," *Los Angeles Times,* December 10, 1989, sec. Q; Jesus Sanchez, "A Longer Road Now Takes Toll," *Los Angeles Times,* October 17, 1989, p. A1; and Tracy Wilkinson, "Southern California Commute Time Lengthening, Study Finds," *Honolulu Advertiser,* June 15, 1990, p. E2; and James M. Lents, "Businesses Running Away from Smog Will Not Change L.A.'s Air," *Los Angeles Times,* September 16, 1990, p. M5.

Page 24. The Long Beach commuter flight is discussed in Paul Feldman, "Sky's the Limit when You Want to Avoid Traffic," *Los Angeles Times,* July 5, 1989, pt. II, p. 3. See, too, Ted Johnson, "Freeway Alternates," *Los Angeles Times,* October 21, 1990, p. B1.

Page 24. For a report on California's schools, see Michael Reese and Jennifer Foote, "California: American Dream, American Nightmare," *Newsweek,* July 31, 1989, p. 23.

Page 25. Dean Richard Weinstein is quoted in Frederick Rose, "Urban Lab: Los Angeles Offers a Future Glimpse," *The Wall Street Journal Centennial Edition,* 1989, p. A15. See also Frederick Rose, "The City of the Future Is a Troubling Prospect If It's to Be Los Angeles,"

The Wall Street Journal, June 12, 1989; Richard J. Stern and John H. Taylor, "Is the Golden State Losing It?" *Forbes,* October 29, 1990, p. 86; and Carl T. Hall, "Experts Debate State's 'Decline,'" *San Francisco Chronicle,* October 22, 1990, P. C1.

Page 25. Jack Kyser is quoted in Kenneth Labich, "The Best Cities for Business," *Fortune,* October 23, 1989, p. 66. See, too, Patricia Sellers, "The Best Cities for Business," *Fortune,* October 22, 1990, p. 48.

Page 25. The UCLA report on metropolitan segregation is considered by Patt Morrison, "L.A. vs. O.C.: A Special Report," *Los Angeles Times Magazine,* June 17, 1990, p. 10.

Page 25. Professor Allen Scott is also quoted in Rose, "Urban Lab," p. A17.

Page 25. Various reports on L.A. residents' dissatisfaction may be found in Morrison, p. 10. See also Robert Reinhold, "San Diego Eyes Its Bad Neighbor," *The New York Times,* July 7, 1989, p. A10; "Coming Soon: Regional Power," *Los Angeles Times,* February 11, 1990, p. M6; and Joel Kotkin, "The Laid-Back View of Hard Times, California Style," *Washington Post National Weekly Edition,* August 6–12, 1990, p. 20.

Page 25. The L.A. exodus is described by Anne Taylor Fleming, "A Collective Yearning: Leaving Paradise Behind," *The New York Times,* August 30, 1989, p. G7. See also Paul Nussbaum, "Lifestyle in Southern California Spurs Exodus," *Honolulu Sunday Star-Bulletin & Advertiser,* August 13, 1989, p. A29.

Page 26. David Hensley is quoted in Daniel B. Wood, "Los Angeles Joins National Slump," *Christian Science Monitor,* December 4, 1990, p. 8.

Page 26. For more on the business exodus from Los Angeles, see Scott Armstrong, "Economic Slump Strains California," *Christian Science Monitor,* May 18, 1990, p. 8. Also, Marc Beauchamp, "Made in Los Angeles," *Forbes,* November 13, 1989, p. 69.

Page 26. Bernard Frieden, "American Business Still Wants to Go Downtown," *The Wall Street Journal,* January 10, 1990, p. A17. (Reprinted by permission of *The Wall Street Journal,* © 1990. Dow Jones & Company, Inc. All Rights Reserved Worldwide.) See also Frieden and Lynne B. Sagalyn, *Downtown, Inc.: How America Rebuilds Cities,* MIT Press, Cambridge, Mass., 1989, and Lucia Mouat, "Cities Quietly Revitalize Downtown," *Christian Science Monitor,* August 30, 1990, p. 8.

Page 26. Carole Rifkind is quoted in Renata von Tscharner and Ronald Lee Fleming, "Making Cities Memorable," *World Monitor,* February 1990, p. 36.

Page 26. Drucker, *The New Realities,* pp. 258–259.

Page 27. George Rossi is quoted in Alan S. Oser, "Japanese Help Fill Trade Center," *The New York Times,* May 16, 1990, p. C16. See also Randolph Walreius, "Japanese Banks Boost a Role in New York," *The Wall Street Journal,* June 22, 1990, p. B-7A.

Page 27. Laurence Simmons is quoted in John Hillkirk, "The Pocket High-Profile Properties," *USA Today,* December 1, 1989, p. 1B.

Page 27. For popular reactions to the taxicab program, see James Barron, "Scary City, Answer May Be Courtesy," *The New York Times,* February 28, 1990, p. A21.

Page 28. For more on New York's loss of manufacturing jobs, see "New York's Future: Bright Lights, Big Trouble," *Business Week,* November 20, 1989, p. 108, and Levine, p. C19; and Levine, "100,000 Jobs Lost in New York Region, U.S. Study Discloses," *The New York Times,* December 21, 1990, p. A1.

Page 28. L.A.'s loss of manufacturing jobs is discussed in Steve Bergsman, "Small L.A. Businesses Find Nicer Climates Elsewhere," *The New York Times,* April 29, 1990, p. F12. Also, see Rodolfo Acuna, "And Then There Were No Blue-Collar Jobs," *Los Angeles Times,* May, 6, 1990, p. M7.

Page 28. Professor Saskia Sassen's perspective is presented in "The New America," *Business Week,* September 25, 1989, p. 152.

Page 28. See Herbers, *The New Heartland,* p. 25.

Page 28. See Spencer Rich, "Our Very Segregated Cities," *Washington Post Weekly National Edition,* August 28–September 3, 1989, p. 37, and Jason DeParle, "Suffering in the Cities Persists as U.S. Fights Other Battles," *The New York Times,* January 27, 1991, p. 1. For a powerful discussion of Detroit's segregation problems, see Ze'ev Chafets, *Devil's Night: And Other True Tales of Detroit,* Random House, New York, 1990.

Page 29. David C. Walters, "Big Cities, Bolts and All," *Christian Science Monitor,* May 24, 1990, p. 13.

Page 29. Professor Scott's notion of "biogeneous" societies is discussed in Patt Morrison, "L.A. vs. O.C.: A Special Report," p. 37. Also, Jamie S. Hirsh and Suzanne Alexander, "Middle-Class Blacks Quit Northern Cities and Settle in the South," *The Wall Street Journal,* May 22, 1990, p. A1, and Scott Armstrong, "Los Angeles Faces Black Exodus," *Christian Science Monitor,* August 13, 1990, p. 6.

Page 29. See David R. Francis, "Cures for Inner-City Black Poverty: Bootstraps and Aid," *Christian Science Monitor,* January 12, 1990, p. 8.

Page 30. Alan Farnham, "Migratory Habits . . .," pp. 400–401. For an excellent discussion of recent out-migration, see also "Corporate Headquarters Are on the Move," *Area Development,* April 1990, p. 16, and Solomon, "Corporate Elite . . .," p. B1.

Page 31. William Whyte's views on small companies are discussed in his *City: Rediscovering the Center,* Doubleday, New York, 1989, p. 297.

Page 31. L. Clinton Hoch and Alan Farnham are quoted in Farnham, "Migratory Habits . . .," p. 400.

Page 32. Louis H. Masotti, "Corporate Dynamics Complicate the Market," *The New York Times Special Report: In the Nation,* May 14, 1989, p. 18.

Page 32. Professor Sternlieb is quoted in Andrew Kupfer, "New York: Down but Hardly Out," *Fortune,* February 26, 1990. p. 94. See, too, Eben Shapiro, "Hard Edges Aside, Manhattan Still Lures the Ambitious," *The New York Times,* January 6, 1991, p. F12.

Page 33. Jerry Kolb is quoted in Lee Burton, "Deloitte to Move Its Headquarters from Manhattan," *The Wall Street Journal,* June 18, 1987. See, too, Stuart Meyers, "A Company Gives Up on New York," *The New York Times,* November 4, 1990, p. F13.

Page 33. Renato Ruggieo is quoted in Thomas J. Lueck, "New York City Is Challenged as Giant of Global Economy," *The New York Times,* June 27, 1988, p. A1.

Page 33. John G. Heinmann is also quoted by Lueck, "New York City Is Challenged . . .," p. C10.

Page 33. For a discussion of Detroit's demise in automaking, see Robert W. McElwaine, "The End of an Era," *Auto Age,* May 1990. Also, David Broder, "Goodbye to All That," *Washington Post Weekly National Edition,* December 18–24, 1989, p. 6; Bill Vlasic, "For Automakers, Motown Is Becoming No Town for Business," *Washington Post Weekly National Edition,* July 3, 1989, p. 22, and Chafets, *Devil's Night: And Other True Tales of Detroit,* Random House, N.Y., 1990.

Page 33. Quotes on Hollywood's decline are from Lockwood and Leinberger, "Los Angeles Comes of Age," *Atlantic Monthly,* January 1988, p. 34.

Page 34. Drucker, *The New Realities,* pp. 258–259.

Page 34. For more on specialized nodes, see Herbers, *The New Heartland,* pp. 11 and 25.

Page 34. Whyte's quote is from his *City: The Rediscovery of the Center,* p. 341.

Page 34. See Joel Oppenheimer, "Cities, This City," *The New York Times Magazine,* July 4, 1976, p. 30.

Page 35.   See Jon Bowermaster, "Seattle: Too Much of a Good Thing?" *The New York Times Magazine,* January 6, 1991, p. 26.

Chapter 3: From
Suburbia to Penturbia

Page 36.   For a comprehensive history of suburbia, see John R. Stilgoe, *Borderland: Origins of the American Suburb,* 1820–1939, Yale University Press, New Haven, 1988; Jackson, *Crabgrass Frontier,* and Fishman, *Bourgeois Utopias.*

Page 36.   Jackson, *Crabgrass Frontier,* p. 188.

Page 36.   Roberta Brandes Gratz, *The Living City,* Simon and Schuster, New York, 1989, p. 202.

Page 37.· Lessinger, *Snow Country,* p. 68.

Page 37.   For population changes, see Fishman, *Bourgeois Utopias,* p. 182, and Herbers, *The New Heartland,* pp. 76–77, 159–160, 166–168, and 207–208. For more information on blacks in suburbia, see Jackson, *Crabgrass Frontier,* p. 301.

Page 37.   Professor Wilbur Rich is quoted in David Broder, "Goodbye to All That," p. 7. For more on the black exodus, see Priscilla Painton, "You Can Go Home Again," *Time,* December 24, 1990, p. 72.

Page 38.   See, for example, William K. Stevens, "Beyond the Mall: Suburbs Evolving Into 'Outer Cities,'" *The New York Times,* November 8, 1987, p. E-5; Bernard Wysocki, Jr., and Michael J. McCarthy, "Latest New Frontier: Exurban Boom Towns," *The Wall Street Journal Centennial Edition,* vol. CXX, no. 122C, 1989, p. A7; Daniel B. Wood, "Driving Themselves to Extremes," *Christian Science Monitor,* September 20, 1990, p. 6; and Rodney Ferguson and Eugene Carlson, "Distant Communities Promise Good Homes but Produce Malaise," *The Wall Street Journal,* October 25, 1990, p. A1.

Page 38.   Anthony DePalma, "New York Suburbs Spilling Westward," *The New York Times,* February 14, 1988, Section 8, p. 1.

Page 38.   Tom Furlong, "The Inland Migration," *Los Angeles Times,* February 11, 1990, p. D1. See, too, Ellen Paris, "Trading Free Time for Better Housing," *Forbes,* July 23, 1990, pp. 88–89, and Ferguson and Carlson, "Distant Communities . . .," *The Wall Street Journal,* October 25, 1990, p. A1; Tim Schreiner, "National Trend Favors 'Bedroom Cities,'" *Honolulu Star-Bulletin,* February 5, 1991, p. A10; and "Desert, Foothills Areas Lead California Population Gains," *Honolulu Star-Bulletin,* January 28, 1991, p. A10. Elizabeth Hoag is quoted in Schreiner, "National Trends . . .," *Honolulu Star-Bulletin,* February 5, 1991, p. A10.

Page 38.   Sean Quinn is quoted in Kevin Drew, "San Francisco's Rising Costs Prompt Business Exodus," *Christian Science Monitor,* May 25, 1989, p. 7.

Page 39.   Dave Anderson of Anderson-Barrows Metal Corporation is quoted in Paris, "Trading Free Time . . .," *Forbes,* July 23, 1990, p. 90.

Page 39.   Economist Michael Greenwood's sentiments are from William Dunn, "Sun Belt Soaks Up '90 Census," *USA Today,* August 27, 1990, p. A1.

Page 39.   See Ross Atkin, "The 'Mallification' of America," *Christian Science Monitor,* October 25, 1989, p. 12, and Roberta Brandes Gratz, "Malling the Northeast," *The New York Times Magazine,* April 1, 1990, p. 34.

Page 39.   Peter Muller is quoted in "The New America," *Business Week,* September 25, 1989, p. 98.

Page 39.   Gratz, "Malling the Northeast," p. 54.

Page 40.   Professor Muller's remarks are from "The New America," p. 98.

Page 40.   See Fishman, *Bourgeois Utopias,* p. 16.

Page 40.   For more on the Coral Gables story, see my "Global Cities of Tomorrow," *Harvard Business Review,* May–June 1977, pp. 79–92.

Page 42.   Peter deVise is quoted in John McCormick and Peter McKillop, "The Other Suburbia," *Newsweek,* June 26, 1989, p. 22.

Page 42.   Jackson, *Crabgrass Frontier,* p. 312. See also Herbers, *The New Heartland,* p. 73.

Page 42.   See "Washington, D.C., Survey," *Economist,* April 16, 1988, p. 5.; Carroll Doherty, "Washington Area Suburbs Face Development Snags," *Christian Science Monitor,* January 18, 1990, p. 7; Joel Garreau, "Yes, Virginia, There Is a Mobil Corp.," *Washington Post National Weekly Edition,* June 15, 1987, p. 31; and Jay Matthews, "Urban, Suburban Cowboys," *Washington Post National Weekly Edition,* February 20–26, 1989, p. 34.

Page 42.   "Lessons from Tysons Corner," *Forbes,* April 30, 1990, p. 186.

Page 43.   Jerry A. Tannenbaum, "In Herndon, Va., Growth Elicits Some Mixed Feelings," *The Wall Street Journal,* March 30, 1989, p. B1.

Page 43.   Bernard Wysocki, Jr., "The New Boom Towns," *The Wall Street Journal,* March 27, 1989, p. B1.

Page 43.   Benjamin Weiner's remarks are from his "Please Stay, Morgan Stanley," *The New York Times,* January 10, 1991, p. A19.

Page 43.   Professor Mark Baldassare is quoted in Frederick Rose, "California Towns Vote to Restrict Expansion as Services Lag Behind," *The Wall Street Journal,* November 27, 1987, p. A1. See, too, "Not in My Neighborhood," *Time,* January 25, 1988, p. 24.

Page 44.   Robert Stuart is quoted in Lisa W. Foderaro, "Coping with Growth, and the Troubles It Brings," *The New York Times,* December 12, 1989, p. C19.

Page 44.   John Lynch is quoted in Tannenbaum, "In Herndon, Va. . . .," *The Wall Street Journal,* March 30, 1989, p. B2.

Page 44.   For a discussion of zoning initiatives to help communities preserve open spaces and aesthetic appeal, see Catherine Foster, "Designs for Growing with Grace," *Christian Science Monitor,* May 10, 1989, p. 12; Brian O'Reilly, "The War against Growth Heats Up," *Fortune,* December 5, 1988, pp. 124–130; Nancy Herndon, "Urban Sprawl: A Tale a Thousand Times Told," *Christian Science Monitor,* March 11, 1988, p. 23; Anthony DePalma, "As Suburbs Sprawl, Open Space Shrinks," *The New York Times,* July 31, 1988, Section 8, p. 1.; and Jon Bowermaster, "Seattle: Too Much of a Good Thing?" *The New York Times Magazine,* January 6, 1991, p. 24.

Page 44.   See Rose, "Urban Lab," p. A1.

Page 44.   See William Dunn, "New Hampshire's Boom Leaves Red Carpet Frayed," *USA Today,* March 8, 1990, p. 8A, and George E. Curry, "Rapid Growth Imports Urban Woes to Bucolic New Hampshire," *Chicago Tribune,* September 9, 1990, Sec. 1, p. 13.

Page 44.   John DeGrove is quoted in Anthony DePalma, "A 10,000-Acre City Is Growing in the Everglades," *The New York Times,* October 2, 1988, pp. 4–35. See, too, Tim O'Reiley, "Florida Growth-Control Law Influencing Development," *The New York Times,* August 27, 1989, pp. 4–33.

Page 45.   The California survey on urban sprawl is cited in William Fulton, "Needed: Strong Governor to Solve Growth Gridlock," *Los Angeles Times,* October 15, 1989, p. M1. Also, DePalma, "A 10,000-Acre City . . .," *The New York Times,* October 2, 1988, pp. 4–35.

Page 45.   See Catherine Foster, "Bay State's 'Friends' Want Reserved Growth," *Christian Science Monitor,* September 19, 1989, p. 7.

Page 45.   See Tracy Walmer and Kevin Johnson, "Urban Development Plows Farmland Under," *USA Today,* March 7, 1990, p. 6A. Also, Dick Johnson, "As Suburbs Stretch to Farm, Plowing Can Become a Crime," *The New York Times,* June 9, 1990, p. 1, and Peter

Applebourne "In North Carolina, the New South Rubs Uneasily with the Old Ways," *The New York Times,* July 2, 1990, p. A1.

Page 46.   Robert Gidel is quoted in Anthony DePalma, "Suburbs Losing Ground in Battles for Tenants," *The New York Times Magazine,* sec. 10A, September 10, 1989.

Page 46.   Regina Armstrong's remarks are from Michael deCourcy Hinds, "Comparing Costs: City vs. the Suburbs," *The New York Times,* May 24, 1987, sec. 8, p. 1.

Page 46.   The Cushman & Wakefield Survey is reported in DePalma, "Suburbs Losing Ground in Battles for Tenants," p. 13.

Page 46.   The Metropolitan Consulting Group's findings may be found in "Pricey Suburbs," *Economist,* September 18, 1989, p. 28.

Page 46.   The *New York Times*/Runzheimer International Study is discussed in Hinds, "Comparing Costs . . .," *The New York Times,* May 24, 1987, sec. 8, p. 1.

Page 46.   For more on the PHH Fantas report, see Michael Selz, "Firms Battling Labor Shortages Call the Movers," *The Wall Street Journal,* January 30, 1990, p. B1.

Page 47.   David Birch's remarks are also from "Firms Battling Labor Shortages Call the Movers," p. B2.

Page 47.   See Fishman, *Bourgeois Utopias,* pp. 16–17, 206.

Page 47.   William J. Levitt is quoted extensively in Michael T. Kaufman, "Tough Times for Mr. Levittown," *The New York Times Magazine,* September 24, 1989, pp. 43–92.

Page 47.   The Gallup results are discussed in Herbers, pp. 188–189, and Dirk Johnson, "Population Decline in Rural America: A Product of Advances in Technology," *The New York Times,* September 11, 1990, p. A12.

Page 48.   Felicity Barringer, "Census Data Show Sharp Rural Losses," *The New York Times,* August 30, 1990, p. A16. See also her "What America Did After the War: A Tale Told by the Census," *The New York Times,* September 2, 1990, p. E1, "The Clustering of America, Part II," *The New York Times,* January 27, 1991, p. E7, and "Population Gains in State Capitals," *The New York Times,* January 26, 1991, p. 1. See, too, Barbara Vobejda, "A Shift of Humanity That's Straight from the Heart," *Washington Post Weekly Edition,* September 10–16, 1990, p. 12.

Page 49.   See Elaine Greene, "The Country Look Is Big Business as Cities Seek the Quaint and Cozy," *The New York Times,* May 26, 1988, B7. For more on the minimalist movement, see Caryn James, "Fiction's New Twist: Small-Town Realism," *The New York Times,* May 4, 1989, p. B1; Roberta Smith, "Minimalism on the March: Less Is Again More," *The New York Times,* January 26, 1990, p. B1; "The Heartland Is Hot," *Newsweek,* December 19, 1988, p. 39; Joan Kron, "It's Not Chic. It's Not Plain. It's Homey," *The New York Times,* July 26, 1990, p. B1; "Coming Home to America," *Metropolitan Home,* July 1990, p. 45; and Merle Rubin, "America's Rural Mansions," *Christian Science Monitor,* November 6, 1990, p. 15.

Page 49.   Scott Donaton is quoted in "Magazines Embracing Rural Virtues," *The New York Times,* August 20, 1990.

Page 50.   Many recent articles describe penturban growth. For instance, see "America's New Boom Towns," *U.S. News & World Report,* November 13, 1989, pp. 54–66; Peter Applebourne, "The South Has Its Second Cities, and They Thrive," *The New York Times,* April 23, 1989, p. E5; "America's Hot Cities," *Newsweek,* February 6, 1989, p. 42; Fred S. Worthy, "Booming American Cities," *Fortune,* August 17, 1987, p. 30; William Dunn, "Boom Towns—on a Smaller Scale," *USA Today,* December 11, 1989, p. 9A; "Boom Town, '80s-Style," *Los Angeles Times,* May 12, 1989, pt. 2, p. 10; Bernard Wysocki, Jr., "The New Boom Towns," *The Wall Street Journal,* March 27, 1989, p. B1; Eugene Carlson, "New Hot Cities for Industry Are Emerging," *The Wall Street Journal,* June 8, 1988, p. A25; Kenneth Rosen, "Which Cities Will Be Hot—And Not," *Fortune,* March 26, 1990, p. 150; Stuart Gannes, "Some Real Comers among the Midsize U.S. Cities," *Fortune,* October 23, 1989, p. 74; Andrea Stone, "'Best-Kept Secret' in USA Is Out," *USA Today,* September 20, 1990,

p. A1; Antony J. Michels, "The Allure of Smaller Cities," *Fortune,* October 22, 1990, p. 50; "Where the Booms Are," *USA Today,* December 12, 1990, p. A11; and David Shribman, "Mobility of U.S. Society Turns Small Cities into Giants," *The Wall Street Journal,* February 8, 1991, p. B1.

Page 50. Stanley Litsinger is quoted in William Dunn, "Naples, Fla., Grew Up in '80s, Report Says," *USA Today,* February 14, 1990, p. 6A.

Page 51. Pamela Plumb, Jay Taylor, and Donald Doudna are quoted in "America's New Boom Towns," p. 66. See also Worthy, "American Boomtowns," pp. 35–36.

Page 52. For more on Wilkes-Barre's renaissance, see Gannes, "Some Real Comers . . .," p. 74.

Page 52. William Wyer's remarks are from "America's New Boom Towns," p. 62.

Page 52. See William Giese, "Fort Collins Is a Shipshape City," *USA Today,* September 9, 1987, p. 4D.

Page 53. See Herbers, *The New Heartland,* p. 57.

Page 53. Mayor Maloof's remarks are from "Peoria: A Faster Heartbeat in the Heartland," *Economist,* June 4, 1988, p. 26.

Page 54. See George D. Hack, "Business Parks: The New Amenity-Packed Mini-Cities," *Area Development,* March 1990, pp. 30–35. See, too, Steve Bergsman, "Business Parks Go Upscale," *Area Development,* December 1990, p. 70, and G. Scott Thomas, *The Rating Guide To Life In America's Small Cities,* Prometheus, Amherst, N.Y., 1989.

Page 55. Fishman, "America's New City: Megalopolis Unbound," *Wilson Quarterly,* Winter 1990, p. 41.

Page 55. Todd Zimmerman is quoted in "The Quest for Community," *U.S. News & World Report,* April 9, 1990, p. 75. Also see Philip Langdon, "A Good Place to Live," *The Atlantic Monthly,* March 1988, pp. 39–60; Paul Goldberger, "A More Perfect Union," *The New York Times Magazine,* pt. 2, April 22, 1990, p. 41; "Can a New Suburb Be Like a Small Town?" *U.S. News & World Report,* March 5, 1990, p. 32; and Laura Van Tuyl, "Planners Look Ahead to the Past," *Christian Science Monitor,* May 30, 1990, p. 12. For a contrary description of one neotraditional community, see Anthony DePalma, "New Vision of Suburbia Is at Stake in New Jersey," *The New York Times,* August 15, 1989, p. C18.

Page 57. Curtis L. Carlson is quoted in William Souder, "Minneapolis: No More Mr. Nice Guy," *The New York Times Magazine,* April 1, 1990, pt. 2, p. 64.

Chapter 4: The Case for
the New Corporate Frontier

Page 60. Philip Restifo is quoted in Farnham, "Migratory Habits of the 500," *Fortune,* April 24, 1989, p. 400. (© The Time Inc. Magazine Company. All rights reserved.)

Page 61. William I. Miller's quote is from Robert Johnson, "With Its Spirit Shaken but Unbent, Cummins Shows Decade's Scars," *The Wall Street Journal,* December 13, 1989, p. 4.

Page 61. Al Egbert's remarks are in "Utah: America's Choice," videotape prepared by the Utah Department of Community and Economic Development, Salt Lake City, 1989.

Page 61. David Birch is quoted in Donald L. Henry, "Quality-of-Life Considerations in Site Selection," *Area Development,* December 1987, p. 32. For greater definition of lifestyle attributes, see "What's in a Lifestyle? Plenty, If You're Staffing Corporate Facilities, Say Executives," *Site Selection,* August 1989, p. 948.

Page 61. See Jack Lyne, "Firsthand Observation, Education Rank as Key Elements in Quality-of-Life Equation," *Site Selection,* August 1989, p. 946.

Page 61.   Finn Caspersen is quoted in James L. Shepherd, "Looking for Utopia in a 19th Century Town," *Business Month,* June 1990, p. 78.

Page 62.   Robert Ady's remarks are from Charles F. Harding, "Why Offices Move," *Area Development,* March 1987, p. 30.

Page 62.   3M's Allen Jacobson is quoted in "Education, the Deficit Are the Biggest Problems," *USA Today,* June 7, 1989, p. 114.

Page 62.   Daniel Krumm's remarks are from "Iowa Brainpower Pays," an advertisement in several national periodicals, 1989.

Page 63.   See Julian M. Weiss, "Companies Seeking New Locations Set Their Sites on Education," *Christian Science Monitor,* October 8, 1987, p. 12.

Page 63.   From "Iowa Brainpower Pays," 1989 advertisement.

Page 64.   Thomas Jablonsky and Marc and June Munger are quoted in Rebecca LaValley, "Californians Pack Up Dreams and Move Away," *Honolulu Star-Bulletin,* November 27, 1989, p. A12. (Copyright 1989, *USA Today.* Excerpted with permission.) See, too, Leslie Dreyfoos, "Weary Professionals Start Over by Dropping Out," *The Sunday* (Honolulu) *Star-Bulletin & Advertiser,* February 10, 1991, p. C4; Ramon G. McLeod, "Californians Now Flocking to Trendy Oregon," *Honolulu Star-Bulletin,* December 25, 1990, p. D20; William Dunn, "Affordable Housing Key to Livability," *USA Today,* July 31, 1990, p. 1A; and Sarah Lyall, "Fed Up, Long Island's Young Are Turning to Florida as Land of Opportunity," *The New York Times,* June 20, 1990, p. A1.

Pages 64–65.   Professors Shi and McCable are quoted in Anita Manning, "City Slickers Uproot for the Quiet Life," *USA Today,* March 28, 1989, p. 20. (Copyright 1989, *USA Today.* Excerpted with permission.)

Page 65.   Jim Crawford's remarks are from Nancy Gibbs, "How America Has Run Out of Time," *Time,* April 24, 1989, p. 67.

Page 65.   Christopher Banus is quoted in Sue Shellenbarger, "Rural Enterprise: Tough Row to Hoe," *The Wall Street Journal,* September 12, 1989, p. B1.

Page 65.   Mary McGrory's remarks are from "Iowa Brainpower Pays," 1989 advertisement.

Page 66.   R. Mark Lubbers and Mitchell Daniels, Jr., are quoted in Rushworth M. Kidder, "Think Tank in Corn Country," *Christian Science Monitor,* March 9, 1989, p. 12.

Page 66.   Mr. Templeton's incredible career is examined in John Train, *The Money Masters,* Harper, New York, 1980.

Page 67.   Warren Buffett is quoted in L. J. Davis, "Buffett Takes Stock," *The New York Times Magazine,* pt. 2, April 1, 1990, p. 64. For more information about America's preeminent investor, see John Train, *The Midas Touch,* Harper, New York, 1987.

Page 67.   Anthony Correra's remarks are from "Life After the Correction," *Financial World,* September 19, 1989, p. 15.

Page 67.   Robert Prechter is quoted in Russell Shaw and David Landis, "Prechter Flees Wall Street for Georgia Hills," *USA Today,* October 9, 1987, p. B1.

Page 68.   Jim Stack's quote is from Dennis Canchon, "Newsletter Chief: Forget Long Term," *USA Today,* January 4, 1988, p. B3.

Page 68.   Compliment Van's executive is quoted in Stephen Advocat, "Office Gear on the Go," *Nation's Business,* November 1989, p. 57. See, too, Jerry Flint and Ellen Paris, "Land Yachts," *Forbes,* April 2, 1990, p. 172.

Page 68.   For more on the Nissan-Hitachi venture, see Jacob M. Schlesinger, "Nissan and Hitachi Team Up to Create a 'Mobile Office,'" *The Wall Street Journal,* December 13, 1990, p. A9.

Page 69. Thomas R. Riedinger of Boeing is quoted in Ann E. LaForge, "Offices That Fly and More Telephones in the Sky," *The New York Times*, December 25, 1988, p. E7. See also Calvin Sims, "Challenging Airfare's Monopoly," *The New York Times*, September 15, 1989, p. C1, 8, and John Hillkirk, "In-Flight Plans Office in the Sky," *USA Today*, December 18, 1989, p. 1A.

Page 69. Mike Schelenberger's remarks are from David Craig, "Closed-Circuit Meetings Save Time," *USA Today*, June 6, 1988, p. 6E. See, too, Neal E. Boudette, "'Meet Me On the Screen,'" *Industry Week*, November 20, 1989, p. 37. See, too, Guy Halverson, "Videoconference Industry Booms," *Christian Science Monitor*, October 3, 1990, p. 7.

Page 69. David Glass is quoted in "Wal-Mart Stores Penny Wise," *Business Monitor*, December 1988, p. 42.

Page 70. See Michael Fritz, "Schwan's Song," *Forbes*, April 3, 1989, p. 43.

Page 70. See "Dream Team," *INC.*, April 1989, p. 111.

Page 71. For more on the Fields' mobile office, see William Andrew, "The Facts About the Mobile Executive," *Vis à Vis*, July 1988, p. 74. Also, Jeffrey Ferry, "The Wired World," *Vis à Vis*, May 1990, p. 25.

Page 71. Debbi Fields quote is from Fields and Furst, *One Smart Cookie*, p. 148.

Page 71. See Stanley Davis, *Future Perfect*, Addison-Wesley, Reading, Mass., 1987, p. 89.

Chapter 5: Boise:
The Cowboy Capital

Page 75. Ernest Hemingway's quote appears in various national advertisements for the state of Idaho.

Page 75. See David Lamb, "Riddle of the Rockies: Just Where Is Idaho?" *Los Angeles Times*, July 13, 1988, pt. 1, p. 1.

Page 75. Governor Andrus is cited in Lamb, "Riddle of the Rockies," *Los Angeles Times*, July 13, 1988, pt. 1, p. 1.

Page 78. See L. J. Davis, "Unlikely, But Boise Means Big Business," *The New York Times Magazine*, June 11, 1989, p. 24. (Copyright 1989 by The New York Times Company. Reprinted by permission.)

Page 78. Leland Smith is quoted in Davis, "Unlikely . . .," p. 24.

Page 78. Joseph Parkinson is quoted from a segment of Adam Smith's *Money World*: "Making Chips in Idaho: A High-Tech Cinderella Story," Journal Graphics, New York, May 12, 1989, p. 3.

Page 79. See William Dunn, "Boom Towns—On a Smaller Scale," *USA Today*, December 11, 1989, p. 9A.

Page 79. Randy Nelson is quoted in Dunn, "Boom Towns . . .," p. 9A.

Page 79. Tom Korpalski is quoted in Rebecca LaValley, "Californians Pack Up Dreams and Move Away," *Honolulu Star-Bulletin*, November 27, 1989, p. A12.

Page 80. Gene Harris's remarks are from Joe Morgenstern, "The Blues Man from Boise," *The Wall Street Journal*, June 6, 1988, p. 17.

Page 80. Governor Andrus is quoted in "The Business Climate in the U.S. West," a special advertisement series, *The Wall Street Journal*, April 7, 1988, p. 9.

Page 82. J. R. Simplot is quoted in Adam Smith's *Money World*, p. 3. See also Roger Lowenstein, "Micron Technology Gets Novel 'Boost' from Potato King," *The Wall Street Journal*, March 2, 1989, p. C1.

Page 83. Background information on Micron Technology's survival after Japanese "dumping" may be found in Lawrence M. Fisher, "The Rescue of a U.S. Chip Company," *The New York Times*, April 6, 1988, p. C1. See also Carrie Dolan, "It's Thanksgiving at Christmas for Micron," *The Wall Street Journal*, December 18, 1987, p. 28, and "Joseph Parkinson," *INC.*, July 1988, pp. 43–48.

Page 83. Joseph Parkinson is quoted in Dolan, "It's Thanksgiving . . .," *The Wall Street Journal*, December 18, 1987, p. 28.

Page 84. Mr. Agee's return to Boise as CEO of Morrison Knudsen is chronicled in Carrie Dolan, "Agee Puts Morrison Knudsen in the Black," *The Wall Street Journal*, February 2, 1990, p. A7C. See also Christopher Knowlton, "Bill Agee Gets a Second Chance," *Fortune*, March 27, 1989, pp. 94–96; L. J. Davis, "Born Again," *Business Month*, January 1990, pp. 22–34; Peter Waldman, "Agee Becomes Morrison Knudsen Chief; Ex-Bendix Head May Shake Things Up," *The Wall Street Journal*, August 8, 1988, p. 25; and Tim W. Ferguson, "A Working Woman's Network into Motherhood," *The Wall Street Journal*, September 4, 1990.

Page 84. William Agee is quoted in L. J. Davis, "Born Again," *Business Month*, January 1990, p. 24.

Page 84. See Waldman, "Agee Becomes Morris Knudsen Chief," *The Wall Street Journal*, August 8, 1988, p. 25.

Page 86. See "Joseph Parkinson," *INC.*, July 1988, p. 48.

Chapter 6: Heartland Heroes

Page 87. For complete biographical information on Herbert H. Dow and the Dow Chemical Company, see Don Whitehead, *The Dow Story*, McGraw-Hill, New York, 1968, and Murray Campbell and Harrison Hatton, *Herbert H. Dow: Pioneer in Creative Chemistry*, Appleton, New York, 1951. The quote is from Whitehead, p. 5. Note: Although Dow Chemical headquarters is in Midland, Michigan, the official head office of Marrion Merrell Dow is in Kansas City, Missouri.

Page 88. See Stephen W. Quickel, "The Five Best Managed Companies: Dow Chemical's Explosive Mix," *Business Month*, December 1987.

Page 89. Dow's competitive strategies are discussed in "Has Dow Chemical Found the Right Formula?," *Business Week*, August 7, 1989. See also Randolph B. Smith, "Dow Chemical Targets Ambitious Growth," *The Wall Street Journal*, December 20, 1989, p. A4, and Stephen Quickel, "Uncle!" *Financial World*, May 15, 1990, p. 25; and "Is Dow Chemical About to Start Bubbling Again?" *Business Week*, February 11, 1991, p. 70.

Page 89. J. Lawrence Wilson is quoted in Claudia H. Deutsch, "Dow Chemical Wants to Be Your Friend," *The New York Times*, November 22, 1987, p. F6. (Copyright 1987 by The New York Times Company. Reprinted by permission.)

Page 90. Dow's global vision is discussed in John S. McClenahen, "Thinking Globally," *Industry Week*, August 21, 1989.

Page 91. Mr. Popoff's sentiments are presented in McClenahen, "Thinking Globally," *Industry Week*, August 21, 1989, pp. 14–15.

Page 91. Popoff's "success breeds inertia" remarks are found in Deutsch, "Dow Chemical . . .," *The New York Times*, November 22, 1987, p. F6.

Page 91. See Smith, "Dow Chemical . . .," *The Wall Street Journal*, December 20, 1989, p. A4.

Page 91. See Quickel, "The Five Best Managed Companies," *Business Month*, December 1987, p. 28.

Page 91. See Whitehead, *The Dow Story*, McGraw-Hill, New York, 1968, p. 9.

Page 91. Ted Doan is quoted in Charles C. Mann, "The Town of Dow," *Business Month,* December 1987, p. 66.

Page 92. Herbert H. Dow's remarks are from Campbell and Hatton, *Herbert H. Dow,* Appleton, New York, 1951, p. 142.

Page 92. See Deutsch, "Dow Chemical . . .," *The New York Times,* November 22, 1987, p. F6. For additional information and discussion on Dow's changing image, see also John S. McClenahen, "Dow's Opened Door," *Industry Week,* January 2, 1989, and John Bussey, "Dow Chemical Tries to Shed Tough Image and Court the Public," *The Wall Street Journal,* November 20, 1987, and "We Were Arrogant," *Industry Week,* April 16, 1990.

Page 92. See Bussey, "Dow Chemical . . .," *The Wall Street Journal,* November 20, 1987, pp. 1 and 10.

Page 93. Mr. Popoff is quoted in Deutsch, "Dow Chemical . . .," *The New York Times,* November 22, 1987, p. F6.

Page 93. See Mann, "The Town of Dow," p. 62.

Page 94. Popoff's interview comments are supplemented by Mann, *ibid.,* p. 63.

Page 94. See Mann, *ibid.,* p. 59.

Page 94. Ted Doan's remarks are expanded in Mann, *ibid.,* p. 63.

Page 94. See Daniel Forbes, "The Flip Side of Baghdad," *Business Month,* December 1987, p. 67.

Page 95. Cited in Kathleen M. Schultz's letter to the editor, *Business Month,* March 1988, p. 7.

Page 95. Mary Sinclair's remarks are from Mann, "The Town of Dow," p. 68.

Page 95. Will Kellogg's remarks are found in "W. K. Kellogg (1860–1951)," *Fortune,* March 13, 1989, p. 135.

Page 96. William LaMothe is quoted in Wendy Zellner, "Kellogg Rides the Health Craze," *1989 Business Week Top 1000,* p. 29.

Page 96. LaMothe's remarks are from, "Kellogg," *Business Month,* December 1988, p. 54.

Page 97. Kellogg's marketing strategies are discussed in Patricia Sellers, "How King Kellogg Beat the Blahs," *Fortune,* August 29, 1988. See also Claudia H. Deutsch, "Has Kellogg Lost Its Snap?" *The New York Times,* September 9, 1989.

Page 97. William LaMothe is quoted in Sellers, "How King Kellogg . . .," *Fortune,* August 29, 1988, p. 58.

Page 98. Philip Caldwell's impressions are found in Sellers, *ibid.,* p. 37.

Page 98. Robert L. Nichols' quote is from Richard Gibson, "Personal Chemistry Abruptly Ended Rise of Kellogg President," *The Wall Street Journal,* November 28, 1989, p. A8.

Page 99. Mr. LaMothe's remarks are in Gibson, p. A8. In December 1990, Kellogg named Arnold G. Langbo president and chief operating officer, ending a year-long search for the cereal giant's next CEO. Mr. LaMothe has indicated that he will retire in 1991.

Page 99. A comprehensive analysis of the Kellogg-Battle Creek crisis may be found in Richard E. Lovell, *To Merge or Not to Merge: A Weighty Decision for the City of Battle Creek and Battle Creek Township,* unpublished master's thesis, Western Michigan University, Kalamazoo, Mich., April 14, 1983.

Page 100. For a history of the Kellogg Foundation, see *For the People of Battle Creek,* W. K. Kellogg Foundation, Battle Creek, 1985, and also Meg Cox, "Snap, Crackle, Give," *The Wall Street Journal,* May 13, 1988.

Page 100. Mr. Mawby is quoted in Michael A. McBride, "Battle Creek, Mich.: Kellogg Foundation Comes Back to Town After Two Decades in a Suburban Campus," *The New York Times,* May 15, 1988, sec. 13, p. 22.

Chapter 7: Mail-Order Marvels

Page 103. See William Safire, "America's New Direction: Out of Town, All the Way," *International Herald Tribune,* September 26, 1989.

Page 103. Safire, *ibid.*

Page 104. See "It's a Lot Tougher to Mind the Store," *Business Week,* January 8, 1990, p. 85.

Page 104. For industry growth estimates, see Guy Halverson, "Mail-Order Retailers Poised for Growth," *Christian Science Monitor,* March 25, 1990, p. 9.

Page 105. For more on the Bean philosophy, see James C. Collins and Jerry I. Porras, "Making Impossible Dreams Come True," *Stanford Business School Magazine,* July 1989, p. 12.

Page 106. Gary Comer is quoted in an advertisement in *Forbes,* January 8, 1990, p. 2.

Page 107. See Brent Bowers, "Companies Draw More on 800 Lines," *The Wall Street Journal,* November 9, 1989, p. B1.

Page 107. Catherine Hartnett's estimates are cited in "Delivery Industry's Happy Marriage," *The New York Times,* December 23, 1989, p. 27.

Page 108. Richard Anderson is quoted in Ronit Addis, "Big Picture Strategy," *Forbes,* January 9, 1989, p. 72.

Page 108. Russ Gaitskill is quoted in "A Mail-Order Romance: Lands' End Courts Unseen Customers," *Fortune,* March 13, 1989, p. 45.

Page 109. See M. R. Montgomery, *In Search of L. L. Bean,* Little, Brown, Boston, 1984, p. 217.

Page 109. Chet Dalzell and Kilton Andrew are quoted in Tom Walker, "She's on the Line to Give Great Service with a Smile," *USA Today,* November 22, 1989, p. 4D.

Page 109. Richard Anderson's remarks are from Barbara Rudolph, "The Chic Is in the Mail," *Time,* July 17, 1989, p. 74.

Page 109. Russ Gaitskill is quoted in "A Mail-Order Romance," *Fortune,* March 13, 1989, p. 45.

Page 110. Chairman Comer's remarks appear in various national advertisements.

Page 110. Catherine Hartnett is quoted in "We Guarantee It! And They Really Do," *Christian Science Monitor,* August 15, 1988, p. 10. (Reprinted by permission from *The Christian Science Monitor* 1988. The Christian Science Monitor Publishing Society. All rights reserved.)

Page 110. For more on L. L. Bean's service record, see Joseph Pereira, "L. L. Bean Scales Back Expansion Goals to Ensure Pride in Its Service Is Valid," *The Wall Street Journal,* July 31, 1989, p. B3, and Barbara Hetzer, "Going Out on a Limb to Keep Customers Happy," *Business Month,* November 1990, p. 25.

Page 111. Mr. Comer is quoted in "Listening Is Key to Management at Mail-Order Firm," *USA Today,* December 26, 1989, p. B3.

Page 111. For discussions of the competitive responses of both companies, see: "Lands' End Looks a Bit Frayed at the Edges," *Business Week,* March 19, p. 1990, p. 30; Eric N. Berg, "Standout in the Land Of Catalogues," *The New York Times,* December 8, 1988, p. C1; Paul

Farhi, "L. L. Bean: Boots, Backpacks and Big Bucks," *Washington Post Weekly National Edition,* December 19–25, 1988, p. 22; Jana Pewitt, "Lands' End's New Tack: Firm Struggles to Weather Financial Squall," *USA Today,* December 26, 1989, p. B3; Francine Schwadel, "Lands' End Stumbles as Fashion Shifts Away from Retailer's Traditional Fare," *The New York Times,* April 27, 1990, p. B1; "Catalog of Woes," *Forbes,* June 11, 1990, p. 10; and Francine Schwadel, "Catalog Firms Court Cautious Shoppers with a Bounty of Christmas Promotions," *The Wall Street Journal,* November 1, 1990, p. B1.

Page 112.   Comer is quoted in several national advertisements.

Page 112.   Comer's quote is from Eric N. Berg, "Lands' End Drifts into the Doldrums," *The New York Times,* August 18, 1989, p. C2.

Page 112.   Ms. Hartnett is quoted in Ellen Neuborne, "Catalog Firms Unwrap Revenue Gains," *USA Today,* January 10, 1990, p. B1.

Page 113.   Leon Gorman is quoted in Pereira, "L. L. Bean Scales Back . . .," *The Wall Street Journal,* July 31, 1989, p. B3.

Page 113.   See Montgomery, *In Search of L. L. Bean,* Little, Brown, Boston, 1984, p. 5.

Page 114.   See Rob Morse, "L. L. Bean: A Catalog of Horror," *San Francisco Examiner,* August 19, 1989, p. A3. See, too, John Gould, "Freeport before Bean," *Christian Science Monitor,* October 12, 1990, p. 17.

Page 114.   Francis Chiarini's remarks appear in Lynn Riddle, "Paying the Price for Growth," *The New York Times,* August 23, 1987, p. 1.

Page 114.   The L. L. Bean manager's quote is from Montgomery, *In Search of L. L. Bean,* Little, Brown, Boston, 1984, p. 213.

Page 115.   David L. Birch, "RFD Inc.: Where to Go When You Want to Start a Business in a Remote Location," *INC.,* February 1988, pp. 14–15. Note, too, that the country's leading direct-marketing experts, Bill Jamie and Heikki Ratalahti, are based in penturban Sonoma, California. See Randall Rothenberg, "Junk Mail's Top Dogs," *The New York Times Magazine,* August 5, 1990, p. 27.

Chapter 8: The Rise of the Minimalist Corporation

Page 120.   See Robert M. Tomasko, *Downsizing: Reshaping the Corporation of the Future,* Amacom, New York, 1987.

Page 120.   The Louis Harris poll is cited in Selwyn Feinstein, "Views of Younger Managers Suggest New Way for U.S. Business to Compete," *The Wall Street Journal,* October 11, 1988, p. C23.

Page 120.   Eric Greenberg is quoted in Amanda Bennett, "Business Takes Out Its Trimming Shears," *The Wall Street Journal,* October 5, 1989, p. A2.

Page 121.   See Tom Peters, "New Products, New Materials, New Competition, New Thinking," *Economist,* March 4, 1989, p. 19–22.

Page 121.   The New Jersey Labor Department quote is from Guy Halverson, "First the Merger, Then the Job Cuts," *Christian Science Monitor,* August 4, 1989, p. 9.

Page 121.   Professor Kaplan's research is cited in "Management Buy Outs: No Staying Power," *Economist,* November 18, 1989, p. 79.

Page 122.   See Henry R. Kravis, "LBOs Can Help Restore America's Competitive Edge," *Financier,* August 1989, pp. 34–35. See also Michael C. Jensen, "Eclipses of the Public Corporation," *Harvard Business Review,* September–October 1989, pp. 61–74. For a rejoinder, see Alfred Rappaport, "The Staying Power of the Public Corporation," *Harvard Business Review,* January–February 1990.

Page 122. See Stephen Taub, "LBO's: The Next Lap," *Financial World,* October 31, 1989, p. 35, and "There's Still Life in the Old LBO," *Business Week,* January 21, 1991, p. 76.

Page 122. Shoshana Zuboff, *In the Age of the Smart Machine,* Basic Books, New York, 1988.

Page 122. See Drucker, "The Coming of the New Organization," *Harvard Business Review,* January–February 1988, pp. 45–53.

Page 122. Drucker, *The New Realities,* Harper, New York, 1989, p. 207. (Reprinted by permission of Harper & Row, Publishers, Inc.)

Page 122. See Raymond C. Miles, "Adapting to Technology and Competition: A New Industrial Relations System for the 21st Century," *California Management Review,* Winter 1989, p. 9. (Copyright 1989 by The Regents of the University of California. Reprinted from the *California Management Review,* vol. 31, no. 2. By permission of The Regents.) See, too, Brian Dumaine, "Who Needs a Boss?" *Fortune,* May 7, 1990, p. 52.

Page 123. See Drucker, *The New Realities.*

Page 123. Jack Welsh is quoted in Noel Tichy and Rava Charon, "Speed, Simplicity, and Self-Confidence: An Interview with Jack Walsh," *Harvard Business Review,* September–October 1989, p. 114.

Page 123. Tom Peters is quoted in John S. McClenahen, "Flexible Structures to Absorb the Shocks," *Industry Week,* April 18, 1988, pp. 41–44.

Page 123. Gordon Forward of Chaparral Steel is quoted in James O'Toole, *Vanguard Management,* Doubleday, New York, 1985, p. 318.

Page 124. John Young's remarks on computer integration are from John H. Sheridan, "Toward the CIM Solution," *Industry Week,* April 18, 1988, pp. 46–47. See, too, Jeremy Main, "Computers of the World, Unite!" *Fortune,* September 24, 1990, p. 113.

Page 124. For more on Caterpillar's "Plant with a Future," see "Can Caterpillar Tech Its Way Back to Heftier Profits?," *Business Week,* September 25, 1989, pp. 57–78; Jeremy Main, "Manufacturing the Right Way," *Fortune,* May 21, 1990, p. 54; and Eric N. Berg, "Thinking Long Term Is Costly to Caterpillar," *The New York Times,* November 24, 1989, p. C1, and Wes Iversen, "Information Systems: Tying It All Together," *Industry Week,* August 20, 1990.

Page 124. McKinsey's Steve Walleck is quoted in John H. Sheridan, "Attacking Overhead," *Industry Week,* July 18, 1988, p. 50.

Page 125. See Drucker, *The New Realities,* p. 209.

Page 125. See George Gilder, "Truth, Light, Salvation and Microelectronics," *Washington Post National Weekly Edition,* September 18–24, 1989, p. 35.

Page 125. Paul Saffo is quoted in "Escape from the Office," *Newsweek,* April 24, 1989, p. 58.

Page 125. For estimates of America's computer literacy, see Mark L. Goldstein, "The Networked Organization," *Industry Week,* April 18, 1988, pp. 46–47.

Page 125. Global strategic partnerships are examined in Howard V. Perlmutter and David A. Heenan, "Cooperate to Compete Globally," *Harvard Business Review,* March–April, 1986, pp. 136–152.

Page 126. Gerald Greenwald is quoted in "Driving Toward A World Car?" *Newsweek,* April 1, 1989, p. 48.

Page 126. See Kenichi Ohmae, "Only 'Triad Insiders' Will Succeed," *The New York Times,* September 2, 1984, p. 2F. See also Bernard Wysocki, Jr., "Cross-Border Alliances Become Favorite Way to Crack New Markets," *The Wall Street Journal,* March 26, 1990, p. A1.

Page 127. See also Douglas Cannon, "Keeping Outsourcing in Hand," *Chief Executive,* November–December 1989, p. 38. Robert Bauman is quoted in Joann S. Lublin, "Smith, Kline, Beecham Honeymoon's Over as Two U.S. Competitors Also Tie Knot," *The Wall Street Journal,* July 31, 1989, p. A10.

Page 128. "The Caribbean: A Back Office Paradise," *Business Week,* April 11, 1988, p. 84, and Melissa C. Forbes, "Case By Case: Expanding Firms Go Global," *Plants, Sites & Parks,* May–June 1990, p. 92.

Page 128. Lawson Narse is quoted in John Burgess, "Exporting Our Office Work," *Washington Post National Weekly Edition,* May 1–7, 1988, p. 22. See, too, Barnaby, J. Feder, "Repairing Machinery from Afar," *The New York Times,* January 30, 1991, p. C7.

Page 128. D. Quinn Mills is cited in Steve Lohr, "The Growth of the Global Office," *The New York Times,* October 18, 1988, p. C1. See, too, "All the World's an Executive Suite," *Economist,* December 8, 1990, p. 72.

Page 129. See Neal E. Bondette, "Tempted By Temps," *Industry Week,* August 7, 1989, p. 20. See also, Kanter, pp. 302–304; Claudia H. Deutsch, "The Allure of Temporary Work," *The New York Times,* April 15, 1990, p. F25; and Michael Barrier, "Temporary Assignment," *Nation's Business,* October, 1989, p. 36.

Page 129. Samuel Sacco's quote is from Bondette, "Tempted by Temps," *Industry Week,* August 7, 1989, p. 20.

Page 129. Edgar Landis is quoted in Stephen Kindel, "Rent-A-Techie," *Financial World,* November 14, 1989, p. 54. See also "Rent-an-Exec Firms: Field Demand Soaring as Corporations Revamp Companies," *The Wall Street Journal,* August 4, 1988, p. 1; "Hire an Executive by the Hour," *Working Woman,* August 1989, p. 29; Ronald J. Diorio, "How to Rent a CEO," *Leaders,* July–August–September 1990, p. 77; John H. Sheridan, "'Just Passing Through,'" *Industry Week,* July 2, 1990, p. 20, and Dyan Machan, "Rent-An-Exec," *Forbes,* January 22, 1990, p. 132.

Page 129. See Edward M. Katz, "Save More—Lease Your Staff," *Leaders,* January–February 1989, p. 175. See, too, Albert B. Crenshaw, "The Trend toward Rent-a-Staff," *Washington Post Weekly National Edition,* January 22–28, 1990, p. 21, and Stanley Katz, "Outsourcing the Mail Room," *Chief Executive,* June 1990, p. 32.

Page 130. Stephanie Pinson's remarks are from Michael A. Verespej, "The New Work Week," *Industry Week,* November 6, 1989, pp. 12 and 14.

Page 130. Richard Belous sentiments are found in "Part-Timers Could Be Handing Foreign Companies an Edge," *Business Week,* November 11, 1988, p. 20.

Page 130. The Link Resources data is presented in Donald C. Bacon, "Look Who's Working at Home," *Nation's Business,* October 1989, p. 22. Also, Joseph F. McKenna, "Have Modem Don't Travel," *Industry Week,* November 20, 1989, p. 26, and Tim Race, "Going It Alone, Bit by Bit," *The New York Times Magazine,* December 2, 1990, p. 19.

Page 131. The Edwardses are described in Marilyn Hoffman, "Home Is Where the Office Is," *Christian Science Monitor,* June 20, 1989, p. 14. See also Suzanne Alexander, "More Working Mothers Opt for Flexibility of Operating a Franchise from Home," *The Wall Street Journal,* January 31, 1991, p. B1.

Page 131. Sunny Bates's remarks are from "Escape from the Office," p. J8.

Page 132. Dorothy Denton is quoted in Bacon, "Look Who's Working at Home," *Nation's Business,* October 1989, p. 20.

Page 132. Gil Gordon's comments are from Bacon, *ibid.,* p. 26. See, too, Deidre Fanning, "Fleeing the Office and Its Distractions," *The New York Times,* August 12, 1990, sec. 3, p. 25, and Laurent Belsie, "Telecommuting Catches on in U.S.," *Christian Science Monitor,* January 3, 1991, p. 6.

Page 132. See John Markoff, "Here Comes the Fiber-Optic Home," *The New York Times,* November 5, 1989, p. F1.

Page 132. Nick Sullivan is quoted in Laura Van Togyl, "Clocking In at Home," *Christian Science Monitor,* November 18, 1988, p. 23.

Page 133. Robert Grayson's comments are from "Rise and Shine: Another Day of Work and Play," *USA Today,* July 20, 1989, p. 2E.

Page 134. Ylonda Davis is quoted in Kathy Rebello, "Bay Area Workers Commute by Wire," *USA Today,* October 30, 1989, p. 1A. See also Barbara J. Risman and Donald Tomaskovic-Devey," The Social Construction of Technology: Microcomputers and the Organization of Work," *Business Horizons,* May–June 1989, pp. 71–75, and Michael Alexander, "Travel-Free Commuting," *Nation's Business,* December 1990, p. 33.

Page 134. Edward Uchida's remarks are contained in Susan Hooper, "Bringing Work Home," *Hawaii Business,* June 1989, p. 23.

Chapter 9: Redefining the Center

Page 135. Ralph H. Kilmann, "Tomorrow's Corporation Won't Have Walls," *The New York Times,* June 18, 1989, p. D3.

Page 135. See David A. Heenan and Howard V. Perlmutter, "Subsidiaries Come of Age," *New Management,* Winter 1987, p. 19.

Page 135. For an original discussion of the M-form organization, see Gilbert H. Clee and Alfred di Scipio, "Creating a World Enterprise," *Harvard Business Review,* November–December 1959, p. 80.

Page 136. Rosabeth Moss Kanter, *When Giants Learn to Dance,* Simon and Schuster, New York, 1989, p. 88.

Page 137. Kenichi Ohmae, "Planting for a Global Harvest," *Harvard Business Review,* July–August 1989, p. 137.

Page 137. George E. Hall, "Reflections on Running a Diversified Company," *Harvard Business Review,* January–February 1987, p. 85.

Page 138. Professor Porter is quoted in "The New Breed of Strategic Planner," *Business Week,* September 17, 1984, p. 68.

Page 138. See Benjamin B. Tregoe and Peter M. Tobia, "Getting Everyone to Think Strategically," *Chief Executive,* September–October 1989, p. 65. See also Tom Peters, "The New Builders," *Industry Week,* March 5, 1990, p. 27, and Christopher A. Bartlett and Summantra Ghoshal, "Matrix Management: Not a Structure, a Frame Of Mind," *Harvard Business Review,* July–August 1990, pp. 138–145.

Page 138. GE's Jack Welsh is quoted in Noel Tichy and Rava Charon, "Speed, Simplicity, Self-Confidence: An Interview with Jack Welsh," *Harvard Business Review,* September–October 1989, p. 114. See also Steve Schlosstein, "U.S. Is the Leader in Decentralization," *The New York Times,* June 3, 1990, p. F13, and Thomas F. O'Boyle, "From Pyramid to Pancake," *The Wall Street Journal,* June 4, 1990, p. R37.

Page 138. Kanter, *When Giants Learn to Dance,* Simon and Schuster, New York, 1989, p. 94.

Page 139. Dennis Lowe is quoted in Terence P. Paré, "How to Cut the Cost Of Headquarters," *Fortune,* September 11, 1989, p. 196. See also "Positioning the Corporate Staff for the 1990's: A Survey of Top Executives of U.S. Corporations," Towers, Perrin, Forster and Crosby, Inc., New York, 1986.

Page 139. Henry V. Quadracci, "The Corporate Cruise Missile," *Success,* June 1988, p. 8.

Page 141. Tom Peters, "Cheating the Fleet-Footed Organization," *Industry Week,* April 18, 1988, p. 89.

Page 141. See my "The Downside of Downsizing," *Journal of Business Strategy,* November–December 1989, pp. 18–23. See, too, Ronald Henkoff, "Cost Cutting: How to Do It Right," *Fortune,* April 9, 1990, p. 40; Carol Hymowitz, "When Firms Slash Middle Management,

Those Spared Often Bear a Heavy Load," *The Wall Street Journal,* April 5, 1990, p. B1; and Brian O'Reilly, "Is Your Company Asking Too Much?" *Fortune,* March 12, 1990, p. 39.

Page 142. On managing strategic alliances and collaborative ventures, techniques, see Perlmutter and Heenan, "Cooperate to Compete Globally," pp. 143–144.

Page 142. Elizabeth Hass Edersheim is quoted in John S. Sheridan, "Sizing Up Corporate Staffs," *Industry Week,* November 21, 1988, p. 46.

Page 144. Paul O'Neill is quoted in "Positioning the Corporate Staff . . .," p. 14.

Page 145. Professor John Kotter's remarks are from Walter Kiechel III, "Hold for the Communicaholic Manager," *Fortune,* January 2, 1989, p. 107.

Chapter 10: Building a Frontier Culture

Page 149. The *Time*-CNN Poll is referred to in Janice Castro "Where Did the Gung-Ho Go?" *Time,* September 11, 1989, p. 53.

Page 149. The Carnegie Mellon survey is discussed in "Labor Letter: A Special News Report on People and Their Jobs in Offices, Fields and Factories," *The Wall Street Journal,* January 16, 1990, p. A1. A Towers Perrin study showed that almost half of U.S. employees have little or no trust in their bosses. See "Inside Moves," *Business Month,* July 1990, p. 5; and Louis S. Richman, "Why the Middle Class Is Anxious," *Fortune,* May 21, 1990, p. 106; Harold Morrison, "When the Lean Machine Acts Mean," *The Globe and Mail,* November 19, 1990, p. A22.

Page 150. Daniel J. Valentino is quoted in Kenneth Labich, "Making Over Middle Managers," *Fortune,* May 8, 1989, p. 58. See also Selwyn Feinstein, "View of Younger Managers Suggest New Way for U.S. Business to Compete," *The Wall Street Journal,* October 11, 1988, p. C-23; Cindy Skrzycki, "Is There Life After Success?" *Washington Post National Weekly Edition,* July 31–August 6, 1989, p. 21; "Farewell, Fast Track," *Business Week,* December 10, 1990, p. 192; and Kenneth Labich, "Breaking Away to Go on Your Own," *Fortune,* December 17, 1990, p. 41.

Page 150. Donald C. Kanter and Philip H. Mirvis, *The Cynical Americans,* Jossey-Bass, San Francisco, 1989. See, too, Amanda Bennett, *The Death of the Organization Man,* Morrow, New York, 1990.

Page 150. See Anne B. Fisher, "The Downside of Downsizing," *Fortune,* May 23, 1988, p. 42.

Page 150. Selwyn Enzer is quoted in Nancy Gibbs, "How America Has Run Out of Time," *Time,* April 24, 1989, p. 60.

Page 151. David Birch is quoted in Nancy Gibbs, "How America Has Run Out of Time," *Time,* April 24, 1989, p. 64.

Page 151. Gerald Celente is quoted in Anita Manning, "Boomers Are Ready to Loll into Decade," *USA Today,* December 13, 1989, p. D1. See also Daniel Levenson, "The Baby-Boomers' Midlife Crisis," *Fortune,* March 26, 1990, p. 157, and William Dunn, "Boomers to Work for Fun, Retire with Class," *USA Today,* February 27, 1990, p. A1.

Page 152. For more on the Department of Labor estimates, see Claudia Wallis, "Onward, Women," *Time,* December 4, 1989, p. 8J; Joel Dreyfuss, "Get Ready for the New Work Force," *Fortune,* April 23, 1990, p. 165; and Dyan Machan, "The Mommy and Daddy Track," *Forbes,* April 16, 1990, p. 162.

Page 152. The *Washington Post*-ABC News Poll is cited in Richard Morin, "Bringing Up Baby the Company Way," *Washington Post National Weekly Edition,* September 11–17, 1989, p. 37. See, too, Fran Sussner Rodgers and Charles Rodgers, "Business and the Facts of Family Life," *Harvard Business Review,* November–December 1989, p. 121, and Claudia H. Deutsch, "Corporate Advocates for the Family," *The New York Times,* November 11, 1990, p. F27.

Page 152. Dana Friedman is quoted in Ronald Henkoff, "Is Greed Dead?" *Fortune,* August 14, 1989, p. 49. See also Alan Farnham, "What Comes After Greed," *Fortune,* January 14, 1991, p. 43.

Page 152. The Bureau of Labor Statistics information is cited in Lavina Edmunds, "On Their Own," *Johns Hopkins Magazine,* October 1989, p. 55. See, too, Michael A. Verespej, "'Shelves' Emptying in Skills Markets," *Industry Week,* November 20, 1989, p. 54.

Page 153. See David W. Rhodes, "Employee Loyalty Is an Attainable Goal," *Journal of Business Strategy,* November–December 1989, p. 52. (Reprinted with permission from the Nov/Dec 1989 *Journal of Business Strategy.* Copyright © by Warren, Gorham, & Lamont, Inc., 210 South Street, Boston, MA 02111.) See also "Family-Oriented Policies Become Competitiveness Advantage," *Challenge,* May 1990, p. 1; Cathy Trost and Carol Hymowitz, "Careers Start Giving in to Family Needs," *The Wall Street Journal,* June 18, 1990, p. B1; Cathy Trost, "Executives' Perspective on Family, Personal Lives Is Said to Have Shifted," *The Wall Street Journal,* August 24, 1990, p. B5A, and Charles R. Stoner and Richard I. Hartman, "Family Responsibilities and Career Progress: The Good, the Bad, and the Ugly," *Business Horizons,* May–June 1990, p. 7.

Page 153. Michael J. Piore is quoted in "The Password Is Flexible," *Business Week,* September 25, 1989, p. 154.

Page 153. "The Password is Flexible," *ibid.* See, too, Ellen Graham, "Flexible Formulas," *The Wall Street Journal,* June 4, 1990, p. R34.

Page 155. See James C. Collins and Jerry I. Porras, "Making Impossible Dreams Come True," *Stanford Business School Magazine,* July 1989, p. 17.

Page 155. For more on Food Lion, see William E. Sheeline, "Making Them Rich Down Home," *Fortune,* August 15, 1988, p. 51. See, too, Charles O'Reilly, "Corporations, Culture, and Commitment: Motivation and Social Control in Organizations," *California Management Review,* Summer 1989, pp. 9–25.

Page 155. Maytag's Daniel Krumm is quoted in Robert Levy, "Hanging Tough," *Business Month,* July–August 1988, p. 92.

Page 155. Tim Smucker's remarks are from Julianne Slovak, "Companies to Watch," *Fortune,* January 16, 1989, p. 80. For an excellent piece on the J. M. Smucker Company, see Andrew F. Malcom, "Of Jams and a Family," *The New York Times Magazine,* November 15, 1987, p. 82.

Page 156. See Kanter and Mirvis, *The Cynical Americans,* p. 208.

Page 156. Tom Chappell's comments are from Tom Richman, "Identity Crisis," *INC.,* October 1989, p. 100. See also Mary Beth Groves, "A Natural Toothpaste Seeks Its Niche," *The New York Times,* November 5, 1989, p. F13.

Pages 156–157. Jim Stack and other employees of Springfield Remanufacturing Center Corp. are quoted in D. Keith Denton and Barry L. Wisdom, "Shared Vision," *Business Horizons,* July–August 1989, pp. 67–69. See also "The Great Game of Business," *INC.,* July 1990, p. 90.

Page 157. Debbi Fields is cited in Collins and Porras, *Making Impossible Dreams Come True,* p. 15.

Page 157. Jim Blair is quoted in Harriet Johnson Brackey, "Tyson Has Recipe for Poultry Power," *USA Today,* April 20, 1989, p. 11B. See, too, "Poultry's Down-Home Potentate," *Fortune,* January 1, 1990, p. 72.

Page 158. For more on *Cliff's Notes,* see Fleming Meeks, "Shakespeare, Dickens & Hillegass," *Forbes,* October 30, 1989, p. 206; Joel J. Gold, "A Pilgrimage to Meet the Patron Saint of Feckless Students, Cliff of Cliff's Notes," *The Chronicle of Higher Education,* September 13, 1989, p. B2; and Karen Peterson, "Paragraphs That Speak Volumes," *USA Today,* May 3, 1988, p. D1.

Page 158. Rubbermaid's Stanley C. Gault is quoted in James Braham, "The Billion-Dollar Dustpan," *Industry Week*, August 1, 1988, p. 46. See also Brian O'Reilly, "Quality of Products," *Fortune*, January 29, 1990, p. 42, and Brian Dumaine, "Who Needs a Boss?" *Fortune*, May 7, 1990. pp. 52–58.

Page 158. Ken Barbee and Jay Myers' comments on Food Lion appear in Sheeline, "Making Them Rich Down Home," *Fortune*, August 15, 1988, p. 53.

Page 159. Tim Smucker is quoted in Benjamin B. Tregoe and Peter M. Tobia, "Getting Companies to Think Strategically," *Chief Executive*, September–October 1989, p. 65.

Page 159. The remarks of Techsonics's Tom Dyer and Jim Belkom are found in Joshua Hyatt, "Ask And You Shall Receive," *INC.*, September 1989, p. 94.

Page 159. Rubbermaid's Stanley Gault is quoted in Braham, "The Billion-Dollar Dustpan," *Industry Week*, August 1, 1988, p. 48.

Page 160. Harry Quadracci of Quad/Graphics explains "Theory Q" in Daniel M. Kehrer, "Doing Business Boldly, the Art of Taking Intelligent Risks," Random House/Times Books, N.Y., 1989, pp. 286–306.

Page 161. For more on Andersen Corporation, see Carl M. Cannon, "Golden Shackles," *Business Month*, September 1988, p. 56.

Page 161. *Ibid.*, p. 61.

Page 162. Rath Manufacturing is discussed in Joel Millman, "Totally Tubular," *Forbes*, June 25, 1990, p. 80.

Page 162. Samuel C. Johnson of S. C. Johnson Wax is quoted in an interview by Joe Kurgman, "Managing When It's All in the Family," *The New York Times*, April 9, 1989, p. F3. (Copyright 1989 by The New York Times Company. Reprinted with permission.)

Page 162. Quad/Graphics' ESOP is described in Kehrer, "The Miracle of Theory Q," p. 49. The company is also cited by Walter Kiechel III in "The Organization That Learns," *Fortune*, March 12, 1990, p. 134.

Page 163. Rick Johnson of Bur Jon Steel is quoted in "Family Ties," *INC.*, August 1989, p. 112.

Page 163. For more on Corning's enlightened practices with family careerists, see Cindy Skrzycki, "Putting Employees on the Family Track," *Washington Post National Weekly Edition*, September 11–17, 1989, p. 20.

Page 163. David C. Schwartz's remarks and a description of R. L. Stowe Mills's rental program are contained in Phoebe Zerwick, "The Old Mill Town Is Revised with a Modern Twist," *The New York Times*, September 10, 1989, p. Y27. (Copyright 1989 by The New York Times Company. Reprinted with permission.)

Page 165. Ralph Stayer of Johnsonville Foods is quoted in Thomas A. Stewart, "New Ways to Exercise Power," *Fortune*, November 6, 1989, pp. 53–54. (© The Time Inc. Magazine Company. All rights reserved.) See, too, "Managing the Journey," *INC.*, November 1990, p. 45, and Ralph Stayer, "How I Learned to Let My Workers Lead," *Harvard Business Review*, November–December 1990, p. 6.

Page 165. Mike Weaver's remarks are from Joshua Hyatt, "Surviving on Chaos," *INC.*, May 1990, p. 70.

Page 166. See Kehrer, "The Miracle of Theory Q," *Business Month*, September 1989, pp. 45–47. See also Brian Dumaine, "Who Needs a Boss?" *Fortune*, May 7, 1990, pp. 53–55.

Page 166. John H. McMillan describes Kellogg's management style in Claudia H. Deutsch, "Has Kellogg Lost Its Snap?" p. 14.

Page 166. Rubbermaid's Stanley Gault's remarks are presented in Braham, "The Billion-Dollar Dustpan," *Industry Week*, August 1, 1988, p. 48.

Page 166. The J. M. Smucker credo was expressed in its 1988 Annual Report, p. 2.

Page 167. For more on the Hershey School, see "The Sweet Smell of Success," *Fortune*, April 24, 1989, p. 30, and "Hershey: Ghosts and Chocolate Kisses," *Business Month*, July–August 1988, p. 93.

Page 167. William Dearden is quoted in Thomas F. O'Boyle, "These Days, Parents of Many 'Orphans' Are Still Very Much Alive," *The Wall Street Journal*, January 11, 1990, p. A1.

Page 167. The Clark Foundation story is presented in William P. Barrett, "The Clarks of Cooperstown," *Forbes*, September 18, 1989, p. 76.

Page 168. The Andersen Corporation's philanthropy is described in Cannon, "Golden Shackles," *Business Month*, September 1988, p. 56.

Page 168. Samuel Johnson is quoted in Kurgman, "Managing When It's All in the Family," *The New York Times*, April 9, 1989, p. F3.

Page 168. Tom Chappell's philosophy of giving is found in Laura Jereski, "Hearts, Minds and Market Share," *Forbes*, April 3, 1989, p. 81.

Page 168. Alan Creditor's quote is from "More Snap and Crackle at Kellogg," *Business Week*, September 19, 1988, p. 160.

Page 169. The takeover defense of Phillips Petroleum is described in Daniel F. Cuff, "Hometown Fights for Phillips," *The New York Times*, February 11, 1985, p. D1. See, too, "Phillips Climbs Up from the Bottom of the Barrel," *Business Week*, January 16, 1989, p. 76.

Chapter 11: Five Frontier Favorites

Page 171. For a description of Sam Walton's austere living habits, see Michael J. Weiss, *The Clustering of America*, Harper, New York, 1988, p. 64, "Sam Moore Walton," *Business Month*, May 1989, p. 38, and Vance H. Trimble, *Sam Walton: The Inside Story of America's Richest Man*, Dutton, New York, 1990, and Janice Castro, "Mr. Sam Stuns Goliath," *Time*, February 25, 1991, p. 62.

Page 171. Mr. Walton is quoted in "Wal-Mart," *Business Month*, December 1987, p. 88. (Reprinted with permission, *Business Month* magazine, December 1987. Copyright © 1987 by Goldhirsh Group, Inc., 38 Commercial Wharf, Boston, MA 02110.)

Page 172. See *In Pursuit of Excellence*, Arkansas Business Council Foundation, Little Rock, 1988, p. 3.

Page 172. Wal-Mart's "Buy American" program is discussed in Michael Barrier, "Walton's Mountain," *Nation's Business*, April 1988, p. 21. See also Karen Blumenthal, "Marketing with Emotion: Wal-Mart Shows the Way," *The Wall Street Journal*, November 13, 1989, p. B1.

Page 173. Mr. Walton is quoted in Barrier, "Walton's Mountain," *Nation's Business*, April 1988, p. 26.

Page 173. David Glass's quote is from Isadore Barmash, "New Moves from Two Grand Old Men of Retailing," *The New York Times*, January 24, 1988, p. 7.

Page 173. Sam Walton's quote appears in John Huey, "Wal-Mart: Will It Take Over the World?" *Fortune*, January 30, 1989, p. 56. See also Sharon Reier, "CEO of the Decade: Sam M. Walton," *Financial World*, April 4, 1989, pp. 56–61.

Page 173. Don Soderquist is quoted in Huey, "Wal-Mart," *Fortune*, January 30, 1989, p. 56.

Page 173. See Abraham Zaleznik, *The Managerial Mystique: Restoring Leadership in Business*, Harper, New York, 1989.

Page 174. CEO Glass is quoted in Huey, "Wal-Mart," *Fortune*, January 30, 1989, p. 56.

Page 174. Herman Miller Inc. is discussed in James O'Toole, "Practicing Leadership," *New Management*, Winter 1988, pp. 2–4. See also O'Toole's *Vanguard Management*, pp. 87–90.

Page 175. Max DePree is quoted in George Melloan, "Herman Miller's Secrets of Corporate Creativity," *The Wall Street Journal*, May 3, 1988, p. 31. (Reprinted by permission of *The Wall Street Journal*, © 1988. Dow Jones & Company, Inc. All Rights Reserved Worldwide.) See also "It Begins with a Belief in People," *The New York Times*, September 10, 1989, p. F3, and "It's Not What You Preach but How You Behave," *Fortune*, March 26, 1990, p. 36. For more on Max DePree's philosophy, see his *Leadership Is an Art*, Doubleday, New York, 1989.

Page 175. For DePree's criticism of U.S. managers, see "Advice to Bosses: Try a Little Kindness," *Time*, September 11, 1989.

Page 175. Max DePree is quoted in O'Toole, "Practicing Leadership," *New Management*, Winter, 1988, p. 3.

Page 175. CEO Richard Ruch's remarks are from Kenneth Labich, "Hot Company, Warm Culture," *Fortune*, February 27, 1989, p. 76. (© The Time Inc. Magazine Company. All rights reserved.)

Page 176. The Miller suggestion system and quotes are from Dana Wechsler, "A Comeback in the Cubicles," *Forbes*, March 21, 1988, p. 56. See also "The Nineties," *Industry Week*, September 18, 1989, pp. 18–19.

Page 176. Max DePree is quoted in Labich, "Hot Company, Warm Culture," *Fortune*, February 27, 1989, p. 76.

Page 176. *Ibid.*

Page 176. Max DePree's remarks on family needs and the deficiencies of contemporary capitalism are from Melloan, "Herman Miller's Secrets of Corporate Creativity," *The Wall Street Journal*, May 3, 1988.

Page 177. See O'Toole, "Practicing Leadership," *New Management*, Winter 1988, p. 4.

Page 177. For an excellent historical overview of Steelcase, see Barbara Flanagan, "Designing a Takeover-Proof Company," *Avenue*, May 1989, pp. 100–116. See, too, Margery B. Stein, "Teaching Steelcase to Dance," *The New York Times Magazine*, April 1, 1990, pt. 2, p. 22.

Page 177. Professor Becker is quoted in Flanagan, "Designing a Takeover-Proof Company," *Avenue*, May 1989, p. 110.

Page 178. *Ibid.* See, too, Dumaine, p. 60.

Page 178. Denise Francis is quoted in Bob Cohn, "A Glimpse of the 'Flex' Future," *Newsweek*, August 1, 1988, p. 39.

Page 178. *Ibid.*

Page 179. Frank Merlotti's remarks are from Flanagan, "Designing a Takeover-Proof Company," *Avenue*, May 1989, pp. 109–110.

Page 180. Ben Cohen is quoted in "Coming of Age," *INC.*, April 1989, p. 38.

Page 181. Mr. Cohen's remarks are from Erik Larson, "Forever Young," *INC.*, July 1988, p. 58.

Page 181. Jerry Greenfield is quoted in Kanter and Mirvis, *The Cynical Americans*, p. 210.

Page 181. Ben Cohen's comments are from Larson, "Forever Young," *INC.*, July 1988, p. 52.

Page 181. Mr. Cohen's philosophy on togetherness and executive compensation are from "Corporate Stars of the Future: Hot Ideas, Blue-Chip Tradition," *The Wall Street Journal Centennial Edition*, 1989, p. A28. See also N. R. Kleinfield, "Wanted: CFO with a Flair for Funk," *The New York Times*, March 26, 1989, p. F4.

Page 182. Fred Lager's quote is from Larson, "Forever Young," *INC.*, July 1988, p. 52.

Page 182. See Kanter and Mirvis, *The Cynical Americans*, p. 216.

Page 183. See Robert Johnson, "With Its Spirit Shaken but Upbeat, Cummins Shows Decade's Scars," *The Wall Street Journal*, December 13, 1989, pp. A1 and 8. (Reprinted with permission of *The Wall Street Journal*, © 1989. Dow Jones & Company, Inc. All Rights Reserved Worldwide.) See, too, David Jeffrey, "A Most Uncommon Town, Columbus," *National Geographic*, September 1978, pp. 383–397.

Page 183. Henry Schacht is cited in Johnson, "With Its Spirit Shaken . . .," *The Wall Street Journal*, December 13, 1989, p. A1.

Page 184. See "Mr. Rust Belt," *Business Week*, October 17, 1988, p. 72.

Page 184. For a discussion of Cummins's recent decline, see Ronald Henkoff, "The Engine That Couldn't," *Fortune*, December 18, 1989, p. 124, and Robert L. Rose, "Cummins Hits Turnaround Roadblocks," *The Wall Street Journal*, September 25, 1989, p. 88.

Page 184. Mayor Robert Stewart's remarks are from "$5 Worth of Loyalty," *USA Today*, July 18, 1989, p. B1.

Page 185. J. Irwin Miller is quoted in Johnson, "With Its Spirit Shaken . . .," *The Wall Street Journal*, December 13, 1989, p. A8.

Page 185. Clementine Tangeman is cited in "$5 Worth of Loyalty," *USA Today*, July 18, 1989, p. B1.

Page 185. Robert Sutherland's remarks are from Rose, "Cummins Hits Turnaround Roadblocks," *The Wall Street Journal*, September 25, 1989, p. B8.

Page 185. Mr. Miller's sentiments on the long-term needs of corporate America are from Sarah Bartlett, "Family Pays $72 Million to Defend a Company," *The New York Times*, July 18, 1989, p. C16. (Copyright 1989 by the New York Times Company. Reprinted by permission.)

Page 185. Henry Schacht is quoted in Jerry Flint, "A Very Japanese Solution," *Forbes*, August 6, 1990, p. 39. See, too, Alison Leigh Cowan, "Cummins Selling 27% Stake to 3," *The New York Times*, July 16, 1990, p. C1, and "Turning Cummins into the Engine Maker That Could," *Business Week*, July 30, 1990, p. 20.

Page 185. Mr. Schacht's remarks on the company's future are from James P. Miller, "Cummins to Sell a 25% Stake to Three Firms," *The Wall Street Journal*, July 16, 1990, p. A3.

Page 186. Vernon Alden's sentiments were offered in "Cummins: Capitalism at Its Best," Letter to the Editor, *The Wall Street Journal*, January 15, 1990, p. A13. (Reprinted by permission of *The Wall Street Journal*, © 1990. Dow Jones & Company, Inc. All Rights Reserved Worldwide.)

Chapter 12: Limitations of Frontier Living

Page 188. For a general discussion of the economic malaise of some small towns, see: William E. Schmidt, "The Depression Deepens in the Mountain States," *The New York Times*, June 26, 1988, Section 4, p. 5. See also Sharon Cohen, "America's Heartland: The Exodus Is Under Way," *Los Angeles Times*, May 7, 1989, pp. 1–6; Alan Murray, "Unemployment Tops 25% in Some Regions Mired in Deep Poverty," *The Wall Street Journal*, April 21, 1988, p. A1; Marj Charlier, "Depressed Rural Towns Develop Jobs from Within as Industrial Lures Fail," *The Wall Street Journal*, August 4, 1988, p. B6; Dennis Farney, "On the Great Plains, Life Becomes a Fight for Water and Survival," *The Wall Street Journal*, August 16, 1989, p. A1; Denise Kalette, "Small Town USA in Trouble," USA Today, September 18, 1989, p. A6; "Battling Rural 'Brain Drain,'" *Newsweek*, December 26, 1988, p. 46; James Howard Kunstler, "Schuylerville Stands Still," *The New York Times Magazine*, March 25, 1990, pp. 48–

60. For an excellent overview, see Griffin Smith, Jr., "Small-Town America: An Endangered Species?" *National Geographic*, February 1989, pp. 186–215.

For more on small-town drug problems, see Jane Mayer, "Seaford, Del., Shows How Crack Can Savage Small-Town America," *The Wall Street Journal*, May 5, 1989, p. A11; Robert P. Hey, "Rural America Fights Traffickers," *Christian Science Monitor*, October 27, 1989, p. 6; Deeann Glamser, "Rural Washington City Becomes a Cocaine Hot Spot," *USA Today*, November 7, 1989, p. A6; John Dillin, "Crack Gangs Extend Reach into Small-town America," November 8, 1989, p. A1; and Jack Kelley, "Cocaine, Other Hard Drugs Invade Rural Areas," *USA Today*, December 20, 1989, p. A11.

The health-care problem is considered in: Frank Maier, "Help Wanted: Boon Docs," *Newsweek*, February 27, 1989, p. 58; "On the Sick List: Rural Hospitals," *Business Week*, March 27, 1989, p. 36.

For more on the difficulties of the frontier schools, see Joseph Berger, "Poignant Problems of the Nation's Rural Schools," *The New York Times*, July 26, 1989, p. B7 and Lee Mitgang, "Rural School Districts Pressured to Raise Standards and Cut Budgets," *The Los Angeles Times*, November 26, 1989, p. A18.

Page 189.   William H. Whyte, *The Organization Man*, Simon & Schuster, New York, 1956.

Page 189.   See "Creating Contention without Causing Conflict," *Business Month*, February, 1990, p. 69.

Page 189.   Dennis Farney, "To the Stresses Faced by a Rural Clergyman, Add His Own Isolation," *The Wall Street Journal*, July 14, 1989, p. A1.

Page 190.   "A Special News Report on People and Their Jobs in Offices, Fields, and Factories," *The Wall Street Journal*, March 28, 1988.

Page 190.   Sue Shellenbarger, "Rural Enterprise: Tough Row to Hoe," *The Wall Street Journal*, September 12, 1989, p. B1.

Page 191.   The Fort Mills quotes are from "Justice in a Company Town," *60 Minutes Transcripts*, vol. 22, no. 17, January 7, 1990, pp. 6–10. (© CBS Inc. 1990. All Rights Reserved. Originally broadcast on *60 Minutes* on January 7, 1990, over the CBS Television Network.) For discussion of a similar incident, see Milo Geyelin, "How a Rural Judge Wielded Kingly Power over Abject Subjects," *The Wall Street Journal*, November 1, 1989, p. A1.

Page 191.   All the quotes on Butte, Montana, are from Sandra Atchison, "A 'Deflated Belt' Town Gets Pumped Up Again," *Business Week*, July 18, 1988, p. 66E. For a mountain community that experienced opposite results, see Jim Robbins, "Some Westerners Prefer Solitude to Economic Power," *The New York Times*, May 29, 1988, p. E8.

Page 192.   Gene Wilcoxson is quoted in Mark Clayton, "Economic Alchemy That Transformed a Town," *Christian Science Monitor*, November 14, 1988, p. 1.

Page 193.   Mayor Willie Casper of Mineral Wells, Texas, is cited in Donald C. Bacon, "Closing a Base Opens Doors," *Nation's Business*, May 1989, p. 9.

Page 193.   The Lowell, Massachusetts, experience is discussed in Laurence Ingrassia, "Recession Haunts City That Believed It Was Saved by High-Tech," *The Wall Street Journal*, January 25, 1990, p. D1, and Christopher Kenneally, "Lowell: City Amid a Renaissance," *Boston Globe*, September 5, 1987, p. 37.

Page 193.   Professor Reed's remarks are from "Revival Bought with Tourist Dollars," *The New York Times*, January 10, 1990, p. C13.

Page 194.   The Orlando quotes are from Fay Fiore, "Disney Co.: A Grinch?" *Honolulu Sunday Star-Bulletin & Advertiser*, March 11, 1990, p. 34. (Copyright, 1990, *Los Angeles Times*. Reprinted by permission.)

Page 195.   See Michael H. Brown, "Hormel's Bitter Legacy," *Business Month*, May 1988, pp. 56–62. Also Dave Hage and Paul Klanda, *No Retreat, No Surrender: Labor's War at Hormel,*

William Morrow, New York, 1989, and Hardy Green, *On Strike at Hormel: The Struggle for a Democratic Labor Movement*, Temple University Press, Philadelphia, 1990.

Page 196. Chairman Robert Boni's quotes are from "Why-Oh, Why-Oh, Did Armco's Brass Leave Ohio?" *Business Week*, February 1, 1988, p. 5.

Page 196. For more on Tokyo's preeminence, see "The Disoriented City," *The Economist*, April 9, 1988, p. 21. (Copyright 1988 The Economist Newspaper Ltd. All rights reserved.) See also Theodore C. Besfor, *Neighborhood Tokyo*, Stanford University Press, Palo Alto, 1989; "The Fast Growing Demand for Office Space and the Redevelopment of Tokyo," Kyowa Bank Economic Report, published in *Japan Update*, Winter 1988, pp. 8–11; "Pity Those Poor Japanese," *Economist*, December 24, 1988, p. 48; Tsuneo Nagase, "Business Concentration in Tokyo Triggers Land Price Increases," *Japan Update*, Summer 1989, pp. 22–26; Clayton Jones, "Japan Tries to Dampen Tokyo Land Prices," *Christian Science Monitor*, March 15, 1990, p. 5, and his "Japanese Take Aim at Soaring Tokyo Land Prices," *Christian Science Monitor*, November 21, 1990, p. 4; Marcus W. Brauchli and Masayoshi Kanabayashi, "Land Prices in Japan Are Getting So Steep the Nation Is Jittery," *The Wall Street Journal*, March 23, 1990, p. A1; and Edward Seidensticker, *Tokyo Rising: The City since the Great Earthquake*, Knopf, New York, 1990.

Page 196. Wakake Hiranaka is quoted in T. R. Reid, "Japan May Move Parliament Out of Troubled Tokyo," *Honolulu Advertiser*, January 2, 1991, p. C2.

Page 196. See "The Disoriented City," *The Economist*, April 9, 1988, p. 21.

Page 198. See Matsuda Katsutake, "A Bold Plan to Reward Tokyo's Business Center," *Japan Echo*, Summer 1988, pp. 28–30. For more on this subject, consider Kazuo Yawata, "A New Capital for Japan?" *Economic Eye*, March 1988, pp. 14–17; "Cramped Tokyo Seeks to Relieve Congestion," *Honolulu Star-Bulletin*, September 15, 1988, p. D1; and James Sterngold, "While Land Prices in Japan Soar, Offices Fight Back with Words," *The New York Times*, March 25, 1990, p. 1.

Page 198. Takao Ogiya's quote is from "Tokyo's Love Affair with High Tech Stops at the Office," *Business Week*, October 10, 1988, p. 112.

Page 199. Professor Shiraki's remarks are from Kathryn Gravan, "Japan's Economic Boon Is Centering on Tokyo and on the Financial Sector," *The Wall Street Journal*, January 5, 1988, p. A10.

Page 199. This research began with my "The Regional Headquarters Decision: A Comparative Analysis," *Academy of Management Journal*, June 1979, pp. 410–415.

Page 199. See Susan Chira, "For Japanese Living in New York City, (Influence Grows)," *The New York Times*, June 6, 1989, p. 18. See also "Japan's Big Property Grab," *Economist*, January 13, 1990, p. 71, and George White, "California Still Popular with Japan Investors," *Los Angeles Times*, January 22, 1991, p. D2.

Page 200. Elizabeth Rubinfien, "Japanese Buyers of U.S. Real Estate Start Shopping for Land Outside the Big Cities," *The Wall Street Journal*, December 29, 1989, p. A4.

Page 200. Hugh Sidey, "A Tapestry of Prairie Life," *Time*, October 9, 1989, p. 30.

Chapter 13: The Re-United States of America: An Action Agenda for Business and Government

Page 202. See David Birch, "RFD Inc.," *INC.*, February 1988, p. 15.

Page 202. Janet Turner is quoted in Ken Slocum, "The Sun Belt Gains Manufacturing Jobs as Nation Loses Them," *The Wall Street Journal*, April 1, 1988, p. 4.

Page 203. The evolution of the Research Triangle Park is discussed in *Public-Private Partnership: An Opportunity for Urban Communities*, A Statement by the Research and Policy Committee of the Committee for Economic Development, Committee for Economic Development, New York, February 1982.

Page 203. The Hampton Roads case is described in "Success Stories of Communities That Solved Economic Problems," *Area Development*, November 1989, pp. 40–86.

Page 204. For more on the choice of private, public, or mixed economic development organizations, see *Leadership for Dynamic State Economies*, A Statement by the Research and Policy Committee for Economic Development, New York Committee for Economic Development, 1986, chap. 6. See, too, "Maintaining Competitive Advantage: Approaches for Advanced Economic Regions," a discussion paper prepared by SRI International (Menlo Park, Calif., July 1990).

Page 204. The Durham, North Carolina, quote is from "The Sun Belt Gains Manufacturing Jobs as Nature Loses Them," p. 4.

Page 205. Ken Smith is quoted in my "Global Cities of Tomorrow," *Harvard Business Review*, May–June 1977, p. 84.

Page 206. See H. Brandt Ayers, "Small Town, U.S.A. Is Going Global," *The New York Times*, January 20, 1990, p. 19.

Page 206. John C. Anderson is quoted in Richard Tharp, "Oregon Turns into a Mecca for High Tech," *The Wall Street Journal*, August 28, 1984.

Page 206. James Hetlinger is cited in Carrie Dolan, "Desperately Wooing Tokyo," *The New York Times*, September 22, 1989, p. R28. See, too, Kirk Johnson, "States Unite to Promote Their Business Abroad," *The New York Times*, December 16, 1990, p. A21.

Page 207. See Ross Atkin, "Winds of Hope Stir in Small Towns," *Christian Science Monitor*, April 27, 1990, p. 12. For other creative solutions, see "Burdens of Government a Strain in Small Towns," *The New York Times*, June 25, 1990, p. A9; Henry Bacus, "Allies for Growth," *Nation's Business*, November 1990, p. 40; Reece C. Wilson, "Establishing Win-Win Relationships," *Area Development*, November 1990, p. 36; and Udayan Gupta, "States Take Different Paths to Spur Small Businesses," *The Wall Street Journal*, January, 9, 1991, p. B2.

Page 209. George Autry is quoted in Marshal Ingwerson, "Jobs Return to Rural South," *Christian Science Monitor*, December 21, 1988, p. 14. See, too, Glenn English, "Rural Development: A New Approach," *Area Development*, December 1990, p. 50.

Page 209. See Henry Anatole Grunwald, "New Challenges of Capitalism," *Fortune*, May 7, 1990, p. 143.

Page 210. For more on the Forward Peoria program, see "A Faster Heartbeat in the Heartlands," *Economist*, June 4, 1988, p. 26.

Page 211. For a discussion of America's different face, see David S. Broder, "Goodbye to All That," *Washington Post Weekly National Edition*, December 18–24, 1989, p. 6; William Dunn, "Kicking Off 'Transitional Decade,'" *USA Today*, December 11, 1989, p. 7A; Otto Friedrich, "Freed from Greed?," *Time*, January 1, 1990, p. 76; Alan Farnham, "The Trust Gap," *Fortune*, December 4, 1989, p. 56; Nicolaus Mills, "90's: The Payback Decade," *The New York Times*, June 26, 1990, p. A19; and Janice Castro, "Hunkering Down," *Time*, June 23, 1990, p. 56.

Page 212. See Robert Levering, "Paradise, Corporate-Style," *Business Month*, July–August 1988, p. 50.

Page 213. William R. Howell is quoted in Willard C. Rappleye, Jr., "Why Penney Is Moving to Dallas," *Financier*, July 1987, p. 28.

Page 214. William H. Whyte discusses "the impulse of the center" in his *City*, pp. 297 and 341.

Page 214. Sioux City's Teresa Wolf is quoted in Judy Keen and Mimi Hall, "Strangers Quickly Turn into Friends," *USA Today*, July 21, 1989, p. 1A. See also "Heroes in Sioux City," *Washington Post National Weekly Edition*, July 31–August 6, 1989, p. 11.

Page 214. Mike Esch's quote is from Andrea Stone and Lori Sharn, "In Iowa, an Outpouring of Support," *USA Today*, July 21, 1989, p. 6A. See, too, Lori Sharn, "Healing Process Continues at Crash Reunion," *USA Today*, July 13, 1990, p. 6A.

Page 215. See Michael J. Weiss, *The Clustering of America*, Harper, New York, 1988.

Selected Bibliography

"America's New Boom Towns," *U.S. News & World Report,* November 13, 1989, pp. 54–66.

Andrew, William: "The Facts about the Mobile Executive," *Vis à Vis,* July 1988, p. 74.

Atkin, Ross: "The 'Mallification' of America," *Christian Science Monitor,* October 25, 1989, p. 12.

———: "Winds of Hope Stir in Small Towns," *Christian Science Monitor,* April 27, 1990, p. 12.

Baldassare, Mark: *Trouble in Paradise: The Suburban Transformation in America,* Columbia University Press, New York, 1986.

Bennett, Amanda: *The Death of the Organization Man,* Morrow, New York, 1990.

Bergsman, Steve: "Small L.A. Businesses Find Nicer Climates Elsewhere," *The New York Times,* April 29, 1990, sec. 3, p. F12.

Birch, David L.: "The Hidden Economy," *Chief Executive,* May–June 1988, pp. 30–35.

———: *Job Creation in Cities,* MIT Press, Cambridge, 1981.

———: "RFD Inc.: Where to Go When You Want to Start a Business in a Remote Location," *INC.,* February 1988, pp. 14–15.

Bluestone, Barry, and Bennett Harrison: *The Deindustrialization of America,* Basic Books, New York, 1982.

"Boom Town, '80s-Style," *Los Angeles Times,* May 12, 1989, sec. 2, p. 10.

Carlson, Eugene: "New Hot Cities for Industry Are Emerging," *The Wall Street Journal,* June 8, 1988, p. A25.

"The Case against Bigsville," *Economist,* December 18, 1988.

Castro, Janice: "Hunkering Down," *Time,* June 23, 1990, p. 56.

Clifford, Frank: "City Office, Home on the Range," *Los Angeles Times,* October 29, 1989, p. 1.

Collins, James C., and Jerry I. Porras: "Making Impossible Dreams Come True," *Stanford Business School Magazine,* July 1989, p. 12.

Davis. L. J.: "Unlikely, But Boise Means Big Business," *The New York Times Magazine,* June 11, 1989, sec. 6, p. 24.

Davis, Stanley: *Future Perfect,* Addison-Wesley, Reading, Mass., 1987.

Denton, D. Keith, and Barry L. Wisdom: "Shared Vision," *Business Horizons,* July–August 1989, pp. 67–69.

DePalma, Anthony: "As Suburbs Sprawl, Open Space Shrinks," *The New York Times,* July 31, 1988, sec. 8, p. 1.

———: "It's Boom Time in What Was Once the Boonies," *The New York Times,* February 10, 1985, sec. 4, p. E22.

Drucker, Peter F.: "The Coming of the New Organization," *Harvard Business Review,* January–February 1988, pp. 45–53.

———: *The New Realities,* Harper, New York, 1989.

Dunn, William: "Boom Towns—On a Smaller Scale," *USA Today,* December 11, 1989, p. 9A.

DuPree, Max: *Leadership Is an Art,* Doubleday, New York, 1989.

The Editors of *Fortune: The Exploding Metropolis,* Doubleday, Garden City, NY, 1957.

Farnham, Alan: "Migratory Habits of the 500," *Fortune,* April 24, 1989, pp. 400–401.

———: "The Trust Gap," *Fortune,* December 4, 1989, p. 56.

"A Faster Heartbeat in the Heartlands," *Economist,* June 4, 1988, p. 26.

Ferry, Jeffrey: "The Wired World," *Vis à Vis,* May 1990, p. 25.

Fields, Debbi, and Alan Furst: *One Smart Cookie,* Simon and Schuster, New York, 1987.

Fishman, Robert: "America's New City: Megalopolis Unbound," *Wilson Quarterly,* Winter 1990, pp. 24–45.

————: *Bourgeois Utopias: The Rise and Fall of Suburbia,* Basic Books, New York, 1987.

Frieden, Bernard, and Lynne B. Sagalyn: *Downtown, Inc.: How America Rebuilds Cities,* MIT Press, Cambridge, Mass., 1989.

Fuguitt, Glenn V., Paul R. Voss, and J. C. Doherty: *Growth and Change in Rural America,* The Urban Land Institute, Washington, D.C., 1979.

Gallup, George, Jr.: "Small Towns, Rural Areas Still Beckon Many Americans," Gallup poll news release, March 24, 1985.

Gannes, Stuart: "Some Real Comers among the Midsize U.S. Cities," *Fortune,* October 23, 1989, p. 74.

Gardner, Richard R.: "New Communities for the Rural Renaissance," *American Land Forum,* Winter 1983, pp. 19–26.

Gibbs, Nancy: "How America Has Run Out of Time," *Time,* April 24, 1989, p. 67.

Glisson, Linda S.: *Main Street: Open for Business,* a three-year special report, National Trust for Historic Preservation, Washington, D.C., 1984.

Gratz, Roberta Brandes: *The Living City,* Simon and Schuster, New York, 1989.

————: "Malling the Northeast," *The New York Times Magazine,* April 1, 1990, sec. 6, p. 35.

Greene, Elaine: "The Country Look Is Big Business as Cities Seek the Quaint and Cozy," *The New York Times,* May 26, 1988, p. B7.

Hack, George D.: "Relocating Corporate Headquarters," *Area Development,* February 1990, pp. 36–139.

Hall, George E.: "Reflections on Running a Diversified Company," *Harvard Business Review,* January–February 1987, p. 85.

Harding, Charles F.: "Why Offices Move," *Area Development,* March 1987, p. 30.

Heenan, David A.: "The Case for Convergent Capitalism," *Journal of Business Strategy,* November–December 1988, p. 54.

————: "Congress Rethinks America's Competitiveness," *Business Horizons,* May–June 1989, pp. 11–16.

————: "The Downside of Downsizing," *Journal of Business Strategy,* November–December 1989, pp. 18–24.

————: "Global Cities of Tomorrow," *Harvard Business Review,* May–June 1977, pp. 79–92.

————: "Is Big Business Heading for Small Town, U.S.A.?" *Journal of Business Strategy,* July–August 1989, pp. 4–10.

————: "The Regional Headquarters Decision: A Comparative Analysis," *Academy of Management Journal,* June 1979, pp. 410–415.

————: *The Re-United States of America,* Addison-Wesley, Reading, Mass., 1983.

Heenan, David A., and Howard V. Perlmutter: "Subsidiaries Come of Age," *New Management,* Winter 1987, p. 19.

Henry, Donald L.: "Quality-of-Life Considerations in Site Selection," *Area Development,* December 1987, p. 32.

Herbers, John: *The New Heartland: America's Flight Beyond the Suburbs,* Times Books, New York, 1986.

Jackson, Kenneth T.: *Crabgrass Frontier: The Suburbanization of the United States,* Oxford University Press, New York, 1985.

Jacobs, Allan B.: *Looking at Cities,* Harvard University Press, Cambridge, Mass., 1985.

Jacobs, Jane: *Cities and the Wealth of Nations,* Random House, New York, 1984.

————: *The Death and Life of Great American Cities,* Random House, New York, 1961.

————: *The Economy of Cities,* Random House, New York, 1969.

Kanter, Donald L., and Philip H. Mirvis: *The Cynical Americans,* Jossey-Bass, San Francisco, 1989.

Kanter, Rosabeth Moss: *When Giants Learn to Dance,* Simon and Schuster, New York, 1989.

Kaufman, Michael T.: "Tough Times for Mr. Levittown," *The New York Times Magazine,* September 24, 1989, pp. 43–44.

Kehrer, Daniel M.: "The Miracle of Theory Q," *Business Month,* September 1989, p. 47.

Kilmann, Ralph H.: "Tomorrow's Corporation Won't Have Walls," *The New York Times,* June 18, 1989, sec. 3, p. D3.

Kowinski, William Severini: *The Malling of America,* Morrow, New York, 1985.

Kristof, Nicholas D.: "Investment in Oregon Spurred by Tax Repeal," *The New York Times,* December 17, 1984, p. D1.

Labich, Kenneth: "The Best Cities for Business," *Fortune,* October 23, 1989, pp. 56–74.

Langdon, Philip: "A Good Place to Live," *Atlantic Monthly,* March 1988, pp. 39–60.

Lessinger, Jack: *Regions of Opportunity,* Times Books, New York, 1986.

Levering, Robert: "Paradise, Corporate-Style," *Business Month,* July–August 1988, p. 50.

Lohr, Steve: "The Growth of the Global Office," *The New York Times,* October 18, 1988, p. C1.

Lueck, Thomas J.: "New York City Is Challenged As Giant of Global Economy," *The New York Times,* June 27, 1988, p. A1.

Lyons, Richard D.: "Scholars Predict a New Era for Small Town, U.S.A." *The New York Times,* September 27, 1987, sec. 8, p. 2.

Macdonald, Michael C. D.: *America's Cities: A Report on the Myth of Urban Renaissance,* Simon and Schuster, New York, 1984.

Mann, Charles C.: "The Town of Dow," *Business Month,* December 1987, p. 66.

Masotti, Louis H., and Jeffrey K. Haddens (eds.): *Suburbia in Transition,* New Viewpoints, New York, 1974.

Matthews, Jay: "Urban, Suburban Cowboys," *Washington Post National Weekly Edition,* February 20–26, 1989, p. 34.

McCormick, John, and Peter McKillop: "The Other Suburbia," *Newsweek,* June 26, 1989, p. 22.

Mumford, Lewis: *The City in History,* Harcourt, New York, 1961.

————: *The Culture of Cities,* Harcourt, New York, 1938.

Naisbitt, John, and Patricia Aburdene: *Megatrends 2000,* Morrow, New York, 1990.

"The New America": *Business Week,* September 25, 1989, p. 152.

"New York's Future: Bright Lights, Big Trouble": *Business Week,* November 20, 1989, pp. 108–109.

O'Reilly, Charles: "Corporations, Culture, and Commitment: Motivation and Social Control in Organizations," *California Management Review,* Summer 1989, pp. 9–25.

O'Toole, James: *Vanguard Management,* Doubleday, New York, 1985.

"The Password Is Flexible," *Business Week,* September 25, 1989, p. 152.

Peirce, Neal R., and Jerry Hagstrom: *The Book of America,* Norton, New York, 1983.

Perlmutter, Howard V., and David A. Heenan: "Cooperate to Compete Globally," *Harvard Business Review,* March–April 1986, pp. 136–152.

"Positioning the Corporate Staff for the 1990's: A Survey of Top Executives of U.S. Corporations," Towers, Perrin, Forster and Crosby, Inc., New York, 1986.

Rappleye, Willard C., Jr.: "Why Penney Is Moving to Dallas," *Financier,* July 1987, p. 28.

Raskin, Eugene: *Sequel to Cities: What Happens When Cities Are Extinct,* Bloch, New York, 1969.

Reese, Michael, and Jennifer Foote: "California: American Dream, American Nightmare," *Newsweek,* July 31, 1989, p. 23.

Rhodes, David W.: "Employee Loyalty Is an Attainable Goal," *Journal of Business Strategy,* November–December 1989, p. 52.

Richman, Louis S.: "Why the Middle Class Is Anxious," *Fortune,* May 21, 1990, pp. 106–112.

Rifkind, Carole: *Main Street,* Harper, New York, 1977.

Rodgers, Fran Sussner, and Charles Rodgers: "Business and the Facts of Family Life," *Harvard Business Review,* November–December 1989, pp. 121–129.

Rose, Frederick: "Urban Lab: Los Angeles Offers Future Glimpse," *The Wall Street Journal Centennial Edition,* 1989, p. A15.

Rosen, Kenneth: "Which Cities Will Be Hot—And Not," *Fortune,* March 26, 1990, p. 150.

Safire, William: "America's Next Direction: Out of Town, All the Way," *International Herald Tribune,* September 26, 1989.

Schlosstein, Steve: "U.S. Is the Leader in Decentralization," *The New York Times*, June 3, 1990, sec. 3, p. F13.

Schmidt, William E.: "The Depression Deepens in the Mountain States," *The New York Times*, June 26, 1988, sec. 4, p. 5.

Seidensticker, Edward: *Tokyo Rising: The City Since the Great Earthquake*, Knopf, New York, 1990.

Shellenbarger, Sue: "Rural Enterprise: Tough Row to Hoe," *The Wall Street Journal*, September 12, 1989, p. B1.

Shepherd, James L.: "Looking for Utopia in a 19th Century Town," *Business Month*, June 1990, p. 78.

Sheridan, John S.: "Sizing Up Corporate Staffs," *Industry Week*, November 21, 1988, p. 46.

Sidey, Hugh: "A Tapestry of Prairie Life," *Time*, October 9, 1989, p. 30.

Smith, Griffin, Jr.: "Small-Town America: An Endangered Species?" *National Geographic*, February 1989, pp. 186–215.

Solomon, Jolie: "Corporate Elite Leaving Home Towns for Headquarters in Faraway Places," *The Wall Street Journal*, February 21, 1990, p. B1.

Starr, Kevin: *Material Dreams: Southern California Through the 1920s*, Oxford University Press, New York, 1990.

Sternlieb, George, and James W. Hughes: "The Changing Demography of the Central City," *Scientific American*, April 1980.

Stevens, William K.: "Beyond the Mall: Suburbs Evolving Into Outer Cities," *The New York Times*, November 8, 1987, p. E5.

Stewart, Thomas A.: "New Ways to Exercise Power," *Fortune*, November 6, 1989, pp. 52–64.

Stilgoe, John R.: *Borderland: Origins of the American Suburb, 1820–1939*, Yale University Press, New Haven, 1988.

Stoner, Charles R., and Richard I. Hartman: "Family Responsibilities and Career Progress: The Good, the Bad, and the Ugly," *Business Horizons*, May–June 1990, p. 7.

Tomasko, Robert M.: *Downsizing: Reshaping the Corporation of the Future*, Amacom, New York 1987.

Tscharner, Renata von, and Ronald Lee Fleming: "Making Cities Memorable," *World Monitor*, February 1990, p. 36.

Vidich, Arthur J., and Joseph Bensman: *Small Town in Mass Society*, Princeton University Press, Princeton, N.J., 1968.

Walters, David C.: "Big Cities, Bolts and All," *Christian Science Monitor*, May 24, 1990, p. 14.

Weiss, Julian M.: "Companies Seeking New Locations Set Their Sites on Education," *Christian Science Monitor*, October 8, 1987, p. 12.

Weiss, Michael J.: *The Clustering of America*, Harper, New York, 1988.

Whyte, William: *City: Rediscovering the Center*, Doubleday, Garden City, N.Y., 1988.

———: *The Organization Man*, Simon and Schuster, New York, 1956.

Wolf, Peter. *The Future of the City: New Directions in Urban Planning*, Watson-Guptill, New York, 1974.

Worthy, Fred F.: "American Boomtowns," *Portfolio*, Fall 1987, pp. 35–63.

Wysocki, Bernard, Jr.: "The New Boom Towns," *The Wall Street Journal*, March 27, 1989, p. B1.

——— and Michael J. McCarthy: "Latest New Frontier: Exurban Boom Towns," *The Wall Street Journal Centennial Edition*, CXX (1989), p. A7.

Index